USING BIBLICAL HEBREW IN MINISTRY

A Practical Guide for Pastors, Seminarians, and Bible Students

Don Parker

University Press of America, Inc.
Lanham • New York • London

Copyright © 1995 by
University Press of America,® Inc.
4720 Boston Way
Lanham, Maryland 20706

3 Henrietta Street
London, WC2E 8LU England

ISBN 0-7618-0124-3 (pbk: alk: ppr.)

Contents

Abbreviations for Biblical Books   v
Preface and Acknowledgments   vii

1   Biblical Hebrew: Questions and Answers   1

2   The Map: The Process of Hebrew Exegesis   17

3   By the Books: Using the Right Tools   39

4   Lightning or Lightning Bug? Word Studies   63

5   Picture This! Figuring Out Figures of Speech   93

6   The Artistry of Biblical Hebrew: Narrative   115

7   The Artistry of Biblical Hebrew: Poetry   145

8   From Text to Life: Bridging the Culture Gap   179

9   From Text to Life:
Bridging the Communication Gap   197

10   Going Further: Progressing in Biblical Hebrew   223

Appendix: Basic 'Brew:
Essential Ingredients to Start "Cooking"   237
Bibliography   257
Index   267

Chapter 1

Biblical Hebrew:
Questions and Answers

Objectives: After reading this chapter, you should be able to:
1. Suggest three benefits of studying biblical Hebrew.
2. Orient Hebrew within a larger language "family."
3. Relate several characteristics of biblical Hebrew.
4. Identify several roadblocks in studying biblical Hebrew.
5. Distinguish a tool-based approach from the traditional approach.
6. Find your way around this book.

A *New Yorker* cartoon shows two men at lunch. One is saying, "I've learned a lot in sixty-three years. But unfortunately almost all of it is about aluminum."

Is biblical Hebrew as unrelated to life as trivia about a specific metal? Regrettably, the traditional approach in teaching biblical Hebrew often leaves that impression.

When I introduce myself as a seminary teacher of biblical Hebrew, men's mouths are stopped, mothers clutch young children to their breast, and extended crucifixes keep me at bay. Well, I exaggerate. But not much.

Perhaps you, too, opened this book with great trepidation, or worry that it will be a waste of time. Yet a decade of teaching ministry-oriented seminarians launched this book. It aims to be a truly *practical* guide to the *use* of biblical Hebrew.

This chapter answers the following questions about biblical Hebrew: Who needs it? Who dreamed up this stuff? Who can do it? Where are we going (in this book)?

Who Needs It? The Importance of Biblical Hebrew

Why is it that many seminary programs require biblical Hebrew? What are some of the benefits?

Biblical Hebrew adds accuracy, depth, and vividness to the study and teaching of the Old Testament.

Years ago, a computer used in a Russian Bible project translated "the spirit is willing, but the flesh is weak" as "the Vodka is strong, but the meat is rotten." Sort of loses something in translation, doesn't it?

The translation process often creates static between the source and target languages. As an Italian proverb observes, "*Traduttore tradittore*," "Translations are treacherous." The ability to go to the source promises greater accuracy in interpretation, as well as heightened appreciation.

Martin Luther, an activist minister and world-changer, can hardly be accused of being an impractical scholastic. Yet Luther advocated studying biblical Hebrew, warning of frequent errors from neglect of the original languages:

> How often does Saint Augustine err in the Psalms and in his other expositions, and Hilary too — in fact, all those who undertake to expound Scriptures without a knowledge of the languages. Saint Augustine himself is obliged to confess that a Christian teacher who is to expound the Scriptures must

know Greek and Hebrew in addition to Latin. Otherwise, it is impossible to avoid constant stumbling; indeed, there are plenty of problems to work out even when one is well versed in the languages.

Luther, of course, was instrumental in the Reformation, which was preceded by the Renaissance with its emphasis on classical languages. Likewise, many students experience their own personal reformation through studying the Bible in the original languages.

Rabbi Hillel Cohn graciously visits our seminary annually and challenges our students: "Who has read the Bible?" Although many students raise their hands, Rabbi Cohn affirms: "You mean you've read a translation; you haven't read the Bible [Old Testament] unless you've read it in Hebrew." Word-plays, sound effects, repetitions, word nuances, sentence emphases, Hebrew idioms[1] and constructions make the text live and breathe.

Take, for example, the Tower of Babel account (Gn 11:1-9). A translation might obscure repetitions, word-plays, and the oppositional patterning of the human and divine actions. God echoes the people's "Come (*habah*), let us build" with "Come (*habah*), let us go down." Whereas the rebels had sought to gain a reputation (*shem*) there (*sham*) at Babel, and reach heaven (*shamayim*), God comes down from heaven and immortalizes their rebellion there (*sham*). The Hebrew mockingly portrays God "confusing" (*balal*) languages at *babel*, the very place the Babylonians esteemed as the gateway to God.[2] Word-play such as that between *nabelah*, God's confounding activity, and *nilbenah* and *nibneh-lanu*, the human brick-making and building, highlights the folly of human pride and disobedience against God.[3]

Of course, because of the challenge of foreign languages and the basic clarity of key biblical doctrines, the biblical languages are not for everyone. Yet the Bible is like the earth, with life-sustaining essentials on the surface and great treasures obtainable by digging deeper. The original languages empower the Bible student and preacher to mine great riches.

Working with the biblical languages also creates an intimacy with the text that promotes lively exposition.[4] The Hebrew poet Haim Nachman Bialik reportedly said: "Reading the Bible in translation is like kissing your bride through a veil."[5]

To use another analogy, a black and white television transmits the same program as a color set. Yet which would *you* rather watch?

Biblical Hebrew aids New Testament study.

Luther put it this way:

> The Hebrew language is the best language of all, with the richest vocabulary.... If I were younger I would want to learn this language, because no one can really understand the Scriptures without it. For although the New Testament is written in Greek, it is full of hebraisms and Hebrew expressions. It has therefore been aptly said that the Hebrews drink from the spring, the Greeks from the stream that flows from it, and the Latins from a downstream pool.[6]

The Old Testament provides background, quotations, allusions, prophecies, types, proper names, loan words, figures of speech, and idioms for the New Testament. Ruefully I recall my Bible college days, when I followed commentators' leads to interpret New Testament passages in a strictly Greek (Hellenistic) context, apart from Biblical Hebrew counterparts.

Old Testament passages have since provided me with clearer perspective. Genesis 38:17 clarifies the "earnest" of the Spirit (Eph 1:14) as a deposit or pledge until receipt of salvation's full benefits. "Daily bread" (Mt 6:11) is another rare Greek term, whose meaning is a day's sustenance (Ex 16:4; Pr 27:1; Jr 52:34). The "poor in spirit" (Mt 5:3) are the afflicted who look to God for help (Ps 18:27; and many references to "the poor" in Psalms); and a "single eye" (Mt.

6:22), in keeping with the context, may refer to generosity (Pr 22:9, 23:6, 15:30).

Thankfully, New Testament interpreters increasingly recognize the Old Testament's contribution. Moltmann maintains:

> We stand today in a remarkable period of transition. On the one side the hellenistically structured form of the Christian faith is ebbing…. On the other side the Christian faith is experiencing what I would like to call a "hebraic wave." About thirty years ago the enduring and prophetic significance of the Old Testament for the Christian faith was discovered. It was realized that the New Testament cannot be read apart from the Old Testament, but that only when both are read together beside and with each other does the fullness of life in the faith unfold.[7]

Biblical Hebrew enables significant theological discussion.

Hear Luther again, regarding the role the original languages played in his struggle to trumpet justification by faith:

> I know full well that while it is the Spirit alone who accomplishes everything, I would surely have never flushed a covey [the papacy] if the languages had not helped me and given me a sure and certain knowledge of Scripture. The devil does not respect my spirit as highly as he does my speech and pen when they deal with Scripture.

Today Christians debate the doctrine of biblical inerrancy. Primarily such debate focuses on details of textual criticism and the New Testament's use of the Old. Also, cultists and critics often bolster deviant views by reference to the original languages. Yet evaluation and engagement with such technical arguments require acquaintance with the biblical languages.

Further, key theological and practical issues extend beyond the bounds of the New Testament. The Old Testament contributes greatly to the doctrines of sin and redemption, election, and eternal security, or issues like abortion, divorce and remarriage, creationism versus evolution, and dispensationalism versus covenantism. A minister discussing theology apart from biblical Hebrew is like a doctor performing surgery without consulting the patient's X-rays or medical history.

Okay, theological issues can be discussed apart from the biblical Hebrew. But fighting from such a handicap calls to mind the progressively de-limbed knight in "Monty Python and the Holy Grail."

So why study biblical Hebrew? Biblical Hebrew increases understanding and appreciation of the Old Testament, aids New Testament study, and enables significant theological discussion. These are a sampling of reasons; you may have others. Often motivation springs from a desire to worthily administer God's inspired Word.

Who Dreamed up This Stuff?
The History of Biblical Hebrew

The Semitic language family

Semitic languages spoken in Western Asia, or generally originating from that area, are characterized by common sounds, forms, vocabulary, and syntax. In ancient times they were the prominent languages of Mesopotamia, Syria-Palestine, and Arabia and Ethiopia. Hebrew belongs to this Semitic language "family."[8]

The character of biblical Hebrew

The "square" script in the Hebrew Bible/Old Testament derives from Aramaic.[9] Early extra-biblical Hebrew inscriptions look quite different.[10]

Jewish scholars of the fourth through tenth centuries A.D. carefully preserved both the written transmission and oral pronunciation of biblical Hebrew. They earned the name *Masoretes* ("masters of the tradition").[11] So the text used today is called the *Masoretic text* or simply MT. It includes a system of vowel signs, or *Masoretic pointing*.[12]

Who Can Do It? The Difficulty of Biblical Hebrew

The challenge of biblical Hebrew

Many students find, much to their surprise and delight, that Hebrew is not particularly complicated. No less a language authority than Tyndale thought:

> The Greek tongue agreeth more with the English than with the Latin [which has no article]. And the properties of the Hebrew tongue agreeth a thousand times more with the English than with the Latin. The manner of speaking is both one; so that in a thousand places thou needest not but to translate into the English, word for word: when thou must seek a compass in the Latin.[13]

Fortunately, biblical Hebrew lacks noun case endings[14] — a major challenge in Greek! Nor are there abundant adjectives and adverbs or multiple verb tenses. Also, proper names (Abraham, David, Moses, Jerusalem) and common religious terms (amen, hallelujah, sabbath) are easily recognizable from English.

Still, biblical Hebrew is generally considered difficult. This apprehension stems from four factors: the Hebrew script, limited English loan-words, the mixed blessing of multifunctional forms, and irregular verb forms.[15] These roadblocks redirect many students to the alternate route offered in this book.

The first roadblock for English speakers is the Hebrew alphabet and vowel system. Besides looking like chicken scratch, Hebrew is written "backwards": right to left!

Yet a colleague's customary admonition may offer hope: "If hundreds of thousands of Israeli children can learn the alphabet, you surely can." Recall some initially frightful or challenging experience which became increasingly pleasurable, perhaps swimming or skiing; such can be your experience with this book's approach to Hebrew.

A second difficulty is that few Hebrew words have been adopted by English, compared with other source languages like Greek, Latin, French, and German. So when memorizing vocabulary or even looking at Hebrew words in a text, the power of association erupts less frequently. Common proper names provide only isolated relief.

Third, while the beginner welcomes Hebrew's limited number of language forms, multiple functions of those forms may confuse the progressing student. Apart from reliable guidance,[16] Hebrew can be a frustrating puzzle where the same piece fits in too many places.

Selecting between subject/object/adverbial functions for a single noun, for instance, may frustrate a student accustomed to English linear word order or Greek case endings. Using Psalm 127:2 as an example, "sleep" may not be *what* God gives His loved ones, but *when* He provides for them, that is, apart from their feverish labors.[17]

Lastly, the greatest bugaboo for traditional biblical Hebrew students is memorizing all the irregular verb forms. While the verb system itself is logical and formally uncomplicated, many individual exceptions occur.

The good news is: This book offers a route that bypasses these roadblocks (apart from some initial wrestling with the alphabet)! Provided you have a fair grasp of English grammar, *you* can learn to use biblical Hebrew in ministry.

Two approaches

1. The traditional approach

Language teachers designate different language proficiency levels, or reading capability levels, apart from speaking fluency.[18] The traditional seminary approach to biblical Hebrew, requiring at least two years, aims for professional mastery or even full reading proficiency. This approach emphasizes memorization of vocabulary and all irregular verb forms, to reduce reliance on dictionaries or other language resources.

When I was a seminary student in the late seventies, all biblical Hebrew analytical tools were forbidden. I was instructed to look at an English translation only as a last resort! The ideal was to so thoroughly learn the language that any translation work (a form of interpretation) would be my own, shaped by the Hebrew text itself.

This traditional approach is time-consuming, rigorous, and expensive. Relying on delayed gratification and bordering on overkill, the acquired language skills are easily lost apart from regular use.

Perhaps the greatest critique of the traditional approach is the number of students who have abandoned hope of expounding the Old Testament. Far too many have answered the traditional approach's call of "All or nothing" by saying "(I'll do) nothing."

Today's busy prospective students are asking, "How much biblical Hebrew is needed?" rather than "How much is biblical Hebrew needed?" While the traditional approach works for some, many seek a better way.

2. The tool-based approach

An alternative practical approach, offered in this book, legitimizes elementary proficiency — the alphabet and some basic concepts — as a starting point, encouraging reliance on language tools. For many, this approach is the answer to the prayer voiced by a child:

Dear God,

Did you have as much trouble learning Hebrew as I am? Are there any easy ways to do it? I know you talk English too, so I am writing in English.

Respectfully, Jerome[19]

At the least, a tool-based approach overcomes inertia and eases groundless fears. (In language study, *un*familiarity breeds contempt.) According to my students, a tool-based approach also stimulates their hunger to learn and use more Hebrew — a striking contrast to the dulled motivation in the traditional approach!

Students who depend on scholarly resources and focus on exposition have a head start toward the right goal. Unquestionably, Hebrew is most productive in ministry when learned well and used correctly. With the help of the language tools and processes presented in this book, however, a student with minimal Hebrew proficiency can score solid exposition.

This book aims to make biblical Hebrew study a rewarding habit rather than a recurring headache and a productive process rather than a perpetual pain. While to misuse or abuse biblical Hebrew is a foul, to ignore biblical Hebrew is too great a forfeit.

Where Are We Going?
What to Expect from This Book

Although you should tailor your study to your own background and aims, this book can lead you from the Hebrew alphabet to the preaching application of biblical Hebrew texts. It presupposes no prior knowledge of Hebrew; a tool-based approach can begin with minimal language proficiency.

Where to Look

If you want...	See:
biblical Hebrew basics	Appendix
an overview of exegesis	Chapter 2
to use biblical Hebrew tools	Chapter 3
a word study process	Chapter 4
to interpret figures of speech	Chapter 5
to understand narrative	Chapter 6
to understand poetry	Chapter 7
to apply the Old Testament	Chapter 8
to craft a sermon	Chapter 9
to plan advanced study	Chapter 10

Action points at the end of each chapter progressively direct you through the Appendix containing biblical Hebrew basics. Also, Chapter 3 contains directions for using helpful resources. For some, these sections may be sufficient to begin using biblical Hebrew in ministry.

Additionally, this book provides direction for working with the biblical text itself. Guidance for blending exegesis and sermon preparation (Chapters 2, 8, 9) comes from essential hermeneutics and homiletics, respectively the crafts of interpretation and preaching.

A separate chapter (4) details the method and cautions for word studies — a primary interest for many beginning expositors. Chapter 5 helps decode figures of speech, and the two primary biblical Hebrew literary styles receive special attention (Chapters 6 and 7).

Numerous notes provide further explanation or resources for those who wish to go deeper. (Multiple works listed for a specific topic appear in a recommended order for consultation.)

Reading the examples, completing the action points, and working with the tools will provide experience and promote confidence in biblical Hebrew exegesis and exposition. Finally, Chapter 10 suggests ways to continue learning and advancing in biblical Hebrew proficiency.

Action Points

1. Can you think of problems ministers have because they don't use the biblical languages?

2. Discuss with several pastors the role biblical Hebrew plays in their ministries. Be prepared for a variety of responses!

3. Tell someone (real or imaginary) why you value biblical Hebrew in ministry.

4. Consider whether a tool-based approach building on elementary Hebrew proficiency is best for you. (This approach can also serve as a port of entry to more traditional language study.)

5. If you've never studied Hebrew, turn to the Appendix and begin learning the alphabet. Try singing it to the tune of "Home on the Range," while adding a final line "and the vowels await you." Sesame Street and Barney have their own musical versions of the Hebrew alphabet; Rabbi Joe Black's 1992 VHS concert tape "Sing Me a Story" includes "Aleph Bet Boogie."

6. Scan the Appendix. Action Points in upcoming chapters assign study of sections other than the alphabet.

Notes

1. As defined in Chapter 5, an idiom is "a language-specific expression whose meaning cannot be determined simply from the meaning of its parts." See Chapter 5, Note 12, for samples and bibliography.

2. Horn suggests: "There was a Babylonian verb *babalu*, 'to scatter,' or 'to disappear,' that may have been the basis of this name [Babel]. The later Babylonians naturally were not proud of such a meaning for the name of their city, and explained it in a different way. By dividing the name into *bab*, 'port' and *ilu*, 'god,' they explained its meaning to be 'port of god'" (Siegfried H. Horn, *The Spade Confirms the Book* [Washington, DC: Review and Herald, 1980], 56).

3. Simplified Hebrew transliteration is used here. For more word-plays and the structure of Genesis 11:1-9, as well as significant historical details, see Allen P. Ross, *Creation and Blessing* (Grand Rapids: Baker, 1988), 234-37.

4. "Languages are the sheath which hides the Sword of the Spirit ... so although the faith of the gospel may be proclaimed without the knowledge of the languages, the preaching will be feeble and ineffective. But where the languages are studied, the proclamation will be fresh and powerful, the Scriptures will be searched, and a faith will be constantly rediscovered through ever new words and deeds" (Luther, cited on the book jacket cover of Kendell H. Easley, *User-Friendly Greek* [Nashville, TN: Broadman & Holman, 1994]).

5. Jacob Milgrom, "An Amputated Bible, Peradventure?" *Bible Review* 10:4 (1994): 17.

6. Pinchas E. Lapide, *Hebrew in the Church* (Grand Rapids: Eerdmans, 1984), frontispiece.

7. Lapide, *Hebrew in the Church*, 202.

8. Sabatino Moscati, ed., *An Introduction to the Comparative Grammar of the Semitic Languages* (Wiesbaden: Harrassowitz, 1980), 1. Semitic languages are divided into eastern, northwestern, and southern regions. The classical Hebrew in the Bible is a northwestern Semitic Canaanite dialect. Some scholars describe the Semitic languages as related dialects rather than a language group. Besides standard reference works, consult H. L. Ginsberg, "The Northwest Semitic Languages," in *The World History of the Jewish People*, ed. Benjamin Mazar, et al. (New Brunswick: Rutgers University, 1970), 2:102-24; William L. Moran and S. J. Moran, "The Hebrew Language in Its Northwest Semitic Background," in *The Bible and the Ancient Near East*, ed. G.

Ernest Wright (Garden City: Doubleday, 1961), 54-72; and Edward Ullendorff, "What Is a Semitic Language?" *Orientalia* 27 (1958): 66-75.

9. In fact, five parts of the Old Testament are in Aramaic: two words in Gn 31:47; Ezr 4:8—6:18, 7:12—26; Jr 10:11; Dn 2:4b—7:28.

10. Klaas A. D. Smelik, *Writings from Ancient Israel* (Louisville, KY: Westminster/John Knox, 1991) provides an introduction, drawing, translation, and discussion of ancient Hebrew inscriptions, within a cultural context, with bibliography. John C. L. Gibson, *Textbook of Syrian Semitic Inscriptions: Volume 1: Hebrew and Moabite Inscriptions* (Oxford: Clarendon, 1971) provides inscriptions in the square script, along with an introduction and philological notes. Or see John H. Eaton, *Readings in Biblical Hebrew I* (Birmingham: Birmingham University, 1982), 114-23. For periodical references, consult Robert W. Suder, *Hebrew Inscriptions* (Susquehanna University, 1984).

11. For a summary of the work of the Masoretes, see A. S. van der Woude, ed., *The World of the Bible* (Grand Rapids: Eerdmans, 1986), 158-64. Standard references are Sid Z. Leiman, ed., *The Canon and Masorah of the Hebrew Bible* (New York: Ktav, 1974); and Christian D. Ginsburg, *Introduction to the Massoretico-Critical Edition of the Hebrew Bible*, repr. of 1879 ed. (New York: Ktav, 1966).

12. The Appendix lists the vowels. The Masoretes also added a system of accent signs.

13. Bruce K. Waltke and M. O'Connor, *An Introduction to Biblical Hebrew Syntax* (Winona Lake, IN: Eisenbrauns, 1990), 236n2.

14. *Case* refers to the relation of nouns (or other nominals like pronouns, adjectives, or participles) to other words in a sentence. For example, a noun functioning as a subject is said to be in the nominative case. While Hebrew nouns function in ways often similar to other languages, these relations are not marked by special changes in a noun's form. Biblical Greek has no less than twenty-four noun case endings which are generally required memory work for students.

15. Henri Fleisch suggests, "Hebrew is not a difficult language but one where one finds some difficulties" (cited by Waltke and O'Connor, *An Introduction to Biblical Hebrew Syntax*, 54n23).

16. Chapters 3 and 10 suggest some reliable guides.

17. Rather than understanding the noun as the direct object and perhaps picturing God as a heavenly Sandman, the second suggestion understands the noun to function adverbially, "while they

sleep." The context favors the latter view by presenting God as the Source of protection, possessions, and progeny. For a technical summary of different views and another suggestion entirely, see Leslie C. Allen, *Psalms 101—150*, Word Biblical Commentary 21 (Waco: Word, 1983), 176n2f.

18. Chapter 10 further outlines the concept of proficiency levels.
19. Eric Marshall and Stuart Hample, *Children's Letters to God* (New York: Pocket, 1966), unpaged.

Chapter 2

The Map:
The Process of Hebrew Exegesis

Objectives: After reading this chapter, you should be able to:
1. Walk through a three-phase process for Biblical Hebrew exegesis.
2. Begin to use this process in an exegetical study.
3. Identify some helpful commentaries, periodicals, and bibliographic resources.

Someone said, "If you don't know where you're going, you'll end up somewhere else." Knowing where you are going — as well as how to get there, and highlights and pitfalls along the way — fosters purposefulness, increases enjoyment, and ensures arrival.

This chapter maps out the exegetical process, presenting steps for the profitable use of biblical Hebrew in ministry. While subsequent chapters serve as guides along the path, the map serves as a constant reference.

Besides marking the general path, maps are often useful when you are in the thick of things. On the other hand, if you are merely planning a brief excursion (for example, you

are interested only in word studies), or if you have frequently made a similar journey (in New Testament studies),
a map may be unnecessary. You may simply wish to
acquaint yourself with the affable travel companions
introduced at the end of this chapter.

Exegesis is "the process by which one comes to
understand a text."[1] A limited view of exegesis seeks the
text's *meaning* for its original audience. A broader view of
exegesis also includes the text's *significance* for others.

According to the broader view, exegetical study poses
three questions:

1. Do I know where my text fits biblically?
2. Am I really certain about what the text is saying?
3. Could anyone benefit from what I have to say about the
    text?[2]

To rephrase these questions methodically: How do you
approach the text? How do you analyze the text? How do
you assimilate and apply the text? These questions represent
three phases of exegesis: overview study, intensive study,
and extensive study.

Interaction between these phases prevents a strictly linear
journey. Your view of the whole affects how you see the
parts, while your perception of the details refines your view
of the whole, and so on. This spiralling refinement of
understanding throughout the process of interpretation is
called *the hermeneutical spiral.*

Two signs along the exegetical path warn travelers.
First, presupposing the text *is* applicable (2 Tm 3:16-17)
does not permit predetermining a specific application (or
interpretation). Second, if a specific application motivates
exegesis, study of the text may require modifications to that
application, or even the selection of a different text altogether. Ignoring these warnings leads down a different path,
the path of eisegesis. *Eisegesis* reads *into* the text something
it does not mean or signify.

Overview Study: Approaching the Text

Once you have chosen a biblical text for study, how should you begin?

Establish the book context.

Preliminary reading(s) of the book in English, or in an interlinear, orient the text. Record your initial observations about tone, repetitions, and structure.

Compose a preliminary idea of the book's theme and purpose. The *book theme* is a single-sentence summary of the content, or *what* the book is about.[3] State the book's subject (what it is talking about) and complement (what it is saying about that subject). The combination of the subject and complement form the *big idea*. A sample big idea for the book of Job is "The proper response of the righteous in suffering is humble faith in a transcendent God who is loving, omniscient, and omnipotent."

The *purpose statement* explains the intent, or *why* the author wrote the book. Frame the purpose statement as a "to do X" phrase. An example from the book of Job might be "to encourage the praise of God in the midst of suffering."

Trace the argument, namely, the advancement of the theme and purpose through each major section of the book. Assigning paragraph or chapter titles, or composing book charts, aids toward this end.[4]

Establish the boundaries of your text within the book (*delimitation*).[5] Do you find a clear beginning and ending bracketing a cohesive topic? Look for binders (repetitions, continuities, pronouns, or conjunctions), or dividers (introductory or concluding conjunctions or adverbs, or changes in topic or setting). Compare the divisions in the Hebrew Bible and in various English translations.

Examine the historical context.

Look for words, persons, places, times, events or ideas that might establish the text's historical setting. Old Testament introductions[6] or handbooks,[7] commentaries,[8] history surveys,[9] Bible dictionaries,[10] Bible encyclopedias,[11] atlases,[12] cultural studies,[13] archaeological studies,[14] study Bibles,[15] and related Old Testament passages shed light on a text's historical background. Compile information regarding authorship, date, social and religious culture, geography, and history. Historical detail may impact exegesis, yet critically evaluate differing opinions and exercise caution in historical reconstructions.

Edom was a rugged area with mountain peaks over 5,000 feet high. In the conduct of ancient warfare, such terrain and high ground was very secure. This historical context informs the Lord's declaration, "Though you soar like the eagle and make your nest among the stars, from there I will bring you down" (Obadiah 4).

Intensive Study: Analyzing the Text

Having gained an overview of the text, what specifics merit detailed study?

Literary analysis comprises the type of literature, major structuring devices in a text, and the immediately surrounding literary context, namely, the preceding and following paragraphs.

No one reads a newspaper account, a love letter, a novel, and a legal brief in precisely the same manner. These different types of literature require different reading strategies. Similarly, the Bible contains various types of literature, or *genres*, which impact interpretation.[16] (Chapters 6 and 7 discuss narrative and poetry.)

Observe the biblical text's content, mood, structure, and context.

Track relations between clauses and identify the main, supporting, and summary sentences in each paragraph. You might try copying the text and presenting it a way that reflects and emphasizes the major structures.[17] Then compose a tentative statement of the text's theme and purpose within its context.

Literary patterning appears clearly in Amos 1:3—2:16. Judgment oracles against eight nations begin with the same formula "Thus says the Lord, 'For three transgressions of nation X and for four I will not relent.'" Lexical and thematic ties link the first six oracles in a stair-step fashion ("exiled...exiled to Edom...brotherhood...sword...ripped open"). These oracles lead to the primary targets, Judah and especially Israel, as shown by the proportionately enlarged last oracle. Imagine the sermon-shock for the Israelites who had probably cheered and "Amen"-ed the first pronouncements.

Textual analysis establishes the very words of the text. The method of Old Testament textual criticism shares much with New Testament textual criticism, but the materials differ significantly in the number and nature of textual witnesses.

Beginning exegetes depend heavily upon Bible translations, commentaries, and other sources, and defer independent textual analysis for advanced study.[18] Differences in English translations and marginal notes in Bibles often point to potential textual research.

Grammatical/Syntactical analysis classifies words by parts of speech (such as nouns and verbs), sentence roles (like subject and object), relations (like coordination and subordination), denominators (like person, gender, and number), and specific functions (for example, a verb indicating a present or future situation). *Grammar* is the study of a language, including its sounds (phonology), forms of words (morphology), and their arrangement into phrases, clauses, and sentences (syntax). *Grammars* are books devoted to this topic.

With the help of tools and grammars such as those listed in Chapters 3 and 10, identify and classify the specific functions of words. Then identify and classify clauses. Note any variations in word order signalling special emphases.[19]

The lead verb in Genesis 2:19 could represent a past perfect situation, as translated by the New International Version: "Now the Lord God *had formed* (all the animals) ... and brought them to the man." Recognizing this attested grammatical function[20] clarifies the narrative sequence. It also relieves a supposed contradiction with the more generalized creation story, which recounts humanity's creation after the animals (1:20-26).

Lexical analysis treats the meanings of words and figures of speech.

Chapter 4 discusses in detail the tools, procedures, and cautions for doing biblical Hebrew word studies. Identify significant words, especially repeated words, rare words, unclear words, or theologically-loaded words (like "grace," "blessing," "praise"). Then locate these words in lexicons. Examine some biblical references listed there or in a concordance, especially seeking concrete, non-theological uses of the word. Conclude by specifying the word's meaning in your text. If you have the time and inclination, do an extended word study following the pattern presented in Chapter 4.

Chapter 5 presents a method for decoding figures of speech. Identify, classify, and explain any figures of speech. Figures can impact both interpretation and application. For example, "soul" sometimes stands for the person, by way of substituting a part for the whole. Recognizing this figurative use might prevent a restrictive view of "soul-winning" that denigrates people's mental, physical, emotional, and social concerns.

Theological analysis correlates the teaching of the text with other areas of theology. Compare the teaching of the text with other revelation. Earlier revelation may inform or infuse the meaning of the text; Kaiser calls this *the analogy of [antecedent] Scripture*. Later revelation may modify or enlighten earlier revelation. (Chapter 8, "Bridging the Culture Gap," provides examples and discusses a theological framework.) Compare later related Old Testament references (*inner exegesis*) as well as New Testament references.

Resolve theological tensions or conflicts that appear in the text. Finally, determine the contribution of the text to biblical and systematic theology. *Biblical theology* examines a specific portion of the Bible in its progressive development, inductively seeking themes, emphases, and organizational categories within that specific biblical portion.[21] *Systematic theology*, based on the total biblical revelation without specific concern for its progressive development, seeks to organize biblical truth in logical and philosophical categories.[22]

"Jacob have I [God] loved, yet Esau I have hated" (Ml 1:2-3) raises questions about God's justice and ability to have emotions. But "love" and "hate" used side by side in Hebrew describe comparison; they are relative terms (Gn 29:30-31; Dt 21:15-17). Malachi 1:2-3 focuses on God's choice of Israel (Jacob) for His purposes, and that election occurred before Jacob and Esau were even born (Gn 25:23; Rm 9:11-13). So this text contributes to understanding both the character of God and the nature of salvation.

Critical analysis employs methods of biblical scholarship promoted over the last several centuries. Advancing students examine the value and use of these methods, which can differ radically in posing and answering questions for biblical texts. A recent anthology discusses thirteen critical methods: historical, source, tradition-historical, form, redaction, social-scientific, canonical, rhetorical, structural, narrative, reader-response, poststructuralist, and feminist criticism.[23] Chapters 6 and 7 ("The Artistry of Biblical Hebrew") employ some elements of modified critical approaches.

Extensive Study: Assimilating and Applying the Text

Having torn apart the text through detailed analysis, you need to pull it together again and share the significance of your study with others.

Assimilating the text

Correlate the particulars of your study into a unified whole. Restate the textual big idea and show how that fits with the book's overall message. Restate the author's purpose for the text and show how that fits with the book's overall purpose.

Time permitting, you may wish to check your synthesis against the history of interpretation of the text. You are then ready to prepare a textual outline that develops the content of the textual idea.

Applying the text

Personal application (devotional, doctrinal, and dutiful), public application (sharable and general), and preaching application are three ways of applying a text. Establish principles and make specific applications from the text.

Consider how to creatively communicate the meaning and significance of the text to others. Chapters 8 and 9 ("From Text to Life") discuss these processes, specifically, "Bridging the Culture Gap" and "Bridging the Communication Gap."

Bon Voyage

The map presents three primary sites — overview, intensive study, and extensive study — and basic steps along the exegetical journey.[24] Although the map presents a stylized journey, each biblical text offers the exegete a unique experience.

The next pages offer a pocket version of the map — an exegetical worksheet.[25] Then the subject of travel companions, otherwise known as commentaries, deserves comment.

A step at a time makes for good walking. Do not settle down at any place on the way; keep moving toward your destination of using biblical Hebrew in ministry.

Exegetical Worksheet

First Phase: *Overview Study: Approaching the Text*

Step 1.   Establish the book context.

Step 2.   Examine the historical context.

Second Phase: *Intensive Study: Analyzing the Text*

Step 3.   Analyze the literary context (genre, structure, and immediate context).

Step 4.   Resolve significant text critical issues.

Step 5.   Examine the grammar and syntax.

Step 6.   Define significant words or figures of speech.

Step 7.   Determine the text's theological contribution.

[Optional Step: Employ critical methods.]

Third Phase: *Extensive Study: Assimilating and Applying the Text*

Step 8.   Form the textual idea, purpose, and outline.

Step 9.   Form a sermon idea, purpose, and outline.

Using Commentaries

Good commentaries make good companions on the exegetical journey. They may even function as seasoned tour guides, pointing out highlights and warning of dangers.

While purely inductive Bible study is fine for personal study, those who presume to instruct God's people should consult commentaries. Spurgeon admonishes:

> In order to be able to expound the Scriptures, ...you will need to be familiar with the commentators: ...Of course, you are not such wiseacres as to think or say that you can expound the Scripture without assistance from the works of divine and learned men who have labored before you in the field of exposition.... It seems odd that certain men who talk so much of what the Holy Spirit reveals to themselves, should think so little of what He has revealed to others.[26]

The role of commentaries

Exegetes disagree over the role of commentaries. Some consult commentaries from the beginning of the process. Others only check commentaries for revision of their own work.

Checking commentaries at the end allows the text to preform the exegete's ideas and enhances the joy of personal discovery. This approach particularly benefits beginning Bible students or those exploring a text for the first time. On the other hand, consulting commentaries along the way saves time since commentaries note key observations and issues.

Whichever approach you choose, mature Bible students and busy ministers guiltlessly benefit from the judicious use of good commentaries.

The variety of commentaries

A variety of commentaries proliferate as commentators emphasize particular steps in the process of exegesis. Clearly, good commentaries can be useful in each of the three phases and the different individual steps. If you highly value or need extra help in any one area, you will gravitate toward that type of commentary. Beyond that, commentaries differ in theological perspective, thoroughness, recency, and bibliographic information.[27]

Recommended commentaries. Purchase the *best individual volumes* after *previewing*. Besides the recommendations in the following charts, consult commentary guidebooks[28] and reviews of books.[29]

Conservative Commentaries

Series	
	Tyndale Old Testament Commentaries (brief, synthetic)
	Expositor's Bible Commentary (recent bibliography; expositionally oriented)
	Word Biblical Commentary (substantive bibliography, often detailed; sometimes less conservative)
	New International Commentary on the Old Testament (some excellent individual volumes)
	Keil and Delitzsch (old and verbose; emphasizes grammar and word studies; helpful for synthesis)
	Soncino (Jewish scholarship)
	Mastering the Old Testament (formerly the Communicator's Commentary; homiletically oriented; the quality varies)
	The Bible Speaks Today (homiletically and applicationally oriented)
Single-volume	
	Bible Knowledge Commentary: Old Testament (by Dallas Theological Seminary faculty)
	New Bible Commentary: 21st Century Edition (also the earlier *New Bible Commentary: Revised*)
	Zondervan NIV Bible Commentary: Volume 1: Old Testament (affordable abridgement of *Expositor's Bible Commentary*)

Non-conservative Commentaries
(Informative and often employing critical methods.)

Series
Anchor Bible (more recent; incomplete)
Hermeneia (technical)
Interpreter's Bible (older)
New Century Bible (continuing paperback series; some fine volumes)
International Critical Commentary (old; yet volumes are gradually being re-written)
Continental Commentary (several fine, erudite initial offerings)
Knox Preaching Guides (homiletically oriented; the quality varies)

Single-volume
Harper's Bible Commentary (by Society of Biblical Literature scholars)
New Jerome Biblical Commentary (Roman Catholic)

Recommended periodicals. Periodical articles often cover much the same ground as commentaries and contain state-of-the-art research. Expositors will want to explore and then subscribe to one or more. Periodical indexes point to articles on specific texts or topics.[30]

The next chart presents about two dozen useful periodicals.[31]

Recommended Periodicals

Periodical	Sponsor	Theology
Andrews University Seminary Studies	Andrews University	Seventh-Day Adventist
Asbury Theol. Journal	Asbury Seminary	Methodist
Bible Review	independent	anti-conservative
The Bible Today	Liturgical	Roman Catholic
Bible Translator	United Bible Societies	N/A[32]
Biblical Archaeology Review	independent publication	N/A
Biblical Illustrator	S. Baptist Convention	Baptist
Bibliotheca Sacra[33]	Dallas Theol. Seminary	evangelical
Bulletin for Biblical Research	Institute for Biblical Research	conservative
Catholic Biblical Quarterly	Catholic Biblical Association	Roman Catholic
Concordia Journal	Concordia Seminary	Lutheran
Criswell Theol. Review	Criswell College	evangelical
Expository Times	T. & T. Clark	non-conservative
Hebrew Union College Annual	Hebrew Union College	Jewish
Interpretation	Union Theol. Seminary	non-conservative
Jewish Quarterly Review	Annenberg Research Institute	Jewish
Journal for the Study of the Old Testament	Sheffield Academic	conservative
Journal of Biblical Literature	Society of Biblical Literature	non-conservative
Journal of Evangelical Theological Society	Evangelical Theological Society	evangelical
Master's Seminary Journal	Master's Seminary	evangelical
Old Testament Abstracts	Catholic Biblical Assn.	N/A
Preaching	independent	conservative
Review and Expositor	Southern Baptist Theological Seminary	Baptist
Southwestern Journal of Theology	Southwestern Baptist Theological Seminary	Baptist
Trinity Journal	Trinity Evangelical Divinity School	evangelical
Tyndale Bulletin	Tyndale House	conservative
Westminster Theological Journal	Westminster Theological Seminary	Reformed

Action Points

1. Decide whether you would delete, add, or rearrange any of the proposed steps in the exegetical process. If so, create your own revised exegetical worksheet. If the proposed process is not far from your own, photocopy the provided worksheet for use in exegesis.

2. Examine and consider purchasing Stuart (Douglas Stuart, *A Guide to Selecting and Using Bible Commentaries* [Dallas: Word, 1991]) or another inexpensive commentary guide (see Note 28).

3. Scan and evaluate several commentaries. Ideally this means spending time in a library and focusing on a particular book or text that you plan to study and teach or preach soon. For which phase (or step) in the exegetical process would they be most helpful? Which ones should be on your priority purchase list?

4. Learn the Hebrew vowel signs and sounds. (See "Vowels" in the Appendix.)

5. Read the section on "Particles" in the Appendix.

6. Practice exegesis on a text, using the exegetical worksheet (or your modified version) and some resources mentioned in this chapter's notes. Or do this after reading Chapters 4-9.

Notes (The bibliography contains full publication data for individual books mentioned in these notes.)

1   L. E. Keck and G. M. Tucker, "Exegesis" in Crim, 296.

2.   Black, *Using New Testament Greek in Ministry*, 64.

3.   Robinson, *Biblical Preaching*, explains, illustrates, and provides practice on developing big idea statements. See also Chapter 9.

4.   Jensen, *Independent Bible Study*, 106-113.

5.   Kaiser provides substantive treatment and examples of delimitation under the rubric "sectional context," although his final example of 1 Corinthians 14:34-35 is suspect (*Exegetical Theology*, 71-77).

6.   Hill and Walton provide a basic conservative survey. Merrill focuses on history. Harrison's introduction is valuable yet verbose. Archer is still a favorite. A fine, recent non-conservative introduction is by Rendtorff.

7.   Beginners appreciate the revised Unger handbook. Related works such as *The World of the Bible*, edited by van der Woude, provide valuable historical background.

8.   The final section in this chapter addresses commentaries. See also Danker, *Multipurpose Tools*, 282-307; Fee and Stuart, *How to Read the Bible*, 246-54; or Goodrick, 13:2-13:7.

9.   Merrill, *Kingdom of Priests* is excellent. Wood, and Davis and Whitcomb are two conservative works. Bright and the works by Kitchen retain value. Non-conservative is Hayes and Miller.

10.   Recent are *The Anchor Bible Dictionary*, edited by Freedman; and the *New Bible Dictionary*, edited by Packer, et al. Still useful is *Interpreter's*, edited by Buttrick; and its supplement, edited by Crim. Older works are those by Hastings; and Unger. Metzger and Coogan edited a similar type of work.

11.   Especially the *International Standard Bible Encyclopedia*, edited by Bromiley; and the *Zondervan Pictorial*, edited by Tenney.

12.   The *Macmillan Bible Atlas* edited by Aharoni, et al., is quite useful. Other helpful atlases are by Baly; Beitzel; Freeman-Grenville; May; Pritchard; Rasmussen; and Paterson, et al.

13.   For cultural aspects, see Thompson; Wight and Gower; Matthews; Matthews and Benjamin; Freeman; Heaton; de Vaux; van der Woude; and Miller.

14.   Archaeological encyclopedias include those edited by conservatives Blaiklock and Harrison; Avi-Yonah and Stern; and Negev. Fritz provides a helpful, brief introduction. More technical and non-conservative are Aharoni; Ben-Tor; Mazar; and Murphy-O'Connor. Biblical correlations are emphasized by conservatives Free; Thompson; Horn; Walton; Livingston; and Winton

Thomas (*Documents*). Pritchard is invaluable, as is the non-conservative work by Keel. Masom and Alexander provide pictures with conservative commentary by Millard, and Mazar (*Views*) contains many fine pictures.

15. Ryrie has his own evangelical and dispensational study Bible. Barker's is evangelical and based on the NIV. Metzger and Murphy provide conservative commentary on the NRSV. Meeks edited the non-conservative *The HarperCollins Study Bible*.

16. For genres, consult the introductory sections of commentaries or see conservative works such as Ryken and Longman; Stein; Inch and Bullock; or Ryken. Non-conservative, but helpful discussions of genre are found in Alter and Kermode; or Eissfeldt.

17. A commonly used Greek diagramming method (John D. Grassmick, *Principles and Practices of Greek Exegesis* [Dallas, TX: Dallas Theological Seminary, 1974]) is difficult and isolates words and sentences, resulting in fragmented texts and non-synthetic outlines. This diagramming method dates back at least to nineteenth century English grammarians like William Dwight Whitney. Such diagramming provides even less help for biblical Hebrew, but is presented by Lee Kantenwein, *Diagrammatical Analysis*. (Warsaw, IN: Lee Kantenwein, 1979). More helpful and less choppy diagramming is used by Walter C. Kaiser, Jr., *Toward an Exegetical Theology* (Grand Rapids: Baker, 1981), 165-73; and applied in his commentary, *Malachi*. (Grand Rapids: Baker, 1984), 115-37. Simpler textual re-writing and paragraph flow charting are the trends in Greek and Hebrew exegesis; see Klein, Blomberg, and Hubbard, 207-210; Wayne McDill, *The 12 Essential Skills for Great Preaching* (Nashville: Broadman & Holman, 1994), 27-39; Richard A. Young, *Intermediate New Testament Greek* (Nashville: Broadman & Holman, 1994), 205-20, 267-77; and Kendell H. Easley, *User-Friendly Greek* (Nashville, TN: Broadman & Holman, 1994).

18. See text critical introductions by Brotzman; McCarter; Klein; Harrison, et al.; or Weingreen. Tov is the standard treatment, supplanting Würthwein. Guides to the critical apparatus are Scott; Vasholz; and Wonneberger. Barthélmy, et al. [HOTTP] helpfully rank textual variants in a fashion similar to the UBS Greek New Testament and include further explanation. Archer and Chirichigno examine *Old Testament Quotations in the New Testament*.

19. Initially consult the appendix and the tools mentioned in Chapter 3. Then see technical commentaries and standard grammars such as listed in Chapter 10.

20.   Waltke and O'Connor, 552-53. For the contrary view disallowing the lead verb in Genesis 2:19 as past perfect, see Randall Buth, "Methodological Collision between Source Criticism and Discourse Analysis," in *Biblical Hebrew and Discourse Linguistics*, ed. Robert D. Bergen (Winona Lake, IN: Eisenbrauns, 1994), 148-49.

21.   For the history and issues in biblical theology, see Hasel; Hayes and Prussner; Goldingay; Ollenburger, et al.; or Smith. Helpful introductory books are by Zuck; Sailhamer; Kaiser; and Martens. Standards are Eichrodt; von Rad; and Childs. See Clines on the Pentateuch and Kraus on the Psalms. Related is Kaiser (*Ethics*).

22.   Accessible introductory works on systematic theology are Ryrie; Boice; and Henry. Elwell offers a popular reference work and Enns surveys biblical, systematic, historical, dogmatic, and contemporary theology. Three good recent systematic theologies are Erickson; Lewis and Demarest; and Grudem. Standard Reformed works are McNeill/Calvin; Bavinck; Berkhof; Buswell; and Shedd; Berkouwer has a series. Thiessen is a premillennial Baptist; Chafer, dispensational. Watson represents Arminianism; Wiley and Carter, Wesleyanism. Pieper is Lutheran; Ott, Catholic.

23.   McKenzie and Haynes provide examples from the Old and New Testaments, along with suggested reading. See also Hayes and Holladay, or individual volumes in the Fortress Guides to Scholarship series edited by Gene M. Tucker. Klein, Blomberg, and Hubbard, 427-57 provides an evaluation of biblical criticisms.

24.   Popular works on general hermeneutics are Fee and Stuart; Zuck; Sproul; and Henrichsen. Practical general methods may be found in Traina; Wald; and Jensen. The best recent conservative hermeneutics textbooks are Osborne; Klein, Blomberg, and Hubbard; and Kaiser and Silva. Other useful hermeneutics textbooks by conservatives are Johnson; Tate; Virkler; and McQuilkin. Older, yet worth consulting, are Ramm; Terry; and Mickelsen. For more technical and theoretical hermeneutics, look at Silva; Hirsch; Barton; Baker; and Thiselton. Two guides on the Old Testament exegetical process are Stuart; and Kaiser. To understand errors to avoid in exegesis, see Carson; and Sire. Knight and Tucker provide a recent survey of issues in Old Testament research.

25.   A similar worksheet for New Testament exegesis is found in Black, *Using New Testament Greek in Ministry*, 118-20.

26.   Cyril J. Barber, *The Minister's Library* (Grand Rapids: Baker, 1974), xi.

27. Lengthier discussions on evaluating commentaries include Fee and Stuart, 246-49; and Kaiser (*Malachi*), 147-57.
28. Worthy commentary guides include Stuart; and Glynn. Helpful are Longman; Childs; Moo; or Parker. Commentaries themselves make their own recommendations.
29. Besides separate book review sections in many periodicals, consult *Religion Index Two*, the annual *Society for Old Testament Study Book List*, and *Critical Review of Books in Religion*. For a general overview of books in the field, see Danker; Barber; Knight and Tucker; Holtz; or Dockery, Matthews, and Sloan.
30. Key periodical indexes are *Religion Index One* and *Elenchus Bibliographicus Biblicus*. A guide to using the latter is Paul F. Stuehrenberg, "Elenchus Elucidated," *EBB* 57 (1976): xlvi-xlviii. Hagner, 98-99 gives directions for using both indexes; see also Stuart (1984), 128-30. Key Old Testament bibliographies, indexes, and databases are discussed by Stephen G. Burnett, "Finding Bibliographic Resources in Old Testament Studies," *Bulletin of Higher Hebrew Education* 4 (1991): 80-86; and Ronald L. Giese, Jr., "Present Capabilities for Classical Hebrew Bibliography," *Bulletin of Higher Hebrew Education* 4 (1991): 68-72. Theological libraries may have the CD-Rom versions of the ATLA Religion Database, or the Religion Indexes: RIO/RIT/IBRR, 1975-, or Biblical Studies (ATLA Religion Database, Special Series).
31. *Biblica*, *Revue Biblique*, *Vetus Testamentum*, and *Zeitschrift für die alttestamentliche Wessenshaft*, while more technical and less accessible, often prove useful.
32. N/A means "not (readily) applicable" and here suggests that the aim of these publications makes theological labeling less than helpful.
33. Galaxie Software produces a single CD-Rom (for Windows or Macintosh) containing *Bibliotheca Sacra*, 1975-1994; phone 800-Galaxie.

Chapter 3

By the Books:
Using the Right Tools

Objectives: After reading this chapter, you should be able to:
  1. Name six primary tools for working with biblical
     Hebrew.
  2. Identify some commonly used tools.
  3. Use these tools to access desired information.

I recall an encounter with a leaking shower faucet. After a lengthy, valiant struggle, I succeeded in stopping the leak — temporarily. Yet when the plumber arrived, he quickly solved the problem using two special tools.

The right tools enable efficient, quality work, whether the task is plumbing or using biblical Hebrew in ministry. A practical approach, with minimal Hebrew proficiency, demands reliance on the proper tools.

The pragmatic Einstein, when asked his phone number, reportedly said, "I don't know. But I know where to find it."

The goal in a tool-based approach is not to become scholars, but to become better consumers of scholarship.

Over the long haul, the ability to access significant information in available resources often surpasses natural or learned abilities.

This chapter describes recommended books, providing full bibliographic data and instructions for using these books. Additional related or alternative tools receive attention, as does computer software. Consult chapters 2 and 10 for other useful resources.

The Basic Toolkit

The basic toolkit for practical Hebrew exegesis includes an Interlinear, an analytical tool, a lexicon, a concordance, a wordbook, and a grammar. A definition, description, and directions for use of each recommended tool follow.

An interlinear

Kohlenberger, John R., III, ed. *The NIV Interlinear Hebrew-English Old Testament,* Four Volumes in One. Grand Rapids: Zondervan, 1987. [Interlinear]

An *interlinear* provides a text with a translation beneath each line. This interlinear, besides a word-for-word translation beneath the Hebrew, presents the New International Version (NIV) in the margin.

The Interlinear arranges the biblical books as in English Bibles. Except for a few minor changes presented in brackets, the Hebrew text matches the standard critical Hebrew Bible (described later in the section on related tools).

Besides guiding the user to Hebrew words, the suggested English translation beneath the Hebrew (sometimes called a *gloss*) helps with grammatical analysis. Occasionally, it can mislead the unwary.[1]

For example, word-for-word translation can fragment word-groups, phrases, and sentences. Will everyone correctly assemble the Interlinear sub-text "on-hill-of holiness-of-you" as "on Your holy hill?" The same "literal" word-for-word equation can hide the multiple senses of words, synonymous constructions, and deliberate ambiguities.[2]

To use the Interlinear, locate a text by book-chapterverse, as in English. The marginal NIV translation provides a good starting point for locating a Hebrew text.

The Hebrew text and the corresponding English sub-text read from *right-to-left*. Still proceed top-to-bottom between lines of text.

An analytical tool

Owens, John Joseph. *Analytical Key to the Old Testament.* 4 vols. Grand Rapids: Baker, 1989-92. [AKOT]

An *analytical tool* provides lexical and grammatical information for words in a text, enabling a non-proficient reader to discern shades of meaning. Useful in determining the components of Hebrew words and as a basis of grammatical analysis, AKOT analyzes every word in the Hebrew text and cross-references the standard lexicon and grammar. Although any such work contains some errors and distortions,[3] this key resource largely supplants alternative analytical tools.

AKOT's analysis emphasizes traditional grammatical and morphological categories (rather than functional syntactic analysis), yet groupings of words frequently point in the direction of syntactic roles.

Morphology describes the forms of words, such as Hebrew noun endings indicating gender and number; AKOT provides this type of information. *Syntax* refers to word functions in relation to other words in a phrase, clause, or sentence. For example, a Hebrew noun may function as a subject, object, or adverbial modifier in a sentence; AKOT often does not provide such analysis.

AKOT and other tools often identify a proposed *root*. In Semitic languages a specific combination of letters, usually three, can express a general idea and is considered the source, or root, of related words. A rough comparison in English involves word sets like act-actor-acted-acting.

Words are easily located in AKOT by book-chapter-verse, in the order and form in the biblical text. An entry presents grammatical analysis, cross-references (and root, for verbs) in parentheses, and the Revised Standard Version or a more "literal" translation. Page numbers refer to the standard lexicon; numbers preceded by "GK" refer to paragraphs in the standard advanced reference grammar.

For future reference, note that AKOT's "conj." with a perfect tense may be functionally either a *waw* conjunctive or *waw* consecutive.[4]

A *lexicon*

Brown, Francis, S. R. Driver, and Charles A. Briggs. *The New Brown-Driver-Briggs-Gesenius Hebrew and English Lexicon with an Appendix Containing the Biblical Aramaic*. Peabody, MA: Hendrickson, 1979. [BDB]

A *lexicon* is an expanded dictionary that provides definitions and examples of the usage of words. BDB is the standard Hebrew lexicon. Twenty-three years in the making, BDB contains a wealth of information on Hebrew and Aramaic words used in the Bible. The new edition of BDB cross-references *Strong's Concordance*.

BDB has these drawbacks: (1) While generally reliable, it is old (1907). BDB is particularly dated for study of a word's early history and overemphasizes South Semitic, especially Arabic. (2) A liberal theological persuasion manifests itself frequently. Watch for assumptions of historical criticism (designating some texts as late, or "New Hebrew") and source criticism (identifying hypothetical sources behind the present biblical text, such as documents J, E, D, and P). (3) Predominantly listing words under a proposed root — rather than alphabetically — complicates locating specific words from a biblical text. The noun עֵצָה needs to be found in BDB under the root יעץ !

Hebrew words also take suffixes and prefixes due to change of person, number, gender, state, and tense, and may have prepositions, the conjunction, and the article prefixed. Some letters drop out altogether in certain usages! So the *textual form* of the Hebrew word in the Interlinear may substantially differ from the entry form in BDB (the *lexical form*).

Although BDB lists some irregular forms alphabetically (with internally cross-referenced index entries), entries appear by root — primarily by the verb when it occurs — and contain related words alphabetically arranged underneath. So students may need help from AKOT, which lists the page number for BDB's treatment of a specific textual form. Discussion of other resources for accessing BDB (Einspahr's *Index*, the *Parsing Guide,* or a cross-referenced concordance) follows subsequently.

The general format of a BDB entry includes: root or verb,[5] etymology,[6] morphology, and usage divided into verb patterns[7] and categories of meaning. Derivatives[8] appear in smaller type after the section on verb patterns or, if no verb forms occur in the Bible, after the etymology section.

The end of an entry is signalled by: 1) a new root, in larger type size, or 2) a listing of another form or forms, followed by "v." (= see the following root). Ignore outdated interspersed bibliographic information, except in cases of special interest.[9]

Locate BDB's comments on the specific use of the Hebrew word in your text. Compare the proposed meaning with other verses listed in that usage category. (BDB uses Hebrew verse numbers.[10]) Also survey the entire entry to check whether other categories of meaning fit your text.[11]

Note any obelus (dagger sign) at the start of an entry. This indicates "all biblical references are cited in this entry." Since such an entry lists every biblical use of the word, recourse to a concordance may be unnecessary.

Become familiar with BDB's guide to abbreviations (xiii-xix).[12]

A *concordance*

Wigram, George V. *The New Englishman's Hebrew Concordance: Coded to Strong's Concordance Numbering System.* Peabody, MA: Hendrikson, 1984. [Englishman's]

A *concordance* is "an alphabetically arranged index showing where in the text of a book or books each principal word is used."[13] Uses of biblical concordances include studying words, tracing a specific writer's emphases, constructing biblical theology, following progressive revelation, or identifying the historical significance of biblical allusions.

For beginning students, Englishman's concordance is an important tool for word studies. The new edition cross-references *Strong's Concordance.*

Englishman's displays the biblical uses of a Hebrew word with an English translation in context. Every major word appears alphabetically and verbs are separated into verb patterns.[14]

In earlier editions, the Hebrew to English index shows how a word has been translated. Also, the English to Hebrew index directs to synonyms and antonyms.

Locate the lexical form alphabetically and then the textual form underneath.

A *wordbook*

Harris, R. Laird, Gleason L. Archer, and Bruce K. Waltke, eds. *Theological Wordbook of the Old Testament.* 2 vols. Chicago: Moody, 1980. [TWOT]

A *wordbook* contains a series of word studies. TWOT is a helpful, affordable tool for word studies, representing a conservative theological perspective. It discusses words of theological significance, plus briefly defines all other words in BDB. Keyed to *Strong's Concordance*, TWOT contains over 1,400 articles by forty-three authors, plus some 400 subentries with definitions only.

Look up a word by its lexical form (not including vowels). A cross reference number will help locate an entry by root. Alternatively, an Index cross-referenced to Strong's provides another means of access.

A grammar

Williams, Ronald J. *Hebrew Syntax: An Outline.* 2d ed., Toronto: University of Toronto, 1976. [WHS]

Waltke, Bruce K. and M. O'Connor. *An Introduction to Biblical Hebrew Syntax.* Winona Lake, IN: Eisenbrauns, 1990. [IBHS]

A *grammar* describes how a language operates: typical word forms and functions, relations in sentences and discourses, and general rules for forming and using words. Appreciation for a grammar, even as for certain people, requires sensitivity and repeated association.[15]

WHS still may be the best "starter" reference grammar, quite helpful for particles. (*Particles*, in traditional grammar, include parts of speech — especially adverbial modifiers like prepositions — which are not grouped under the other two broad categories of words, namely, nouns and verbs.) Thoughtfully working through the examples will pay dividends.

However, students may quickly outgrow WHS' concise outline and want Waltke and O'Connor's excellent intermediate grammar, IBHS.[16] IBHS presents a contemporary linguistics perspective and contains extensive bibliographic information. A third corrected printing was issued in 1991.

The table of contents and subject and scripture indexes in IBHS lead to pertinent information.

Alternative and Related Tools

Since the end — using biblical Hebrew in ministry — justifies the means, and as a check on this author's biases, this section describes some alternative resources. If you have decided to use the recommended basic toolkit, you may want to skip ahead to the section on computer software.

Bible texts

In addition to the Hebrew text, consulting various translations can pinpoint problems, suggest different interpretations, and aid in determining meaning. Personal preferences often color evaluations of Bible translations.[17] The recommended Interlinear contains the New International Version [NIV].

Green, Jay P., ed. *The Interlinear Bible: Hebrew-Greek-English*. Peabody, MA: Hendrickson, 1986.

This alternative interlinear places Strong's *Concordance* reference numbers above the Hebrew and Greek words, yet some find the crowded format distracting. Although Strong's provides lexical and grammatical information, a more direct approach uses other tools.

Elliger, Kurt and Wilhelm Rudolf, eds. *Biblia Hebraica Stuttgartensia*. Stuttgart: German Bible Society, 1984. [BHS]

In conjunction with an interlinear, the Hebrew student should be aware of the current standard critical text. This more conservative revision of Kittel's earlier *Biblia Hebraica* [BHK] is available in large and small-size editions from the American Bible Society.

The highly-regarded Leningrad Hebrew manuscript, dated approximately A.D. 1000, serves as the textual basis. A cryptic critical apparatus lists major textual variants, their sources, and evaluative comments. BHS includes German, English, French, Latin, and Spanish versions of the preface.

Regular use of BHS may be reserved for advanced study.

The Comparative Study Bible. Grand Rapids: Zondervan, 1987.

The Complete Parallel Bible. New York: Oxford University, 1993.

Vaughan, Curtis, ed. *The Word: The Bible from Twenty-Six Translations.* Moss Point, MS: Mathis, 1993.

Kohlenberger, John R., III, ed. *The NIV Triglot Old Testament.* Grand Rapids: Zondervan, 1981.

Brenton, Lancelot C. L. *The Septuagint with Apocrypha: Greek and English.* Repr. of London: Samuel Bagster & Sons, 1851 ed., Grand Rapids: Zondervan, 1982.

Ximenes, Francisco, ed. *Biblia polyglotta.* Complutum, Spain: Industria Arnaldi Guillelmi de Brocario, 1514-17.

The Comparative Study Bible presents the King James Version, New American Standard Bible, NIV, and Amplified Bible in four columns to the double page. *The Complete Parallel Bible* presents four modern translations: New Revised Standard Version (1989), Revised English Bible (1989), New American Bible (1970), and the New Jerusalem Bible (1985). *The Word* uses the King James Version as its base text, and lists significant translation departures given in many English versions underneath.

The NIV Triglot presents the Hebrew (MT), Greek (Septuagint or LXX), and English (NIV), although it is has a limited text critical basis. Brenton's is similar, a parallel English-Greek LXX. *Biblia polyglotta* is old, yet still a convenient compilation of ancient versions.

Alternative analytical tools[18]

Einspahr, Bruce. *Index to the Brown, Driver and Briggs Hebrew Lexicon.* Rev. ed. Chicago: Moody, 1977. [Einspahr]
This index pinpoints the location in the standard lexicon for most words in the Hebrew text. However, Einspahr indexes only those words explicitly mentioned in BDB.

Usually words *not* indexed are very common words that can be located through AKOT or concordances. Unfortunately, Einspahr does not reflect the order or form of Hebrew words in a verse; lexical forms appear alphabetically, minus any vowels.

Einspahr's most valuable feature is the listing immediately after the BDB page reference. A/B/C/D refers to approximate imaginary quadrants on a page, visualized in the following manner:

$$\begin{array}{c|c} A & C \\ \hline B & D \end{array}$$

Check for your text and word by book-chapter-verse. Using Einspahr to locate the lexicon's view of a word's specific use saves time and eyesight (although scanning the entire BDB entry is a good habit to cultivate).

Davidson, Benjamin. *The Analytical Hebrew and Chaldee Lexicon.* Repr. of London: Samuel Bagster & Sons, 1850 ed. Grand Rapids: Zondervan, 1981. [Davidson]

Davidson lists alphabetically (omitting any prefixed conjunction *waw*) and analyzes all the biblical Hebrew forms. This older work contains some errors and proposed roots sometimes differ from more informed recent lexicons.

Beware of terminology differences for verb tenses:[19]

Davidson's Terms	Contemporary Terms
"pret" = preterite	perfect (or suffixed) tense
"fut" = future	imperfect OR one of the volitives
"pret… w conv.(conversive)"	*waw* consecutive plus perfect
"fut… w conv.(conversive)"	*waw* consecutive plus preterite

To use Davidson, simply look up the textual form alphabetically.[20]

Beall, Todd S., William A. Banks, and Colin Smith. *Old Testament Parsing Guide.* 2 vols. Chicago: Moody, 1986, 1990. [Parsing Guide]

Parsing describes the elements of a verb form. A complete parsing of a Hebrew verb includes its root, verb pattern, tense or mood, person, gender, and number, and any attached prefixes and/or suffixes.[21]

The Parsing Guide lists and parses verb forms in order of biblical occurrence, incorporating recent scholarship and providing ready access to BDB. Thus, the Parsing Guide shares benefits of both Davidson and Einspahr.

The Parsing Guide is particularly valuable for analyzing different functions of the conjunction on verbs. However, it deals only with verb forms and contains no Hebrew vowels. Also, the Parsing Guide's "wci" (*waw* consecutive imperfect) is better termed *waw* consecutive plus preterite.[22]

To use the Parsing Guide, look up the Scripture reference, find the consonants of the verb's textual form, and read across the columns.

Alternative lexicons

More recent lexicons serve as supplements or alternatives to BDB.

Koehler, Ludwig and Walter Baumgartner. *Lexicon in Veteris Testamenti Libros*. Leiden: Brill, 1958. [KB]
___. *Supplementum Ad Lexicon in Veteris Testamenti Libros*. Leiden: Brill, 1958.
Holladay, William L. *A Concise Hebrew and Aramaic Lexicon of the Old Testament*. Grand Rapids: Eerdmans, 1971.

Koehler and Baumgartner, originally written in German (1953), contains both English and German, and comes with a supplementary volume. KB, which was 40 years in the making, has been criticized for containing too many text critical emendations. Positively, KB alleviates some of the difficulties with BDB by providing more recent etymological information, listing entries alphabetically — or, for verbs, by root with alphabetic derivatives underneath — and seldom mentioning hypothetical sources (J/E/D/P). Further, common biblical words which can not be treated exhaustively are provided with frequency counts.

Holladay is a convenient abridgment of KB.[23] So it falls between a simple dictionary and a full lexicon. Holladay lists entries alphabetically and is relatively easy to use. Holladay omits bibliography, extensive citation of passages, and related foreign words (except for providing biblical Hebrew cognates for biblical Aramaic words).

Koehler, Ludwig, Walter Baumgartner, and J. J. Stamm, eds. *The Hebrew and Aramaic Lexicon of the Old Testament: The New Koehler/Baumgartner in English*. Translated and edited under the supervision of M. E. J. Richardson. Leiden: Brill, 1994-. [New KB]
Clines, David J. A., ed. *The Dictionary of Classical Hebrew: Part 1: Aleph*. Sheffield: Sheffield Academic, 1993. [DCH][24]

Two in-progress, expensive lexicons may also be useful.

The first volume of a four-volume English edition of KB is much more up-to-date than BDB. The New KB includes recently discovered cognates, Dead Sea Scroll material, and recent bibliography. Strict alphabetical organization simplifies locating textual forms.

The first of eight projected volumes designed to replace BDB, DCH includes data from Hebrew inscriptions, the Dead Sea Scrolls, and Ecclesiasticus. Alphabetical order (as well as mention of proposed root), morphological and syntactic breakdowns, the treatment of particles, and word frequencies are helpful features. While extensive, DCH is daunting and less helpful than other lexicons for determining specific meanings of Hebrew words.

Alternative concordances

Strong, James. *The New Strong's Exhaustive Concordance of the Bible*. Nashville: Nelson, 1984. [Strong's]

Popularly considered the standard Bible concordance, Strong's is an English-based concordance with numbered indexes for the biblical language words. The Hebrew Dictionary/Index does not provide frequency counts or divide verb usage according to verb patterns.

The new edition subdivides entries, gives full biblical book names and pronunciation for proper names, adds a topical index, and deletes the key-verse comparison chart.

Use of Strong's is more time-consuming than Englishman's: 1) Find the number assigned to the English word. 2) Look in the index to find the corresponding biblical language word. 3) Look up all the English translations listed in the index for that word and matching that number.

Young, Robert. *Analytical Concordance to the Bible*. Grand Rapids: Eerdmans, n.d. [Young's]

Young's is analytical in incorporating a break-down of the original language roots into the English word listing itself. So, taking the English word study route, some information appears more readily in Young's than in Strong's.

Young's has some similarities in format and use to *Englishman's*. For general word studies, first find the transliterated Hebrew word in the "Index-Lexicon to the Old Testament." English translation(s) and frequency counts appear there (as well as verb translations according to verb pattern). Then look up each of the English words to find the references for the Hebrew word. Collect synonyms by this same process.

Even-Shoshan, Abraham, ed. *A New Concordance of the Old Testament Using the Hebrew and Aramaic Text.* 2d ed. Grand Rapids: Baker, 1989. [Even-Shoshan]

Although almost entirely in Hebrew and daunting for beginners, Even-Shoshan contains a number of unparalleled features, such as ready frequency counts for different uses, common constructions using a particular word, and listed synonyms. The textual basis has minor variations from BHS. A helpful "Introduction" by John H. Sailhamer explains how to use the concordance.

Mandelkern, Solomon. *Veteris Testamenti Concordantiae: Hebraicae atque Chaldaicae.* Jerusalem: Schocken, 1967.

Lisowsky, Gerhard. *Konkordanz zum Hebräischen Alten Testament.* 2d ed. Stuttgart: Würtemburgische Bibelanstalt, 1958.

These two expensive, traditional concordances are not integral to a practical approach.

Mandelkern's concordance separately lists various forms, so its primary use is for tracing a particular grammatical form. Just a glance shows that the third masculine plural imperfect of אמן in Moses' objection ("What if they don't *believe* me?" Ex 4:1) recurs three times in the Lord's answer, namely, the bestowal of three authenticating signs (Ex 4:5, 8, 9).

Lisowsky unfortunately contains non-block Hebrew script, completely Hebrew citations in context, handprinting, and a few Latin-influenced book abbreviations. The focus is on nouns and verbs, with grammatical notes at the bottom of each page providing a major benefit. These notes include information such as the subject of a verb or the antecedent of a pronoun.

Use caution as the note letters change on each page. A helpful single page of "Explanatory References" shows the elements of the entries in Lisowsky.

Kohlenberger, John R., III and Edward W. Goodrick. *The NIV Exhaustive Concordance*. Grand Rapids: Zondervan, 1990.

Thomas, Robert L., ed. *The New American Standard Exhaustive Concordance of the Bible*. Nashville: Holman, 1981.

These two useful alternative concordances are based on modern Bible translations.

Supplemental wordbooks

Botterweck, G. Johannes and Helmer Ringgren, eds. *Theological Dictionary of the Old Testament*. Grand Rapids: Eerdmans, 1974-94. [TDOT]

Kittel, Gerhard and Gerhard Friedrich, eds. *Theological Dictionary of the New Testament*. Translated by Geoffrey W. Bromiley. 10 vols. Grand Rapids: Eerdmans, 1964-76. [TDNT/Kittel]

Brown, Colin, ed. *The New International Dictionary of New Testament Theology*. Rev. ed. 3 vols. Grand Rapids: Zondervan, 1975-1986. [NIDNTT]

TDOT is a valuable Old Testament series on key words, corresponding to TDNT. TDOT manifests a liberal perspective generally and is incomplete — seven volumes, through ליץ . Look up the Hebrew word (or synonyms) alphabetically by volume and by table of contents.

TDNT and NIDNTT treat biblical Hebrew words as well as Greek. Vol. X of TDNT contains the index, including an "Index of Hebrew and Aramaic Words." NIDNTT has an "Index of Hebrew and Aramaic Words" in each volume. Optionally, locate the English concept in the individual volume's Table of Contents and scan the Old Testament background section at the start of relevant entries. David

Townsley and Russell Bjork compiled a separate volume scripture index for NIDNTT.

Supplemental grammars

Kautsch, E., ed. *Gesenius' Hebrew Grammar*. Revised in accordance with the twenty-eighth German edition (1909) by A. E. Cowley. Repr. of 1910, 2d English ed. Oxford: Clarendon, 1976. [GKC]

Joüon, Paul. *A Grammar of Biblical Hebrew*. Translated and revised by T. Muraoka. Vol. 2, Part Three: Syntax, Paradigms and Indices. Rome: Biblical Institute, 1991.

Continuing students will want to purchase the dated but standard comprehensive advanced grammar, GKC. Use the indexes for "Subjects," "Hebrew Words and Forms," and "Passages," as well as the table of contents.

Volume two of Joüon's grammar is another worthwhile reference work.[25] Unfortunately, volume one is less helpful for exegesis and the volumes sell as a set.

(*** indicates not approved,   marks primary works)

Type	Book Title	Abbreviation	Date Published	Theological Bent	Arrangement	Entry Form	Cross-Referenced
Interlinear	*NIV Interlinear Hebrew-English OT	Interlinear	1987	N/A	English Bible	text	X
Analytical	*Analytical Key to the OT	AKOT	1989-1992	N/A	English Bible	textual	BDB, GKC
	Einspahr Index to BDB	Einspahr	1977	N/A	English Bible	textual (no vowels)	BDB
	OT Parsing Guide	Parsing Guide	1986, 1990	N/A	English Bible	textual (verbs)	BDB
	Analytical Hebrew & Chaldee Lexicon	Davidson	1850/1981	N/A	alphabetical	textual	X
Lexicon	*New Brown-Driver-Briggs Hebrew & English Lexicon	BDB	1907/1979	liberal	root (primarily)	lexical	Strong's
	Lexicon in Veteris Testamenti Libros	KB	1958	liberal	alphabetical & root (verbs)	lexical	X
	Concise Hebrew & Aramaic Lexicon	Holladay	1971	N/A	alphabetical	lexical	X
Concordance	*New Englishman's Hebrew Concordance	Englishman's	1843/1984	N/A	alphabetical	lexical	Strong's
	New Concordance of the OT	Even-Shoshan	1989	N/A	alphabetical	lexical	X
Wordbook	*Theological Wordbook of the OT	TWOT	1980	conservative	alphabetical	lexical	Strong's
	Theological Dictionary of the OT	TDOT	1979-	liberal	alphabetical & root (verbs)	lexical	X
Grammar	*Hebrew Syntax: An Outline	WHS	1976	N/A	topical	N/A	X
	Introduction to Biblical Hebrew Syntax	IBHS	1990	N/A	topical	N/A	X
	Gesenius' Hebrew Grammar	GKC	1910/1976	N/A	topical	N/A	X

Computer Software for Biblical Hebrew

In 1993, computer sales surpassed color television sales. Computer hardware and software sales have exceeded five hundred billion dollars, and perhaps thirty percent of American homes contain a computer. This spread of computers has led to more available and affordable software for biblical studies.

Computer software exists for biblical language fonts, multilingual word processors, ancient biblical versions and Bible translations, concording work, grammatical analysis, resource tools, lesson and sermon planning, bibliographic databases, and complete Bible research systems. *Christian Computing Magazine* provides a ready update on such offerings. Jeffrey Hsu, *Computer Bible Study* (Dallas, TX: Word, 1994) surveys much available Dos/Windows software.[26] Kay Hall, *The Ministry Macintosh* (Durham, NC: Church Bytes, 1995) covers many different Macintosh applications.

A *biblical Hebrew research system* is software that includes the biblical language text, search and concording capabilities, and grammatical analysis. Additional modules may provide other features.

The following ranked chart of current biblical Hebrew research systems serves as an invitation into a new dimension of study. Certainly, personal priorities vary (speed, finances, user interface, a primary use, or some combination of these factors). Read the promotional material, and watch or use a demo prior to any purchase. If price is a factor, consider the total cost of all desired modules.

	Software	Contact
PC	1. *Bible Works for Windows 3.0*[27]	Hermeneutika (406) 837-2244
	2. *Logos Bible Software 2.0 (Windows)*	Logos (800) 87-LOGOS
	3. *Bible Windows 3.0*	Silver Mountain (800) 214-4000
	4. *The Word Advanced Study System 3.0 (Dos/Windows)*	Wordsoft, Nelson Word (800) 251-4000
MAC	1. *acCordance*	Gramcord Institute (206) 576-3000
	2. *AnyText*	Linguists (206) 775-1130

Action Points

1. Prepare your list of "priority" tools to purchase after completing the following exercises. The recommended basic toolkit included the Interlinear, AKOT, BDB, Englishman's, TWOT, and WHS or IBHS. As a minimum, a tool-based approach to biblical Hebrew requires an interlinear, an analytical tool, and a lexicon. (Read aloud this chapter's title as a *double-entendre*.)

2. Read the "Nouns" section of the Appendix.

3. Look at Genesis 1:6 in the Interlinear. Supposing you want to know more about the "expanse" (KJV "firmament"), where is it in BDB? Use AKOT, but compare Einspahr for a precise location.

3. What meaning do BDB give to "expanse"? How does this relate to the verbal concept of the root, given at the start of the BDB entry?

4. How often does the Hebrew word for "dry ground" (Gn 1:9) occur in the Old Testament? Identify the Hebrew noun from the Interlinear and AKOT, before looking in Englishman's. Then check Even-Shoshan to compare these concordances.

5.   Look at Genesis 2:7 in the Interlinear. Compare the
      sound of the Hebrew words for "man" and "ground."
      (Try writing out the Hebrew words in transliteration.)
      English translations often obscure such Hebrew word
      associations.

      "man"= _____   "ground" = _____

      Key difference in sound: _____

6.   Parse the first verb in Genesis 3:1. Check AKOT, the
      Parsing Guide, and Davidson. (You might scan the
      "Verbs" section of the Appendix. The purpose of this
      action point, however, is to examine these tools.)

7.   Look up the word נָחָשׁ in TWOT for some insight on
      Genesis 3:1.

8.   Review the alphabet by looking at Zephaniah 3:8 in the
      Interlinear. This verse contains all the Hebrew letters,
      including final forms, except for *shin*. Can you find all
      of them?

9.   Practice "reading" the Hebrew of Genesis 1 in the In-
      terlinear. Do not worry about dots and dashes; concen-
      trate on consonants and vowels. Unless they are the
      vowel signs, assume marks above and below con-
      sonants are accents and disregard them for now.[28]

Notes

1. A so-called literal translation of Hebrew is misleading for idioms (see Chapter 5, Note 12), contextually construed meanings (see Chapter 4 on word studies), construct chains, and infinitive absolutes combined with a finite verb (see the Appendix).

2. Chapter 5 discusses multiple senses of words and synonyms in word studies. Chapter 7 discusses synonymous parallelism and deliberate ambiguities in poetry.

3. AKOT does not always indicate *Kethiv-Qere* readings or which of those readings is analyzed. A *Kethiv-Qere reading* is a specific text critical variant written one way according to the consonants and read another way according to the vowels (see introductions to Old Testament textual criticism). Also, the use of the Revised Standard Version as the translation — even when it seemingly contradicts the analysis! — can be confusing, especially when the RSV renders a variant textual reading. For example, in Proverbs 10:24, AKOT analyzes יִתֵּן as Qal imperfect, yet translates "will be granted." (The latter represents a text critical variant reading or perhaps AKOT intends a rare indefinite usage. But simply pairing this analysis with this translation is unclear.)

4. The Appendix, as well as biblical Hebrew grammars, AKOT's Preface, and the Parsing Guide's Introduction discuss these terms. The caution warns of a drawback of the tool, but do not worry about these terms right now.

5. BDB assigns homonyms (different roots with the same spelling) distinct Roman numerals.

6. See Chapter 4 for a definition and discussion of etymology in word studies.

7. The Appendix, as well as biblical Hebrew grammars, describes the basic verb patterns.

8. For more on derivatives, see Chapter 4 on word study method.

9. An exception concerns references to the standard reference grammar described in this chapter, GKC. BDB refers to this grammar as "Ges," and includes some references not listed in AKOT.

10. Contrast the assertion and example in John Edward Gates, *An Analysis of the Lexicographic Resources Used by American Biblical Scholars Today* (Missoula, MT: Society of Biblical Literature, 1972), 126. The last two pages in Englishman's Concordance provide a convenient listing of differences between Hebrew and English verse numbers and may be worth copying for ready reference.

11. See Chapter 4 on word study method.

12. Edward W. Goodrick, *Do It Yourself Hebrew and Greek*, 2d ed. (Grand Rapids: Zondervan, 1980), 17:2 decodes abbreviations in a sample BDB entry.

13. William H. Grentz, ed., *The Dictionary of Bible and Religion* (Nashville: Abingdon, 1986), 214.

14. The Appendix, as well as biblical Hebrew grammars, describes the basic verb patterns.

15. Frederick W. Danker, *Multipurpose Tools for Bible Study* (Minneapolis, MN: Fortress, 1993), 139 gives a less inclusive version of this analogy borrowed from A. T. Robertson's anecdote.

16. Dawson correctly evaluates IBHS as more of an updated traditional grammar focusing heavily on semantics and not specifically syntax (as the title indicates). Yet this does not devalue its contents as much as Dawson's critique might suggest (David Allan Dawson, *Text Linguistics and Biblical Hebrew* [Sheffield: Sheffield Academic, 1994], 24-28).

17. Brief evaluations of Bible translations include David Alan Black, *Using New Testament Greek in Ministry* (Grand Rapids: Baker, 1993), 37-43; and Frederick W. Danker, *Multipurpose Tools for Bible Study* (Minneapolis, MN: Fortress, 1993), 177-95. For more detail, see Philip Wesley Comfort, *The Complete Guide to Bible Versions* (Wheaton: Tyndale, 1991); S. Kubo and W. F. Spech, *So Many Versions?* rev. ed. (Grand Rapids: Zondervan, 1983); or even William J. Chamberlin, *Catalogue of English Bible Translations* (Westport, CT: Greenwood, 1991).

18. This chapter only discusses analytical tools that deal directly with the Hebrew text. *The Complete Word Study Old Testament* (Chattanooga, TN: AMG, 1994) provides Hebrew grammatical analysis above an English text, as well as cross-references to Strong's and additional lexical information.

19. The Appendix, AKOT's Preface, and biblical Hebrew grammars discuss these terms. Do not worry about these terms now, but make a mental note or copy this page to insert in the front of Davidson if you decide to use that tool.

20. In Davidson, "id" (= "as above") directs attention to a preceding line, sometimes several lines above, for the bulk of the analysis. Goodrick provides a helpful introduction to the use of Davidson.

21. The Appendix discusses Hebrew parsing and the separate elements involved in parsing a Hebrew verb.

22. This is reference information for after you work through the Appendix, as guided by the action points.

23. Holladay is based upon and advances beyond the third and second editions of KB (from *'ayin* onward).

24. An electronic version is available, initially in Macintosh format.

25. Francis I. Andersen considers Joüon "the best overall general reference grammar for biblical Hebrew." His review is *JBL* 112 (1993):123-26.

26. Steve Hewitt, "Revolution in Bible Study," *BAR* 20:6 (1994): 63-66 discusses Windows software. Tim Walker, "Original Language Bible Study Software Review," *Christian Computing Magazine* 6:11 (1994): 18-25 discusses Dos and Windows products. Kay Hall, "Choosing the Right Bible Software for Your Macintosh," *Christian Computing Magazine* 6:3 (1994): 14-19 covers that platform.

27. The latest version makes *BibleWorks* the frontrunner; see the review by Tim Walker, "BibleWorks for Windows, Version 3.0," *Christian Computing Magazine* 7:5 (1995): 20-22. *Bible Companion/Hebrew Gramcord for Windows* is projected to ship in January 1996.

28. See the treatment of accents in Samuel R. Levin, *Hebrew Grammar* (Binghamton: State University of New York at Binghamton, 1966), 48-68; Jacques B. Doukhan, *Hebrew for Theologians* (Lanham, MD: University Press of America, 1993), 182-90; Israel Yeivin, *Introduction to the Tiberian Masorah* (Missoula: Scholars, 1980), 157-296; and M. B. Cohen, *The System of Accentuation in the Hebrew Bible* (Minneapolis: Milco, 1969). BHS includes a printed card identifying the accents.

Chapter 4

Lightning or Lightning Bug?
Word Studies

Objectives: After reading this chapter, you should be able to:
1. Distinguish a word's range of attested meanings
   from its current and specific textual meaning
   (diachronic versus synchronic linguistics).
2. Distinguish selection from arrangement as factors in
   word meaning (paradigmatic versus syntagmatic
   relations).
3. Guard against common word study abuses.
4. Describe the basic steps for a word study.
5. Employ useful tools for studying Hebrew words.
6. Begin studying a biblical Hebrew word.

Mark Twain observed, "The difference between the *almost*-right word and *right* word is really a large matter — it's the difference between the lightning bug and the lightning."

Words make a difference. "We live by words, love by words, pray with words, and die for words."[1]

In exegesis, word studies add color, depth, and precision. Often, words form the foundation of biblical and systematic theology. So the payoff from word studies motivates beginning exegetes.

In language acquisition, word studies serve as a "Swiss cheese" approach. They effectively "punch holes" into biblical Hebrew's vocabulary and stimulate an acquired taste.

In sermons, word studies flash or fizzle depending on selectivity, sound methodology, clarity, and relevancy. So this chapter presents basic issues of word meanings, as well as the tools and a method for biblical Hebrew word studies.

Semantic Issues and Cautions

Two primary concepts of modern semantics suggest cautions when studying words. Semantics, or more precisely, *lexical semantics*, is that branch of linguistics concerned with the ways words convey meanings.[2]

Diachronic vs. synchronic linguistics[3]

The Swiss linguist Saussure distinguished two semantic approaches. *Diachronic*, or evolutionary, linguistics traces a word's development through history. *Synchronic*, or static, linguistics focuses on a word's usage current in a particular time period.[4]

Saussure also asserted the priority of the synchronic over the diachronic. For a suggested meaning to be appropriate in a particular context, it must have been a then-current meaning. However, Bible students have often followed a diachronic approach — with misleading results. (See, after the next sub-section, "The ABCs of sound word studies.")

The word study method presented in this chapter might be labeled *panchronic*, examining both diachronic and synchronic issues. A word's range of biblical uses provides material for explaining different texts. Yet exposition typically centers on a single text and should spotlight a word's specific textual usage (*usus loquendi*).

Paradigmatic vs. syntagmatic relations[5]

To create a sentence an author often selects words from groups of related words, typically involving synonyms and antonyms. Substitutable words in a given set or syntactic role constitute *paradigmatic relations*. "Paradigmatic relations are relations of similarity and opposition with other words which might have been chosen in place of the word which was chosen."[6]

Notice, in the following diagram, the interchange of words for creating in Genesis 1—2:4. In this case, the author's intertwining usage mutes differences between these words and warns against emphasizing subtle distinctions.

	Ch. 1					Ch. 2		
בּרא	1		21		27thrice			3	4
עשׂה		7	16	25	26		31	2twice	3	4

A group of related words for a given concept forms a *semantic field*. As the following sample shows, Hebrew words for holiness and cleanness demonstrate overlap, contrasts, and similarities.[7] An "unclean" object was ritually unclean and unholy; but a "(ritually) clean" object might be either holy or unholy, depending on its consecrated status. Study of such semantic fields adds interpretive precision.

קָדוֹשׁ	"holy"		טָהוֹר	"(ritually) clean"
חוֹל	"not holy"		טָמֵא	"unclean"

On the other hand, the arrangement of words in a phrase or sentence often conditions their meaning. Their specific meaning depends on words used in combination with them. Linguists refer to these combinations as *syntagmatic* relations, "the relations of this word to the other words which are used in contiguity with it, in (let us say) the same sentence."[8]

Syntagmatic relations often determine meaning.[9] Even a single word in the context may affect the meaning of another word. In English, "fat chance" means "slim chance!"

ברך normally means "bless;" but it can mean the very opposite when God is the object (Jb 1:5, 11; 2:5, 9; 1 K 21:10-13).[10] Rather than actually saying "curse God," "bless God" is sometimes substituted as a euphemism. In these cases, the direct object contributes to a polarized, or opposite, meaning for the verb.[11]

Both word selection and arrangement influence meaning. Thus, paradigmatic and syntagmatic relations operate interactively on vertical and horizontal planes. In the following example, substitutable words for the subject noun constitute paradigmatic relations, while relations between words in the sentence are syntagmatic.

	paradigmatic relations	
The	boy girl man woman	<u>painted the fence white</u>. *syntagmatic relations*

The ABCs of sound word studies (cautions)

The modern distinctions between synchronic and diachronic linguistics and between paradigmatic and syntagmatic relations have practical ramifications for ministers doing word studies.

1. Avoid an "etymological fallacy." [12]

A word's *etymology*, either its component parts or early attested meaning, is often *not* part of an author's intended meaning. Insisting on an etymological meaning, without support beyond the historical fact of ancient usage, overemphasizes diachronics and abuses a word. Word etymologies merit the same skepticism as "memories of past lives" and often serve as little use.

Just a few examples suffice to demonstrate the irrationality of this too-common word study abuse.[13] "Mrs." originally meant "mistress!" And who suggests that a pineapple is an apple produced by pine trees, or that a butterfly is a floating dairy product? Even assuming לֶחֶם ("bread" or "food") relates to מִלְחָמָה ("war"), not every war was fought over a loaf of bread.

Additionally, sometimes ministers impose English word etymologies upon biblical words. For example, the oft-proclaimed Latin derivation of "sincere" is "(a statue) without wax."[14] Apart from the difficulty of accurately tracing a word's origins and the lack of English speakers' cognizance of such etymologies, English etymologizing summons the otherwise trite reminder: The Bible was written in the biblical languages.

A related abuse, *reverse etymologizing*, imposes an anachronistic meaning upon a word.[15] Saying "The gospel is the dynamite (*dunamis*) of God," imposes an eighteenth-century English meaning on Romans 1:16. Further, this could misleadingly suggest unfocused destruction; whereas the gospel is the constructive, life-giving power of God.

Transparency (clearly applicable meaning derived from the components of a compound word) and context determine the legitimacy of any claimed etymological meaning for a word's usage.[16] The revelation of God's presence prompted Jacob's naming of Beth-el ("house of God," Gn 28:19); its description as the house of '*elohim* (Gn 28:17) confirms the intentional etymology. In Psalm 4:2 [4:1 English], the accompanying verb "make room for/relieve," indicates the significant etymology of "distress" as a "narrow place."[17]

Show the textual relevance of any purported etymologi-cal meaning. Or leave the etymology in the dust of ancient history.

2. **B**eware of "illegitimate totality transfer!" [18]

Words often convey different meanings in distinct uses. For example, the English word "trunk" has distinct mean-ings when used with reference to a car, an elephant, clothes, or a tree. In 1 Samuel 1:9-10, the same Hebrew preposition עַל communicates sitting "upon" a seat, "beside" the temple doorpost, and praying "to" God.

Words may also carry specific *connotations*, or asso-ciated emotive meanings, in a particular context or for a particular group. The Hebrew word for "subtle" in Genesis 3:1 carries negative connotations as a description of the tempter, unlike the positive description of a wise person in Proverbs 12:23. (See BDB 791A and compare the connota-tions in "slick salesman" or the colloquial "slick response.")

But no single use of a word bears all the possible mean-ings of that word; suggesting otherwise deserves the label *illegitimate totality transfer*.

Kelsey's comments aptly characterize this word study abuse:

> [The interpreter] proceeds as though a concept, biblical or otherwise, were (a) a kind of container that lugs the selfsame meaning-content into every context, and (b) a kind of onion that accumulates layers of meaning from its several contexts of use in the past, interrelates them systematically, and thereafter bears them in all contexts whatsoever, so that all uses of the concept are present when any one is explicitly used ....[19]

Imposing a technical sense of a word — apart from clear contextual indicators — is a form of illegitimate totality transfer. The term *satan*, or adversary, refers to humans (1 K 11:23) or even the angel of the Lord (Nm 22:22). Reading (the) Satan into such passages is inappropriate.

Be explicit about the word's *specific* meaning in a given text, as opposed to providing encyclopedic information on all its possible uses.[20]

3. Consider the limits of word studies in Bible study and theology.[21]

A dear woman, face aglow, told her pastor that one word in the Bible especially inspired her, "The wonderful word, Mesopotamia."[22] Apparently she associated some great personal significance to this single word. Granted, "Mesopotamia" is a melodious mouthful; but would the biblical world or any specific biblical text share her associations?

Words should not be viewed like the rock which struck the statue in Nebuchadnezzar's dream, becoming a huge mountain and filling the whole earth (Dn 2:35). Individual words do not necessarily communicate a theological concept.

Ideas ultimately come in word combinations, specifically, phrases, sentences, paragraphs, and larger units. Twenty-five years ago, a Jehovah's Witness challenged me to show that *'el gibbor* refers to *the* mighty God in Isaiah 9:6; only then would he agree that Jesus is God and the Trinity is a biblical doctrine. Unfortunately, I naively accepted his parameters — there is no definite article — and I had no response. Had I considered the entire phrase and book context, however, I might have discovered Isaiah 10:21. There (the very next chapter!) the same indefinite phrase *'el gibbor* refers to *the* mighty God, the LORD.

Studying the individual words in the phrase "dear John letter" would not be particularly productive. Concentrating on the "myrtle" in Zechariah's vision of the four horsemen (1:8, 10, 11) could distract from the text's own interpretation of the vision (1:14-17).[23]

Additionally, theological concepts extend beyond individual words. Messianic passages typically do not contain the word "Messiah."

Yet overvaluing and overloading words is an ancient problem. The medieval humanist scholar Erasmus related his encounter with word abuse:

> I know of another monk of eighty years of age who was so scholarly that it was often said that Scotus, himself, was re-born in him. He expounded the mystery of the name of Jesus, showing with admirable subtlety that the letters of the name served to explain all that could be understood about Him. The fact that the name can be declined in three different cases — *Jesus, Jesum,* and *Jesu* — clearly illustrate the threefold nature of God. In one case the name ends with "s," this showing that He is the sum; in the second case it ends with "m," illustrating that He is the middle; and finally, in the third case we find the ending "u," this symbolizing that He is the ultimate. He amazed his audience even more when he treated the letters of the name mathematically. The name Jesus was equally divided into two parts with an "s" left in the middle. He then proceeded to point out that this lone letter was שׁ in the Hebrew language and was pronounced Schin or Sin, and that furthermore this Hebrew letter was a word in the Scottish dialect that means *peccatum* (Latin for sin). From the above premises he declared to his audience that this connection showed that Jesus takes away the sins of the world. His listeners, especially the theologians, were so amazed at this new approach that some of them came near to being overtaken by the same mysterious force that transformed Niobe to stone.[24]

Words constantly tempt the exegete to overuse and abuse them. Yet words have specific meanings in particular contexts.

As a guideline, individual biblical words do not settle theological issues. Nor do they often provide the substance for an entire sermon.

Further, while liberating your dependence on others and increasing your precision and confidence in ministering the Word, personal word study is not magic. Do not expect to "pull a rabbit out of the hat" that all other ministers and scholars missed.

Moule balances the promise and problems of word studies:

> Words are feeble things — never adequate for the job; yet
> priceless things — seldom dispensable. They are dangerous
> things, for they are so fascinating that they tempt the user to
> linger with them and treat them as ends instead of means.[25]

Mind these cautionary ABCs and word studies can
enhance ministry: Avoid an etymological fallacy. Beware of
illegitimate totality transfer. Consider the limits of word
studies.

Hebrew Word Study Tools[26]

The primary word study tools in a practical approach
include an interlinear (with the Hebrew text and a good
English translation), a Hebrew lexicon (BDB, KB,
Holladay), and a Hebrew-based concordance (like
Englishman's).

Secondary tools are English-based concordances
(Young's, Strong's) and wordbooks (TWOT, TDOT). For
extended studies, consult additional lexicons (such as
Jastrow[27] and DWSI[28]), concordances (Even-Shoshan or
Hatch and Redpath[29]), and wordbooks (TDNT, NIDNTT,
Richardson,[30] Snaith,[31] Girdlestone[32] or Vine, Unger, and
White[33]).

Chapter 3 provided descriptions and directions for using
many of these books. The word study method prescribed
below provides additional guidance in the use of such tools.

Hebrew Word Study Method

A general method for word study consists of four parts:
checking the word's etymology, studying the word's usage,
verifying your results, and synthesizing your conclusions.
Individual words, as well as the training, time, and inclination of the minister, may require adaptations to this representative method.

As principles of sound method become second-nature, the need for full inductive word studies lessens and other tools — lexicons, wordbooks, or commentaries — can be used critically and profitably. Also, a single word study potentially affects many different texts where it or related words occur, and so exponentially increases exegetical momentum.

Not every word can or should be studied at length. Time constraints and the goal of using Hebrew in ministry restrict word studies to *significant words*.

Four criteria mark a word as potentially significant:

1) A rare biblical word may pose an interpretive problem, since few parallel references clarify its meaning.
2) A repeated word may provide a key to a text's message. The Gentile sailors' increasing "fear" (Jonah 1:5, 10) grows into reverence for the LORD as the Sovereign of creation (Jonah 1:16).
3) An ambiguous word may need further study. Variations in English Bible translations often point to unclear words.
4) A theologically-loaded word is worth studying. Stained glass words like "sin," "grace," "worship," or "love," need clear focus because such traditional church words are viewed with a variety of meanings.

Try sniffing out significant words with the saying, "I smell a *r-r-a-t* (a rare, repeated, ambiguous, or theologically-loaded word)." Then your study begins.

The remainder of this chapter proposes a word study method and illustrates each of the steps with a sample word (the Hebrew root יצר).

Check the etymology.

Etymology recounts a word's origin or early development. *Cognates*, similar words in other Semitic languages such as Ugaritic, Aramaic, Arabic, or Akkadian, may shed light on a word's history. *Derivatives*, Hebrew words linked to the same root, may point to a shared meaning.

The basic word study tools provide some etymological information worth noting and cautiously evaluating along with a word's usage.[34] Obviously, limited facility with Semitic languages should restrict a focus on etymology. Besides, merely comparing cognates is a notoriously unreliable guide to meaning.[35]

1) Record the ball-park "definition"[36] given in the lexicon (BDB or KB).

2) Note cognates and their meanings found at the beginning of the lexicon's entry. Wordbooks like TWOT or TDOT provide additional information. Occasionally, common meanings in the related languages may be discernable.

3) Then notice the Hebrew derivatives in the lexicon. For this purpose, BDB's listing of derivatives alphabetically under a proposed root is advantageous. Is there a shared element among these derivatives?

Sawyer, among others, has emphasized the continuity of Hebrew into the post-biblical period.[37] Especially when confronted with a rare word, consult Jastrow's dictionary for post-biblical Hebrew usage. Exceptional students might also want to check for inscriptional information in DWSI.

Write a "concluding" paragraph concerning the etymology, attempting to trace the development in related languages and within Hebrew. Revise after completing the next two parts of the word study.

The etymology of יצר . Consider how this step of the process applies to a sample root-word, יצר.[38]

1) In terms of verbal "definitions" for יצר , the lexicons propose "form/fashion/shape/design."[39]

2) Cognates appear in many of the Semitic languages with similar meanings.[40] In particular, the noun meaning "potter" occurs in Akkadian ("As." in BDB), Ugaritic, Phoenician, Punic, and rabbinic Hebrew, even as in biblical Hebrew.[41]

General historical usage appears consistent in related languages, with three *caveats*. Akkadian creation texts rarely use this word.[42] Secondly, an Arabic cognate usage, "contract" (apparently as an agreement formed between parties, a designed relationship), does not occur in biblical Hebrew. Lastly, יֵצֶר as "(good/evil) impulse" is a later development at Qumran and in rabbinic Hebrew.[43]

3) Besides a few related proper names, two biblical Hebrew derivatives occur. The noun יֵצֶר describes formed objects, namely pottery, an idol, and humanity, but also "mental designs/thoughts/purposes." Once (Jb 17:7) a plural noun indicates "body parts" as created, functioning instruments. Also, a common technical usage of the Qal participle for "potter" or "crafter" merits mention with the derivatives. So derivatives within Hebrew, like the cognates, share the idea of forming or designing.

Study usage.

The meanings a word conveys in different contexts are more significant than etymology. Accordingly, an inductive study of biblical uses is ideal. Once the pattern and principles of word study method are understood, the busy minister may judiciously glean from commentaries or other sources.

1.   Check the biblical uses and their distribution.

Before examining various meanings of the selected word, observe the distribution of biblical uses. Does the word, or related forms, occur frequently in particular books or sections of the Bible?

Look up the scripture references and decide upon the word's meaning in each context. A less efficient approach employs an English-based concordance. However, Englishman's is a Hebrew-based concordance that lists all references, organized by verb pattern and tense or mood.

Verb patterns are specific modifications made to the root which often affect meaning. *Tense*, or more precisely, *aspect*, refers to how a speaker conceives the situation conveyed by the verb — primarily as complete or incomplete. The *volitive moods* indicate a speaker regards the action as dependent on someone's will. (The Appendix outlines the Hebrew verb system.)

Follow these guidelines on the number of biblical references to consult during a word study:[44]

If the total number of uses is:	Study ...
less than 25	every use
25-50	the author's uses and/or about 25 uses
50-100	50% of the uses
100+	the author's uses and/or about 50 uses

When doing an abbreviated word study, examine selected references from traditional divisions (like the Pentateuch, Historical Books, Poetic Books, or Prophets), or from time periods (like the era of the judges, the United Kingdom, and the exilic or post-exilic era). Check sufficient references from each verb pattern. Finally, evaluate figurative or other unusual uses of the word.[45] In an abbreviated word study, the fewer references examined the more tentative the conclusions.

The distribution of יצר . Englishman's lists seventy-two uses of יצר .[46] For verbs, all except three occur in the basic verb pattern (Qal). Forty-three examples, or nearly sixty percent, are Qal participles. Almost half of all uses occur in Isaiah and nearly seventy-one percent in the prophetic books.

The significance of such observations often becomes clearer while exploring the usage. The prophets prefer this word when describing God as the Creator of Israel or restored Israel, even as He is the Creator of humanity and the universe.

(For presentation purposes, each of the individual uses of יצר are grouped under categories of meaning, the next step in the process.)

Biblical Distribution of יצר (72 Uses)

		Gn	5
Pentateuch	6	Dt	1
Historical	5	2 S	1
		2 K	1
Books		1 Ch	3
Poetic		Jb	1
Books	10	Ps	9
Prophetic	51	Is	29
		Jr & Lm (1)	14
Books		Other (Am, 2; Hb, 3; Zc, 3)	8

2. *Categorize the range of meanings.*

The following concocted sentence, although politically incorrect, displays multiple meanings of English words: "You are right to assert your right to challenge the right, but having left, and being left alone, you may get little support from the left."[47]

In biblical Hebrew, a "house" may refer, among other things, to a home (Ex 12:7), a palace (1 K 10:12), a temple (1 K 5—7), a tent (2 K 23:7), a place (Neh 2:3), a receptacle (Ex 25:27), a family (Gn 7:1), or a dynasty (2 S 7:11).

1) Group the biblical word's uses into meaning categories — similar to BDB's entries — by semantic nuances, author or time period, type of literature, or even grammatical associations. (For example, some verbs use only certain subjects or objects.) Semantic categories are usually preferable, although some words lend themselves

well to other categories.[48] Compare the categories offered by the lexicon.

2) Pay attention to any non-theological uses of the word in everyday affairs. A form of חָטָא describes unerring marksmen, showing that this common word for "sin" can sometimes indicate "miss a mark" or "err" (Jg 20:16; Pr 19:2; 8:35-36; compare Rm 3:23).

The range of biblical meanings of יָצַר .

1) For meaning categories, the lexicons tend to propose two: human/non-theological and divine/theological uses. Sometimes they subdivide each of those two categories into literal and figurative meanings. Such a categorization scheme emphasizes syntagmatic relations, specifically the grammatical subject or actor function. While the popularity of that scheme testifies to its value, a broader semantic categorization may prove beneficial and incorporate those syntagmatic relations.

Biblical usage of יָצַר typically involves crafting material into a purposeful object. So the English word "design" best represents יָצַר . Individual uses reflect specific aspects of design.

A particular use may focus on the designer, the planning or purpose of the design, the process or act of designing, or the product which results. God and humanity are capable of each of these designing aspects.[49]

Observing the variety of designed objects clarifies nuances inherent in the word itself and guards against unwarranted generalizations.[50] Humans designed idols, weapons, pottery, and plans, even evil. God designed His own purposes (Is 46:11; Jr 18:11), the elements (earth, Is 45:18; dry land, Ps 95:5; mountains, Am 4:13; light, Is 45:7; the seasons, Ps 74:17; all things, Jr 51:19), creatures (animals, Gn 2:19; locusts, Am 7:1; Leviathan, Ps 104:26), humanity (spirit, Zc 12:1; heart, Ps 33:15; eye, Ps 94:9; body, Gn 2:7; bodily parts, Jb 17:7), the nation Israel (Is 43:21), and selected individuals, such as the prophet Jeremiah (Jr 1:5) and the Servant (Is 44:21). Isaiah 43:10 denies the formation of any gods by a divine Creator.

2) A common non-theological use relates to a human potter, or the shaping or objects formed by the craft of pottery. By analogy, God is represented as the Divine Potter. A key passage, involving seven uses of this root, records how a prophet watched the activity at a potter's house and applied it to God's dealing with His people, Israel (Jr 18:2-11). Just as the potter shaped a vessel for his purposes and could exercise his sovereign will over a mis-shapen pot, God could forgive Israel's past or shape its future for good or ill.[51]

The next chart categorizes all the biblical uses of יצר .

Usage of יצר : "design"[52]

	Producer	Planning	Process	Product
H **U**	idol-maker (sculptor, Hb 2:18; engraver, Is 44:9)		shaping idols (Is 44:10,12)	concrete (an idol, Hb 2:18)
M **A** **N**	potter (2 S 17:28; 1 Ch 4:23; Ps 2:9; Lm 4:2; Is 29:16; 30:14; 41:25; Jr 18:2, 3, 4[twice], 6[twice]; 19:1, 11; Zc 11:13[twice])	devising evil (Ps 94:20)	forming a weapon (Is 54:17)	abstract (plans, thoughts Gn 6:5, 8:21; Dt 31:21; 1 Ch 28:9; 29:18; Is 26:3)
D **E** **I** **T** **Y**	Potter/Creator (Ps 33:15; 94:9; Is 22:11; 27:11; 29:16; 43:1; 44:2, 24; 45:7, 9[twice], 11, 18; 49:5; 64:8[7]; Jr 10:16; 33:2; 51:19; Am 4:13; 7:1; Hb 2:18)	planning (Is 46:11; Jr 18:11); even pre-ordaining events (2 K 19:25; Ps 139:16; Is 37:26)	creating (Gn 2:7, 8, 19; Ps 74:17; 95:5; 104:26; Is 43:7, 10, 21; 44:21; 45:18; Jr 1:5; Zc 12:1)	concrete (human body, Ps 103:14; or its parts, Jb 17:7; a human "pot," Is 29:16)

3.   Compare synonyms and antonyms.

Determine the word's uniqueness by comparing synonyms and antonyms.[53]

A *componential analysis* examines content features of related terms. The chart below shows the presence (+) or absence (-) of three features in four related English words.[54]

	"man"	"woman"	"boy"	"girl"
human	+	+	+	+
adult	+	+	-	-
male	+	-	+	-

Sources for synonyms and antonyms, besides lexicons, include concordances and wordbooks. To find synonyms, start with Englishman's indexes. (Unfortunately, the new edition of Englishman's does not include these indexes.) The "Hebrew and English Index" uses the Hebrew script and order, supplying English translations which may then be located in the "English and Hebrew Index."

If using Strong's, Young's, or other English-based concordances, examine other Hebrew words that have the same translation. Strong's has numbered indexes for the biblical language words. Young's lists transliterated Hebrew words alphabetically in an index; synonyms may be found by looking up each of the English translations for those. Similarly, in the *New Wilson's Old Testament Word Studies*, locate English translations for the Hebrew word in the "English and Hebrew Index" and find those in turn.[55]

Although almost entirely in Hebrew, Even-Shoshan conveniently lists synonyms (Hebrew: קרבים) after the preliminary definitions (counted in Hebrew א , ב , ג ...) and before the numbered references. Modern Hebrew dictionaries also may provide limited help in locating synonyms, as long as the words existed in biblical times and do not show significant semantic change.

BDB occasionally note synonyms or antonyms, especially in parallelism (indicated by //).[56] Compare BDB's distinction between two Hebrew words for "dust": "flying" or "lying" (BDB 7B+C).

TWOT, TDOT, TDNT, NIDNTT, and other wordbooks often discuss synonyms and antonyms.

Looking up synonyms, in turn, can lead to additional synonyms. Typically, synonyms are more significant than antonyms in narrowing a word's range of meanings.

Synonyms and antonyms of יצר . Comparing features of the two primary synonyms for יצר (Is 45:18) clarifies this word's specific contributions.[57] In contrast to יצר , ברא describes strictly divine creative action.[58] עשה is a more general and common root. In the next chart, (+) indicates a feature found only in certain contexts.

	יצר	ברא	עשה
forming process	+	+	(+)
purposefulness	+	(+)	(+)
initiation of a new product	(+)	+	(+)
divine action	(+)	+	(+)
human action	(+)	-	(+)
pot-shaping	(+)	-	(+)

Several antonyms also highlight the design and purposefulness in יצר . שחת describes a "marred" or "ruined" and useless vessel (Jr 18:4), namely, a nation deserving "destruction" (אבד ; Jr 18:7). תוהו describes a "formless," useless condition (Is 45:18; Gn 1:2). Idolatry is a "broken" (שבר) cistern that cannot hold water and serves no good purpose (Jr 2:13).

4.   Consult translations and New Testament passages.

Related Greek terms, especially, may provide insights. Recognize, however, that word meanings may change over time and between languages.

1) For the Septuagint [LXX], check Hatch and Redpath for the Greek "equivalents." These show how the LXX translators understood the word.

Hatch and Redpath's "Hebrew Index..." can also point to synonyms by way of Greek terms. For a quick listing of the Greek terms used to translate a Hebrew word, along with their frequencies, dos Santos' *Index* is convenient, although handwritten.[59]

2) The New Testament writings may focus on a particular nuance, enlarge a word's usage, or provide concrete examples. A cited Old Testament text may possess significance for a word study.

Greek terms and New Testament texts related to יצר .

1) Greek terms in the LXX reflect early understandings of יצר . By far the most common translational term is πλασσω, highlighting the activity of shaping or molding. Related translational terms are κτιζω and ποιεω. The former looks especially to creative activity and the latter refers to a more general "making." κεραμευς specifies the potter.

2) New Testament passages repeat or highlight nuances of יצר and suggest applications. Paul quotes Isaiah 29:16, applying the image of the sovereign Potter to God's election of believers (Rm 9:20-21; Is 45:9; Mt 20:15). 2 Corinthians 4:7, in a "new creation" context, refers to the indwelling and enabling Spirit's presence in "clay pots (human bodies)." Galatians 4:19 describes growth in Christian maturity as Christ being "formed" in the believer (compare 2 Cr 3:18). Paul also derives truth about order in the church from the original creation account (1 Tm 2:13).

In particular, Ephesians 2:10 serves indirectly as a commentary on יצר .[60] There Paul describes the church and believers as God's new creation. To a surprising degree (and yet not surprisingly) Paul exhibits the insights uncovered in the word study on יצר :

Ephesians 2:10
God's Sovereign Design

For we are God's [Producer]
workmanship [product],
created in Christ Jesus [process]
to do good works [purposefulness],
which God prepared in advance [preordination] for us to do.

5.   *Conclude the specific meaning in your text.*

If the word study contributes to the exegesis of a particular text, identify, emphasize, and validate the word's *specific* usage. What does the word mean *in that context*?

When evaluating the specific meaning, consider the *circles of context*. Away from the point of impact, water ripples become less visible and farther apart.[61] Likewise, word uses closest to the text (verses, chapters, book), by the same author, or in a similar literary style, are more apt to share the same meaning.

The use of יצר in Genesis 2:7. As an example of a specific textual meaning of יצר , consider Genesis 2:7: "God *formed* the man from the dust of the ground." This is the first use of this root in the Bible.

Humanity's creation is vividly portrayed by this term so frequently used for the shaping of pottery.[62] God, the Divine Designer, skillfully crafted humanity. So we all have "Designer Genes."

Also, the use of יצר in Genesis 2:7 indicates humanity was purposely created and not the result of mere chance.[63] The repetition of יצר in Genesis 2:8 clarifies that purpose as service and worship of the Creator.

Verify your results.

Resources may contain overlooked information, organize the material better, or confirm your work. Consider checking wordbooks, reference works, and periodical articles. As a minimum for verification, see TWOT or TDOT.

Bible dictionaries, Bible encyclopedias, Old Testament theologies, commentaries, and periodical articles often contain useful and more-or-less current information.[64]

Verifying your results from other sources allows for final modifications, guards against grievous errors, and heightens assurance.

(See the Notes for some verification and even contrary views of the results for the sample word study on יצר .)

Synthesize your study.

Conclude with an overall summary.

Emphasize the word's biblical usage. Discuss categories and shades of meaning in a connected essay form, if giving an overview. Synonyms, antonyms, and particular grammatical constructions may add insight. If treating a particular text, state and validate the word's specific use.

Explain applications for theology, life, and ministry.

Application from יצר . Both an overall synthesis and a specific use of יצר have been illustrated. Ideally, specific applications of word studies grow out of specific uses in biblical texts. In Genesis 2:7, יצר presents humanity as God's handiwork and points to the purposefulness of human existence as His servants. Thus, key application areas are God's sovereignty, sanctification and service, and self-image or self-esteem.

Psalm 8 elaborates on these themes from the creation account. Also suggestive of the use of יצר in ministry, the songwriter desires a new creation type of experience:[65]

You are the Potter, I am the clay.
Mold me and make me, this is what I pray.

Build your knowledge base.

Accumulating biblical Hebrew word studies establish a knowledge base for a lifetime of ministry.

Start a file folder on Hebrew word studies. Set up a three-by-five card filing system (Hebrew alphabetical order) for particular words, or note useful word studies in a computerized retrieval system.

Take heart! Word studies become easier and the need for fully inductive studies recedes with developing skills and knowledge.

A Hebrew Word Study Blueprint

1. Check the etymology (in BDB or KB).
   a. Survey definitions.
   b. Search for cognates.
   c. Scan derivatives.
   d. Summarize etymology.
2. Study usage (in BDB, Englishman's, concordances, wordbooks, or Bible translations).
   a. Check the biblical uses and their distribution.
   b. Categorize the range of meanings.
   c. Compare synonyms and antonyms.
   d. Consult translations and New Testament passages.
   e. Conclude the *specific* meaning in your text.
3. Verify your results (in wordbooks, Bible encyclopedias and dictionaries, Old Testament theologies, commentaries, or periodicals).
   a. Research additional information.
   b. Revise conclusions.
4. Synthesize your study.
   a. Summarize your results.
   b. Stress the word's specific use in your text.
   c. Suggest applications for life, theology, and ministry.

Action Points

1. Recall errant word studies you have heard. What principle of sound word study method did they violate?
2. Name the four parts of a Hebrew word study and a useful tool for each. (Check the preceding "A Hebrew Word Study Blueprint.")
3. Read the "Verbs" section of the appendix to get a feel for the biblical Hebrew verb system. Especially note how meanings change in different verb patterns.
4. Study a significant word (a rare, repeated, ambiguous, or theologically-loaded word), preferably in a text you'll be teaching or preaching soon.
5. New Testament authors frequently seem to play upon Hebrew word meanings. Identify possible plays on Hebrew words in Mt 1:21; Mt 1:23; the *praise* of *Jews* (Rm 2:28-29); the *weight* of *glory* (1 Cr 3:18); *turned* to God from idols (1 Th 1:9); and may the God of *peace* Himself sanctify you *entirely ... complete* (1 Th 5:23).
6. Read further examples and cautions in word study method. Start with D. A. Carson, *Exegetical Fallacies* (Grand Rapids: Baker, 1984), 25-66; Grant R. Osborne, *The Hermeneutical Spiral* (Downers Grove, IL: InterVarsity, 1991), 64-92; Moisés Silva, *Biblical Words and Their Meaning* (Grand Rapids: Zondervan, 1983), 34-51; Walter C. Kaiser, Jr. and Moisés Silva, *An Introduction to Biblical Hermeneutics* (Grand Rapids: Zondervan, 1994), 46-64; or William W. Klein, Craig L. Blomberg, and Robert L. Hubbard Jr., *Introduction to Biblical Interpretation* (Dallas: Word, 1993), 183-99.

Notes

1. Haddon Robinson, *Biblical Preaching* (Grand Rapids: Baker, 1980), 177. A revision of this book is in process.

2. For a brief history of semantics related to biblical studies and a helpful summary of types of meaning, see Harold P. Scanlin, "The Study of Semantics in General Linguistics" in *Linguistics and Biblical Hebrew*, ed. Walter R. Bodine (Winona Lake, IN: Eisenbrauns, 1992), 125-36.

3. See further Moisés Silva, *Biblical Words and Their Meaning* (Grand Rapids: Zondervan, 1983), 35-38.

4. Dating portions of the Old Testament is notoriously controversial and theological perspective influences periodization of the biblical texts and their language. However, even conservatives split over dating certain Minor Prophets as pre-exilic or post-exilic, or whether a book ascribed to a specific biblical author may include ancient or updated material.

5. See Silva, *Biblical Words*, 119.

6. James Barr, "Hebrew Lexicography" in *Studies on Semitic Lexicography*, ed. Pelio Fronzaroli (Firenze: Universit à di Firenze 1973), 122. Scanlin, 134, refers to paradigmatic relations as *referential meaning*, meaning derived from related words in a semantic domain. However, since other linguists speak of referential meaning as the "real world" object that the linguistic sign/word identifies, perhaps *selectional meaning* would be a better term.

7. Barr, "Hebrew Lexicography," 122.

8. Barr, "Hebrew Lexicography," 122. Scanlin, 134, refers to syntagmatic relations as *associative meaning*, meaning derived from the grammatical context, and also uses this term for meaning derived from social and discourse factors.

9. "Syntagmatic combinations play the determinative role in language" (Silva, *Biblical Words*, 120).

10. "Bless" is the typical meaning in the Piel verb pattern. The Appendix discusses the primary verb patterns, as well as tense and mood. Any description of a Hebrew verb's meaning(s) must include the verb pattern, since these specific inflections of the root may modify meaning.

11. The pop culture expression, "I'm *bad*," illustrates polarized meaning.

12. James Barr, *The Semantics of Biblical Language* (Oxford: Oxford University, 1961), 107ff.

13. D. A. Carson, "Word Study Fallacies" in *Exegetical Fallacies* (Grand Rapids: Baker, 1984), 25-66 gives these examples and more.
14. Silva discusses this example at length and creates his own outrageous examples to show the danger of English etymologizing (Walter C. Kaiser, Jr. and Moisés Silva, *An Introduction to Biblical Hermeneutics* [Grand Rapids: Zondervan, 1994], 54-56).
15. Silva, *Biblical Words*, 45. This particular abuse is more common with Greek word studies.
16. See further Silva, *Biblical Words*, 48-51.
17. Luis Alonso-Schökel, *A Manual of Hebrew Poetics* (Rome: Biblical Institute, 1988), 104. He translates: "Thou hast given me room when I was in *dire straits.*"
18. Barr, *Semantics*, 218.
19. John H. Hayes and Frederick Prussner, *Old Testament Theology* (Atlanta: John Knox, 1985), 214-15.
20. Linguists distinguish between *langua*, the semantic range of all possible meanings, and *parole*, the specific meaning in a given context. Assume the biblical text intends to clearly communicate a message and seek a primary specific meaning for words. The possibility of deliberate ambiguity exists, particularly in poetic texts; yet the text itself should provide clear indicators of purposeful ambiguity. Ambiguity in the interpreter's mind is distinct from purposeful ambiguity intended by the text.
21. For a brief history and critique of theological lexicography see Silva, *Biblical Words*, 18-32.
22. Graham Maxwell, *Servants or Friends* (Redlands, CA: Pine Knoll, 1992), 112.
23. Jim Townsend, *The Minor Prophets* (Elgin, IL: David C. Cook, 1988), 75.
24. John P. Nolan, trans., *The Essential Erasmus* (New York: American Library, 1964), 151. I am indebted to Dr. Allen Ross for this quotation.
25. C. F. D. Moule, *The Holy Spirit* (Grand Rapids: Eerdmans, 1979), 97.
26. Chapter 3 describes many of these tools.
27. Marcus Jastrow, *A Dictionary of the Targumim...* (Brooklyn: Shalom, 1967).
28. Hoftijzer, Jean and K. Jongeling, eds., *Dictionary of West Semitic Inscriptions* (Leiden: Brill, 1995) [DWSI]. This dictionary references inscriptions, papyri, and ostraca from about 1000 B.C. to A.D. 300 recovered and published by the beginning of 1991. Sources include Phoenician, Punic, Hebrew, Aramaic,

Moabite, Ammonite and material from el-Amarna and Deir Alla
(yet omitting Ugaritic and Dead Sea materials!). DWSI provides
some grammatical analysis, brief translations in context, and
extensive bibliography. Verbs appear by root, and cross-
references index cognate spellings. The Semitic words are necessarily transliterated and unvocalized, yet biblical Hebrew students
can manage when checking on rare words. Finding cited
bibliographic references involves additional research.

29.   Edwin Hatch and Henry A. Redpath, *A Concordance to the
       Septuagint*... (Oxford: Clarendon, 1954).

30.   Alan Richardson, ed., *A Theological Word Book of the Bible*
       (New York: MacMillan, 1978) contains some readable helpful
       entries. However, it exaggerates the contrast of Hebrew and
       Greek thought (Barr, *Semantics*, 197).

31.   Norman H. Snaith, *The Distinctive Ideas of the Old Testament*,
       repr. (London: Epworth, 1983).

32.   Robert B. Girdlestone, *Synonyms of the Old Testament*, repr.
       (Grand Rapids: Eerdmans, 1973). Use this older work with
       caution.

33.   Vine, W. E., Merrill F. Unger, and William White Jr., *Vine's
       Complete Expository Dictionary of Old and New Testament
       Words*, rev. ed. (Nashville: Nelson, 1985).

34.   Cyril Barber, *Introduction to Theological Research* (Chicago:
       Moody, 1982), 105 briefly mentions the standard books used in
       more detailed etymological research.

35.   C. R. Taber, "Semantics" in Keith Crim, ed., *The Interpreter's
       Dictionary of the Bible: Supplementary Volume* (Nashville:
       Abingdon, 1962), 801. Barr's *Comparative Philology and the
       Text of the Old Testament* (Winona Lake, IN: Eisenbrauns,
       1987) sounded a wake-up call on such scholarly abuses when
       first published in 1968. See Silva, *Biblical Words*, 35-51. J. J.
       M. Roberts, "Ps xxii 17c" *Vetus Testamentum* 23 (1973), 252
       suggests guidelines for proposed cognates: 1) well-attested; 2)
       same root consonants, or variations explainable on the basis of
       Semitic phonology; 3) consistent meaning in cognate languages
       and within the contexts of other languages.

36.   For a warning about these "definitions," see James Barr's com-
       ments in Harold P. Scanlin, "The Study of Semantics in General
       Linguistics," 133.

37.   For example, John F. A. Sawyer, *A Modern Introduction to
       Biblical Hebrew* (London: Oriel, 1976), 184.

38.   An unpublished paper by Richard Speece, edited and revised by
       Allen Ross and distributed at Dallas Theological Seminary stim-

ulated the selection of this word. Although the organization, some of the method, and many details of my presentation differ, I acknowledge a debt.

39.   The meaning ("fashioning/casting/molding metal") and the few biblical derivatives of צור III seem related (KB 305; TDOT 6:258; BDB's צור IV; and Loren R. Fisher, ed., *Ras Shamra Parallels, Vol. II* [Rome: Biblical Institute, 1975], 52-53). However, do not confuse יצר with צרר ("distressed"); Englishman's interposed section should be separated. (Notice the different reference number, BDB 864b.)

40.   Contrary to Otzen's overly cautious assessment in TDOT 6:258.

41.   KB, DWSI, and Fisher, *Ras Shamra Parallels,* 2:52-53. The biblical Hebrew participle, used as a substantive, conveys this meaning.

42.   TDOT 6:258. However, the Genesis creation account also limits the use of יצר .

43.   TDOT 6:265, Jastrow 1:590. The linkage to a text like Gn 6:5 is not hard to conceive: "mental design/thought/purpose" grew into an "impulse/inclination." This development parallels the aphorism, "Thoughts shape habits and habits shape actions."

44.   Neal Windham, *New Testament Greek for Preachers and Teachers* (Lanham, MD: University Press of America, 1991) 107.

45.   See Chapter 5 on figures of speech.

46.   Even-Shoshan plausibly adds Is 49:8 with a form which BDB and others link to נצר instead.

47.   Jonathan Magonet, *A Rabbi Reads the Psalms* (London: SCM, 1994), 118.

48.   BDB's usage categories are inconsistent. To a degree, language's flexibility and the broad biblical corpus make this unavoidable. However, categorizing a word's uses according to God and man, theological and non-theological, or literal and figurative, often leaves important aspects of a word's meaning unanswered.

49.   Isaiah 43:10 denies the formation of any gods by a divine Creator.

50.   Contextual meaning is at least as significant as lexical meaning for an expositor. On the legitimacy of including *referent* along with *sense* as part of *meaning* in a practical word study, see Kendell H. Easley, *User-Friendly Greek* (Nashville, TN: Broadman & Holman, 1994), 126-27.

51.   Although applied to Israel/Judah, this principle holds for all nations (vv. 7-10). Unfortunately, Judah chose not to repent and

the Potter-Creator shaped the disastrous events of the exile as the part of His plan (vv. 11-17).

52. These four categories (producer, planning/purposing, process, product) are modifications of semantic functions of subjects, verbs, and objects as identified by so-called "case grammar" (specifically actor, action, and thing produced) and applied to this word.

53. Osborne, *The Hermeneutical Spiral*, 85-87, following Silva, further clarifies the relationships among synonyms as overlap, contiguity, and inclusiveness. Linguists love to point out that there are no absolute synonyms; but few would deny that there are functional synonyms. Other discussions of synonymy include Silva, *Biblical Words*, 159-69; and Stephen Ullmann, *Principles of Semantics* (Oxford: Basil Blackwell, 1957), 141-55.

54. Osborne, 87 cites this common example, providing a cautious endorsement of this type of analysis.

55. William Wilson, *New Wilson's Old Testament Word Studies* (Grand Rapids: Kregel, 1987). Similar is Aaron Pick, *Dictionary of Old Testament Words for English Speakers*, repr. (Grand Rapids: Kregel, 1977).

56. Chapter 7 discusses parallelism.

57. A more complete list of synonyms includes: כנה פעל כון זמה חשב פסל צור קנה חיל קום שית שים קרץ צלם נתן פלס עצב יצג חצב צמד חרש עצה משפט מראה דמות .

58. ברא , contrary to popular opinion, does not of itself indicate creation *ex nihilo* ("out of nothing"). God created male and female, respectively, from dust and a body part (Gn 5:2). However, this one word alone does not determine a doctrine of creation.

59. Elmar Camilo dos Santos, *An Expanded Hebrew Index for the Hatch-Redpath Concordance to the Septuagint* (Jerusalem: Dugith/Baptist House, n.d.).

60. Three translation terms for יצר — other than πλασσω — appear in Ephesians 2:10 and the conceptual associations seem undeniable.

61. Windham (106) uses this analogy, although I recall it from my seminary days. He also prefers the phrase *principle of immediacy*.

62. Most illuminating is a picture of an Egyptian deity at a potter's wheel, fashioning the prince (ANEP #569). Westermann traces the concept of humanity's creation from dust or earth in the

ancient Near East and critiques finding the potter image in Genesis 2:7 (Claus Westermann, *Genesis 1—11* [Minneapolis, MN: Augsburg, 1984], 203-207). Westermann suggests the text rather emphasizes the material (dust), and shows humanity as perishable.

63. Although some see God's more intimate involvement with humanity in this anthropomorphic representation of God as the Divine Potter, יצר also describes the animals' creation. Further, in regard to creationism and evolution, יצר affirms the purposefulness, but not the mode, of creation. (Jr 1:5 refers to a formation in the womb, seemingly a natural process taking about nine months.) This exemplifies the limits of word studies in theological controversies.

64. Chapter 2 recommends specific commentaries, commentary guides, and periodicals. Chapter 3 recommends other reference works. A sampling of non-conservatives showing judicious semantic judgment includes James Barr, William Holladay, David N. Freedman, Marvin Pope, and G. R. Driver. Among conservatives, Walter Kaiser, Bruce Waltke, Allen Ross, Derek Kidner, Leon Morris, Robert Hubbard, and Joyce Baldwin often do exemplary work.

65. Adelaide A. Pollard wrote the earlier hymn, *Have Thine Own Way, Lord*, which was adapted in this chorus.

Likewise, the Bible makes frequent use of figurative speech. One punster warns of a "whale" of biblical figures, suggesting the exact number is "the $64,000 question."[2]

The impact of a figure of speech can be arresting, evocative, and memorable. Like a vehicle's sudden stop or slackening in speed, a figure changes the pace of a discourse.[3] Often, well-crafted figures of speech present a vivid picture.

Biblical figures can also be interpretive booby-traps or leave egg on your face.[4] They create interpretive problems when missed (by taking literally what is figurative), mistaken (by taking figuratively what is literal), or misinterpreted (by mis-taking the point of the figure).[5] On the other hand, figures of speech are fertile ground for the interpreter and communicator.

Understanding Figures of Speech

A *figure of speech* is a purposeful variation in the use of words.[6,7] Figures transfer a word, or words, into a different semantic domain, or equate elements of different semantic domains.[8] They often picture the unfamiliar by means of the familiar.[9]

Also, a figure of speech communicates emotion along with content more economically than prose. Just as "a picture is worth a thousand words," figures typically arouse emotive associations not easily conveyed by "plain vanilla" prose.

> It may be helpful to note that in *turning* the word, the poet often juxtaposes or transfers the word into a semantic field of thought where it is not normally at home. Furthermore, when an author artfully turns his words he does not fully explain his meaning because he is also attempting to create a feeling in his reader. In other words, all figures are elliptical and many are evocative. Because the figure is in a *different than normal* form, then, indicates the author is communicating an unstated thought and unstated feeling (i.e., not explicitly stated).[10]

Because figurative language often involves analogies, some consider it inaccurate or untrue. Such an assumption represents a double error, in light of the emotive function of figures. Figures of speech generally express additional aspects of truth.[11] They compactly present content *and* emotions, connotations *and* denotations.

Figures of speech may be distinguished from idioms, symbols, allegories, and irony. An *idiom* is a language-specific expression whose meaning can not be determined simply from the meaning of its parts.[12] Allegories and symbols carry additional meaning in a single unit, whereas figures typically involve two elements.[13] Irony[14] generally derives from considerations beyond the sentence level and so belongs to rhetorical or discourse analysis.[15]

Biblical figures of speech, however, do not justify the allegorical method of hermeneutics. The *allegorical method* seeks hidden spiritual meaning beyond the historical and literary meaning of the text.[16]

Identifying Figures of Speech

How can you identify figurative language? Bullinger suggests, "When a statement appears to be contrary to our experience, or to known fact, or revealed truth ... then we may reasonably expect that some figure is employed."[17]

Many assume figures are readily recognizable. However, the history of biblical interpretation offers a more sober assessment. Consider, for example, disagreements over the person of Christ, divine attributes, the relationship between Israel and the church, or the nature of the Lord's supper.

General agreement, with some specific disagreements, may be the most that can be hoped for, as in other areas of interpretation. Even so, primarily logical and literary criteria help identify figurative language.[18]

Logical criteria

Is the expression contrary to reality? Metaphysically speaking, two distinct concrete objects can not be one and the same; therefore, a mismatched subject and predicate in "Yahweh is a rock" (2 S 22:2) indicates a figure of speech.[19]

Is the expression contrary to common reason? Mountains are ill-equipped to sing and trees to clap (Is 55:12).

Literary criteria (general hermeneutical principles)

Does the near context (a defining phrase, the character of the speaker, a heightened or dramatic tone, or the situation itself) show the expression is figurative? In 1 Kings 12:4, the Israelites' "yoke" is spelled out as "hard service."

Does the kind of literature warn the interpreter to look out for figures of speech? Poetry, in particular, uses many figures.

Does the style of a particular book or author provide clues? Amos, for example, shows a preference for figurative language: "The LORD roars from Zion" (Am 1:2; 3:8); "Hear this word, you cows of Bashan" (Am 4:1); and "Let justice roll like a river, and righteousness like a never-failing stream" (Am 5:24).

What help does the biblical corpus provide by way of allusions, parallel passages, and similar figures?[20] A basic knowledge of patriarchal history demands a figure of speech in "the high places of Isaac" (Am 7:9).

Do comparable figurative expressions appear in ancient Near Eastern literature and art? In particular, books by Keel and Pritchard are eye-opening (Othmar Keel, *The Symbolism of the Biblical World: Ancient Near Eastern Iconography and the Book of Psalms* [New York: Crossroad, 1985]; James B. Pritchard, *The Ancient Near East in Pictures Relating to the Old Testament*, 2d ed. [Princeton: Princeton University, 1969]).

Classifying Figures of Speech

> Since the author turns his words in various ways, literate people have attempted to analyze and categorize these deviations in the use of words in order to give better control on inferring the intended thought and feeling of the author.[21]

"Figurative" is not a magician's term. It neither conjures meaning nor makes meaning vanish from a text.

Identifying figures is only a first step in interpreting them. As Bullinger warns, "If a word or words be a figure, then that figure can be named, and described."[22]

To classify a particular figure, detect which of four formative processes is at work and then name the specific figure of speech.[23] (Both the four processes and specific major figures appear in following charts.)

General classification (four formative processes)

1. Comparison - Two things of basically unlike nature are linked because they share something in common.
2. Substitution - Something associated (an object, idea, or expression) stands in place of something else.
3. Addition - More is said in order to convey less (more effectively).
4. Omission - Something is not explicitly stated, although communicated.

Specific classification (major figures of speech)

Lengthy lists of figures of speech exist, often with names derived from Greek and Latin.

In his classic work, Bullinger lists about two hundred distinct figures of speech, including several with thirty to forty varieties. (Although sometimes as exhausting as it is exhaustive, consult Bullinger during exegesis by way of the indexes.)[24] However, about a dozen common figures pay great dividends to the exegete and appear in the immediately following charts.

Process	Figure of Speech (see in Bullinger)	Description	Examples (English Bible references)
C O M P A R I S O N	simile (726-33)	an expressed comparison between different items with something in common; uses "like/as;" formula: x is like y	"All people are like grass." (Is 40:6) "He shall be like a tree planted by waterstreams." (Ps 1:3)
	metaphor (735-43)	an implied direct comparison between different items with something in common; English uses a "to be" verb; formula: x is y	"The Lord (is) my shepherd." (Ps 23:1) "You (are) a shield about me, O Lord." (Ps 3:3)
	hypocatastasis (744-47)	an implied comparison with an unexpressed item; a submerged simile; formula: (x is like) y	"Dogs [vicious enemies] have surrounded me." (Ps 22:16) "Let the bones you have crushed [emotions/ inner being] rejoice." (Ps 51:8)
	personification[25] (861-69)	representing an inanimate object, animal, or an abstract truth by personal attributes	"The trees clap their hands." (Is 55:12) "All my bones shall say, 'Lord ....'" (Ps 35:10)
	anthropomorphism (871-82)	representing God in human form or with human attributes	"Your eyes saw my embryo." (Ps 139:16) "The gracious hand of my God was upon me." (Nh 2:8)
	anthropopathism (882-94)	representing God with human emotions or passions	"The Lord mocks them." (Ps 2:4) "The Lord was grieved that he had made man." (Gn 6:6)
	zoomorphism (882-94)	representing God (or someone) in animal form or with animal attributes	"I sing in the shadow of Your wings." (Ps 63:7) "The Lord roars from Zion." (Am 1:2)

Process	Figure (Bullinger)	Description	Examples (English Bible references)
	metonymy (539-608)	substitutes an associated noun; four types:	
S U B S T I T U T I O N		cause (or instrument) for effect	"The earth was of one lip [language]." (Gn 11:1) "Pour out your wrath [judgment]." (Ps 79:6)
		effect for cause	"Two nations [infants] are in your womb." (Gn 25:23) "O Lord, my strength[-ener]" (Ps 18:1)
		subject (container for contents)	"The earth [humanity] was corrupt." (Gn 6:11) "The grave [dead] cannot praise You." (Is 38:18)
		adjunct (the sign for the thing signified)	"I said, 'Days [aged men] should speak.'" (Jb 32:7) "the fear [God] of Isaac" (Gn 31:42)
	synecdoche (613-56)	substitutes an innately associated idea; four types:	
		part for whole	"my soul knows [I know]" (Ps 139:14) "feet [they] run to evil" (Pr 1:16)
		whole for part	"My people [some] will be exiled." (Is 5:13) "They sleep naked [poorly covered]." (Jb 24:7)
		species for genus	"man [humanity]" (Ps 8:4); "eat bread [food]" (Gn 3:19)
		genus for species	"the mother of all living beings [humanity]" (Gn 3:20) "Saul did not say anything at all [about David]." (1 S 20:26)
	merism (435)	two contrasting parts express a totality	"heaven and earth [the universe]" (Gn 14:19); "when you sit/walk [on all occasions]" (Dt 6:7)
	euphemism (684-88)	substituting a mild or less offensive expression	"You shall go to your fathers [die]." (Gn 15:15); "covering his feet [excreting]" (Jg 3:24)

lessness (Ex 15:16; compare 1 S 25:37), firmness or hardness (Jb 41:16; compare "hard hearted"), solidness (Jb 38:30), strength (Jb 6:12), commonness (1 K 10:27), and weightiness or lack of buoyancy (Ex 15:5).[29] Further, possible modern associations for "stone," — like "smoothness," "smallness," or "fragmentary" — might not occur in the Bible or fit many contexts.

Determine the specific thought of the figure in its context. Paraphrasing often clarifies comprehension,[30] as does interacting with different interpretations (such as those proposed in the following extended section of examples).[31]

Conceptual translation offers the "meat" of the figure, but not the whole "cow."[32] While the interpreter's attention generally focuses on the underlying thought or concept, a figure of speech creates additional emotive effects.

Explaining a figure's attendant emotive effects is challenging and more of an art than a science.[33] Nevertheless, capturing the emotive effects heightens the impact of the text and helps interpret surrounding details or the overall message.

Examples[34]

For comparisons, name the figure, identify the two elements (the topic and item of comparison), and specify the common thought and the emotive effects.

"He shall be *like a tree planted by rivers of waters*" (Ps 1:3).
    Figure of speech: simile
    Topic: a person diligent in studying God's Word
    Item of comparison: a plentifully watered tree
    (Common thought: health, productivity)
    (Emotive effect: desirableness, effectiveness)

"All flesh is *as grass*" (Is 40:6).
    Figure of speech: simile
    Topic: "flesh" (humanity)
    Item of comparison: grass or herbage
    (Common thought: transitoriness)
    (Emotive effect: pathos)

"The LORD God is *a sun and shield*" (Ps 84:11).
    Figure of speech: dual metaphor
    Topic: LORD God
    Item of comparison: sun, shield
    (Common thought: safety)
    (Emotive effect: security, confidence, robustness)

"*A lion* has gone up from his thicket" (Jr 4:7).
    Figure of speech: hypocatastasis
    (Topic: contextually, the king of Babylon)
    Item of comparison: a lion
    (Common thought: a vicious attacker)
    (Emotive effect: fear, desire to flee and seek safety)

For substitutions, specify the relationship which occasioned the switch, as well as the emotive effects.

"And the whole earth was of one *lip*" (Gn 11:1).
    Figure of speech: metonomy of cause
    Stated cause (instrument): lip
    (Intended effect: language)
    (Emotive effect: cohesiveness, unity)

"a land flowing with *milk and honey*" (Ex 3:8,17)
    Figure of speech: synecdoche of species
    Stated species: milk, honey
    (Intended genus: produce)
    (Emotive effect: abundance, fertility, prosperity)

"O Thou who inhabitest *the praises of Israel*" (Ps 22:3).
Figure of speech: metonomy of adjunct
Stated adjunct: praises
(Intended subject: the Israelite temple)
(Emotive effect: attending presence of God, joy)

For additions and omissions, state the intended thought and the emotive effects.

"The cities are great, and *walled up to heaven*" (Dt 1:28).
Figure of speech: hyperbole
(Intended thought: very high)
(Emotive effect: awesome impregnability, hopelessness)

"Why do the heathen rage?" (Ps 2:1).
Figure of speech: rhetorical question
(Intended thought: the irrationality or foolishness of unbelieving resistance against God and His will)
(Emotive effect: indignation, confidence in ultimate triumph)

Interpretive cautions

1. *Distinguish dead figures of speech from live ones.*[35]

In *dead figures of speech* the original word-picture has faded.

Notice the dead figure in the baseball announcer's cry, "He hit that *square* ..." — both the ball and bat are round! Another example of a dead figure is: "The ants are making a *bee-line* for the kitchen." Likewise, in Genesis 22:17, "shoreline" does not conjure up the sea's "lip," a more common use of the Hebrew word (BDB 974a).

No mental image is intended by a dead figure. Typically, through extensive use over long periods, that figure has ceased to act as a figure of speech. Such obsolescence of a figurative meaning resembles forgotten or lost etymological meanings.

The absence of related contextual clues pointing to a "live" figure helps diagnose a dead figure of speech. Conversely, interpreting a dead figure as a living image often yields some contextual incongruity — either a contradiction in terms or a mixed metaphor.

2. *Watch for multiple figures of speech and specify the figurative language.*

"All flesh is grass" is a metaphor; yet "flesh" is also a synecdoche for humanity. In Job 29:14, a simile follows a metaphor: "I put on righteousness and it clothed me. Like a robe and turban was my justice."

3. *Avoid restricting figures of speech to one usage.*

Figures, like any words, are quite adaptable. They may apply to different referents and carry different connotations. For example, the lion is often used in biblical figures of speech. Positively, the lion can represent the nation Israel (Ezk 19:1-9) or the powerful and triumphant Christ (Rv 5:5). Negatively, the lion pictures a prowling, voracious Devil (1 Pt 5:8), or vicious, attacking enemies (Ps 22:13).[36]

4. *Do not neglect the context as an interpretive guide.*

Rousing rabbinical discussions attempted to identify an entirely edible tree from the Garden of Eden ("the tree was good for food;" Gn 3:6). Such interpretations choke on the specific mention of "fruit" (Gn 3:2, 3, 6). Genesis 3:6 contains a synecdoche of the whole (tree) for the part (fruit).

The point of the comparison follows immediately in Isaiah 53:6, "All we like sheep have gone astray." In Psalm 1:3-5, chaff and a tree respectively represent the wicked and the righteous in regard to their stability and fruitfulness, according to modifying clauses and a concluding statement.

Again, a following clause in Psalm 22:16 identifies the "dogs" as evil doers.[37]

Elsewhere, parallelism,[38] synonyms, antonyms, or modifiers provide interpretive clues.

Respecting Figures of Speech

Cultural differences

Despite the abundance of biblical figures and a general familiarity with the Bible itself, cultural differences in the modern world complicate understanding and communicating the biblical message. Biblical figures often use objects, places, and customs foreign to modern readers. Even when those elements are familiar, the particular associations created in the biblical world may be quite foreign today.[39]

> The twentieth century urban reader is greatly removed from an Iron Age agrarian man. It is therefore imperative that the modern reader try to steep himself in the culture of the author in order to be able to think and feel with the inspired poet.[40]

Communicative value

Figures of speech have value for communication as well as interpretation. An Arab proverb says, "The best speaker is he who turns ears into eyes."

Vivid figures of speech grab attention and touch the emotions and will. Their picturesqueness seems tailored to an MTV generation.

A figure also promotes heightened understanding. It represents

> a deliberate choice ... to force ... a new awareness of the message. At first, the readers [or listeners] are jarred by the incongruity of the thought, for normal literal meanings do not fit. They are led to a new word picture of reality and forced to rethink the categories of the proposition stated .... A new world of discourse is fashioned, and the reader [or listener] is drawn into it.[41]

Finally, figures of speech provide a sensory experience that anchors revelation to reality. They are well suited for preaching.[42]

> We are to help our congregation to live anew the message God has revealed in the text and to feel its power to change their situation as well. The startling reverberations of meaning inherent in the Bible's figurative language is [sic] the best place to start, for it is alive with powerful, colorful ideas. In recapturing the vitality and forceful presentation of the language, we will help our listeners to place themselves in the shoes of the original hearers and both to relive and to apply anew that eternal message.[43]

Effective communicators, like the biblical writers, employ figures of speech.

Action Points

1. In your own terms, define "figure of speech."
2. Recall several common modern English figurative expressions. (Or find several in the introduction to this chapter.)
3. Can you cite a figurative biblical expression that is ignored or misinterpreted, or a literal expression mistaken as figurative?
4. Practice interpreting figures of speech. At least one figure occurs in each of the following verses: Gn 4:10, 41:57; 1 S 15:29; Jb 12:7, 28:22; Ps 1:4, 6:6, 23:1; Pr 8:1; Is 1:18, 10:7, 40:11.[44] (See Note 44 to compare answers.)
5. Evaluate the treatment of figures in several Bible translations, using the following scale.[45] (Start with the passages listed in Action Point #4.)

Verbatum Translation	Slight Modification	Renders Thought	Renders Thought & Emotive Effects
0	1	2	3

6. Evaluate the treatment of figures in several commentaries, using the following scale. (Start with the passages listed in Action Point #4.)

No Mention of Figure	Identifies Figure	Labels Figure	Decodes Thought	Decodes Thought & Emotive Effects
0	1	2	3	4

7. Review the Hebrew alphabet and vowels.
8. Read the sections on "Syntax" and "Discourse Analysis" in the Appendix.
9. Read more on biblical figures of speech.[46] (Begin with the references in Note 46.)

Notes

1. Ethelbert W. Bullinger, *Figures of Speech Used in the Bible*, repr. of London: Messrs. Eyre and Spottiswoode, 1898 ed. (Grand Rapids: Baker, 1968), xv. C. S. Lewis commented, "The truth is that if we are going to talk at all about things which are not perceived by the senses, we are forced to use language metaphorically" (J. Robertson McQuilkin, *Understanding & Applying the Bible* [Chicago: Moody, 1992], 167).

2. Edward W. Goodrick, *Do It Yourself Hebrew and Greek*, 2d ed. (Grand Rapids: Zondervan, 1980), 22:2-3. Bullinger lists about 8,000 Bible references containing figures (besides the most common, xii).

3. Bullinger, vi. McQuilken suggests figures are often necessary, emphatic, emotive, memorable, illustrative, illuminating, or obscure (166-69).

4. Goodrick, *Do It Yourself*, 22:2-3.

5. Bullinger notes, "Commentators and interpreters, from inattention to the figures, have been led astray from the real meaning of many important passages of God's Word; while ignorance of them has been the fruitful parent of error and false doctrine" (xvi).

6. Quintilian defines a figure of speech as "... a form of speech artfully varied from common usage" (Bruce K. Waltke, Jr., "Figures of Speech," unpublished *Psalms* class notes [Dallas, TX: Dallas Theological Seminary, n.d.]). Quinn objects to the static, passive term "figure of speech" as misleading, preferring "figurings of speech" or even "figuring speech" (Arthur Quinn, *Figures of Speech* [Salt Lake City: Peregrine Smith, Gibbs M Smith, 1982], 2). In Chapter 5, figure of speech refers to *tropes*, or words.

7. While technically belonging to the sphere of rhetoric (E. Wendland and E. A. Nida, "Lexicography and Bible Translating," in *Lexicography and Translation*, ed. Johannes P. Louw [Cape Town: Bible Society of South Africa, 1985], 12), figures of speech involve semantic analysis. Osborne agrees, despite the common treatment of figures as part of special hermeneutics (Grant R. Osborne, *The Hermeneutical Spiral* [Downers Grove, IL: InterVarsity, 1991], 103).

8. Stephen J. Brown, *Image and Truth* (Rome: Catholic Book Agency, 1955), 11. A figure "involves a shift in expectancy ... designating something which belongs to a quite different semantic domain" (Wendland and Nida, 9). So a "literal" reading of figures is the source of humor in many cartoons or puns.

9.   Brown, 19.

10.   Waltke, "Figures of Speech."

11.   Brown, 14, 45.

12.   Wendland and Nida, 10-11. English idioms include "take a seat" and "under the weather." Work still remains in the area of Hebrew idioms. Bullinger uses the term often for individual words and grammatical constructions (819-60). Sterrett admits his examples are more figurative or lexical uses (T. Norton Sterrett, *How to Understand Your Bible* [Downers Grove, IL: InterVarsity, 1974], 123-30). Clinton's attempt to categorize idioms lacks comprehensiveness and rationale (Bobby Clinton, *Figures and Idioms* [Coral Gables, FL: Learning Resource Center, West Indies Mission, 1977], 91). Lamsa is quite uneven, often presenting fanciful or anti-supernatural interpretations (George Mamishisho Lamsa, *Idioms in the Bible Explained and a Key to the Original Gospels* [New York: Harper & Row, 1985]). Samples of biblical Hebrew idioms include: "lift up the hands" = take a solemn oath (Gn 14:22); "laying on of hands" = blessing or approval (Gn 48:14); "hearts melting" = becoming disheartened or discouraged (Js 2:11); "to go out and come in" = lead in warfare (Js 14:11); "be known in the gates" = renowned in the city or public assembly (Pr 31:23); the reciprocal construction "a man to his fellow" = to one another (Jon 1:7); the superlative construction, as in "holy of holies" = the holiest place; "son of quality x" = possessing quality x (Ezk 2:1); and "son of x years" to express age (Gn 21:5; Ex 12:5). Finally, idiomatic uses of individual words occur; one example is "hate" as a relative rather than an absolute term (Ml 1:2-3; Gn 29:30-31; Dt 21:15-17).

13.   "Metaphor is constructed by bringing together two independent semantic units; allegory and symbol are constructed by deepening the meaning of one unit" (Jurij Lotman, *The Structure of the Artistic Text* [Ann Arbor, MI: University of Michigan, 1977], 208). Further, symbols are often relatively stable elements in a discourse which also represent something else, like the cows in Pharaoh's dreams (Gn 41) or the sun, moon, and stars in Joseph's (Gn 37:9-10). Common elements used as symbols are light (Ps 36:9), night (Job 35:10), and water (Jr 2:13). Events and actions, as well as objects, may be symbolic (Ezk 12:4, Is 20:2, Hs 1). See McQuilken, 260-64, for distinctions between symbols and types.

14.   Ryken distinguishes three types of irony: "(1) Dramatic irony occurs when a reader knows more about what is happening than do some of the characters in a story. (2) Verbal irony occurs

when a writer states something but means exactly the opposite. (3) Irony of situation occurs when a situation is the opposite of what is expected or appropriate" (Leland Ryken, *The Literature of the Bible* [Grand Rapids: Zondervan, 1974], 360). The greatest overlap with figures of speech, of course, involves verbal irony (1 K 18:27; 22:15; Am 4:4). A standard work is Edwin M. Good, *Irony in the Old Testament*, repr. of London, 1965 ed. (Sheffield: Almond, 1981). Briefer treatments are: W. G. E. Watson, *Classical Hebrew Poetry* (Sheffield: JSOT, 1984), 306-12 and Luis Alonso-Schökel, *A Manual of Hebrew Poetics* (Rome: Biblical Institute, 1988), 156-65.

15. See the brief comments on discourse analysis in the Appendix.
16. Consult general hermeneutics textbooks for the history of biblical interpretation. Chapter 6 briefly discusses allegorizing as a common error in treating biblical narratives.
17. Bullinger, xv.
18. Walter C. Kaiser, Jr., *Toward an Exegetical Theology* (Grand Rapids: Baker, 1981), 122; repeated in Walter C. Kaiser and Moisés Silva, *An Introduction to Biblical Hermeneutics* (Grand Rapids: Zondervan, 1994), 92-3. On the theoretical insufficiency of identifying criteria, see Brown, 140-50. Stein provides pragmatic suggestions for identifying hyperbole which are often applicable to other figures of speech; hyperbole: 1) is literally impossible; 2) conflicts with what the speaker says elsewhere; 3) conflicts with the actions of the speaker elsewhere; 4 & 5) conflicts with teachings of the OT or NT; 6) is interpreted by another biblical writer in a non-literal way; 7) has not been literally fulfilled; 8) would not achieve its desired goal if taken literally; 9) uses a literary form prone to exaggeration; or 10) uses universal language (Robert H. Stein, *Playing by the Rules* [Grand Rapids: Baker, 1994], 126-28).
19. Linguistically, such a figure breaks selectional rules (or acquires new selectional characteristics); specifically, the subject and predicate do not share the feature of animacy.
20. Interpretive help from the rest of the Bible is sometimes called *the analogy of Scripture*.
21. Waltke, "Figures of Speech."
22. Bullinger, xi.
23. Different schemes are proposed, along with some variety in the relation of specific figures to the processes for "figuring speech." Bullinger's three formative processes are omission, addition, and change; Kaiser's four are comparison, addition, relation, and contrast (122). Snyman and Cronje suggest another four

processes: repetition, omission, shift in expectancies, and mea-
surement of units (Kaiser and Silva, 93n6). Osborne lists six:
comparison, addition, incompleteness, contrast, personal figures,
and association or relation (103). Clinton pares down to three
processes: comparison, substitution, and apparent deception
(including over-, under-, and misstatement; 14). Wendland &
Nida apparently find the two processes of similarity (metaphors)
and association (metonyms) sufficient (10). Brown basically sees
figures as involving substitution with explicit or implicit comparison (1).

24. Bullinger, ix. Another reprint of an older work — Benjamin
Keach, *Preaching from the Types and Metaphors of the Bible*
(Grand Rapids: Kregel, 1972) — requires more judicious sifting.

25. A related rhetorical device, apostrophe, addresses an absent person
or an imaginary object and can involve personification.

26. A fine distinction suggests that overstatement is literally possible, as opposed to hyperbole. Alonso-Schökel, 168, notes
hyperbole is "particularly frequent in comparisons" in biblical
Hebrew.

27. Alonso-Schökel, 168-69, suggests understatement is relatively
rare in biblical Hebrew and "easier to find in negative forms."

28. Judson Jerome, "The Poetry of Concrete" in *The Writer's Digest
Guide to Good Writing*, ed. Thomas Clark, Bruce Woods, Peter
Blocksom, and Angela Terez (Cincinnati, OH: Writer's Digest,
1994), 254.

29. Compare BDB 7a 8. BDB frequently present what they understood to be the point of biblical figures of speech; look for their
abbreviations "fig.," "sim.," "metaph.," and "poet."

30. "'He who sows injustice will reap calamity' (Prov 22:8) can be
aptly re-expressed this way: 'He who acts unjustly will receive
calamity in return.' That clearly does not get all that the original
offered, for the imagery of sowing and reaping makes its own
aesthetic, affective, and exploratory contribution. But the
author's presentative purpose is adequately suggested in the
literal paraphrase" (Peter Macky, *The Centrality of Metaphors to
Biblical Thought* [Lewiston, NY: Mellen, 1990], 182).

31. Debate rages, for example, over the key term in Ecclesiastes,
"Everything is *a vapor/meaningless*." Does this figure represent
irrationality (as the English translation might suggest), or tran-
sience or insubstantialness (as the figure itself might suggest)?
Or is incomprehensibility or unfathomableness, or unsatisfac-
toriness or unacceptability the point? Perhaps usage varies

within Ecclesiastes? Or is there a single idea broad enough to capture this figure?

32.   Goldingay speaks of the problem of delimiting theology strictly in symbolic terms, "...symbolism itself invites or at least is open to, conceptual explication. Though it is concerned to do more than communicate at the cerebral level, it is not concerned to do less than that" (John Goldingay, *Theological Diversity and the Authority of the Old Testament* [Grand Rapids: Eerdmans, 1987], 177-78).

33.   Alonso-Schökel, 100-102, emphasizes the limits of conceptual translation. He also notes the difficulty of capturing the full import of figures: "Images are the glory, perhaps the essence of poetry, the enchanted planet of the imagination, a limitless galaxy, ever alive and ever changing. Is it not presumptuous to attempt to explain such a world created for contemplation and surprised light?" (95).

34.   These examples are adapted from Waltke.

35.   Osborne, 104-105; John Beekman and John Callow, *Translating the Word of God* (Grand Rapids: Zondervan, 1974), 131-35.

36.   Brown, 153.

37.   As a negative example, using Psalm 22:6 to teach a "worm theology" of self-deprecation ignores the context. The worm figure indicates insignificance; yet does not mean that the psalmist had, and we should have, low self-esteem. Although the psalmist's exceptional circumstances might have momentarily affected his self-esteem, the immediately following phrase emphasizes his mistreatment by others, as do the next twelve verses. Similarly, Job 25:6 could represent Bildad's distorted perspective, or more likely, humanity's comparative insignificance next to a holy Creator.

38.   Parallelism, discussed in Chapter 7, often aids interpretation.

39.   Brown, 45-61 discusses the impact of cultural differences for biblical figures of speech and provides numerous examples.

40.   Waltke.

41.   Osborne, 103, interpreting Ricoeur's discussion.

42.   Chapter 9 surveys the preaching application of the biblical text.

43.   Osborne, 108-9.

44.   Did you identify the following figures of speech? personification (Gn 4:10); metonymy of subject (Gn 41:57); metonymy of adjunct (1 S 15:29); personification (Jb 12:7); personification (Jb 28:22); simile (Ps 1:4); hyperbole (Ps 6:6); metaphor (Ps 23:1); personification and rhetorical question (Pr 8:1); simile (Is 1:18); understatement (Is 10:7); and simile (Is 40:11).

45.   The charts in Action Points #5 and #6 are modified from Clinton, 13.

46.   For more on biblical figures of speech, see Osborne, 100-109; Kaiser and Silva, 92-98 (similarly, Kaiser 1981, 121-25); Watson, 251-343; Beekman and Callow, 116-50; William W. Klein, Craig L. Blomberg, and Robert L. Hubbard Jr., *Introduction to Biblical Interpretation* (Dallas: Word, 1993), 241-52; McQuilken, 165-83; Clinton; A. Berkeley Mickelsen, *Interpreting the Bible* (Grand Rapids: Eerdmans, 1963), 179-235; or William E. Mouser, Jr., *Walking in Wisdom* (Downers Grove, IL: InterVarsity, 1983), 80-123.

Chapter 6

The Artistry of Biblical Hebrew: Narrative

Objectives: After reading this chapter, you should be able to:
1. Recall three aspects of the nature of biblical narrative.
2. Suggest some practical benefits of a literary approach to biblical Hebrew narrative.
3. Look for basic narrative devices as an aid in exegeting biblical Hebrew narrative.
4. Avoid common errors in interpreting biblical Hebrew narrative.

Variously considered edifying or embarrassing, the many Old Testament stories seldom fail to engage readers.

About forty percent of the Hebrew Bible is narrative, making it the most common type of literature there.[1] Broadly speaking, *narrative* refers to a story of the life, or episodes in the life, of a person or group.[2] Such narratives occur throughout the Old Testament, but especially in the section commonly called the Historical Books — Genesis through Esther.

Not only are Old Testament narratives popular and prominent, but they can be very productive in ministry. Narratives transform listeners by: 1) catching them off-guard and reversing expectations (as Nathan's parable convicted David of his sin with Bathsheba; 2 S 12:1-6); 2) developing personhood and self-identification (through the story characters and their actions); 3) stimulating imagination and exploration of possibilities (through entrance into the story-world); and 4) authorizing, evaluating, celebrating, and directing certain behaviors and values.[3]

If study of biblical narrative was once "in eclipse,"[4] narrative is now radiant in biblical studies and other disciplines. Narrative theology emphasizes the power of stories for shaping theology and interpreting faith;[5] narrative preaching is a prominent homiletical approach;[6] and narrative counseling is becoming a popular therapeutic treatment.[7]

This chapter promotes a literary approach consistent with biblical narrative's nature, surveys narrative devices influential for exegesis, and warns of common errors in treating biblical narratives.

Tell Me a Story: A Literary Approach to Biblical Hebrew Narrative

The nature of biblical narrative

A holistic conservative view treats biblical narrative as both history and story, and ultimately, His story.

1. Biblical narrative is history.

The Bible is not primarily a history text. Nor does biblical history conform to a modern myth of history writing as totally objective and impartial reporting. But viewing biblical narrative as defective fiction is itself defective.

Christianity, following Christ and the Apostles, has traditionally affirmed the inspiration and historical reliability of the Bible. Many historical details receive confirmation from archaeology, which is still an adolescent science posing problems awaiting future resolution. Therefore, conservative Christians insist on reading biblical narratives as accurate presentations of time and space events.

Greidanus indicates the relation of history to biblical narrative:

> Although there is much to be said for the power of story and how it works apart from the question of historicity, it must also be said that treating all biblical narratives like parables is a gross oversimplification, for not all biblical narratives are non-historical .... The issue here again is the intent or purpose of the text. If that intent ...entails relating historical events, then sidestepping that intent in one's interpretation fails to do full justice to that narrative's meaning.[8]

2. Biblical narrative is story.

Often in ways as crucial for their interpretation as historicity is for their authority, biblical narratives appear as stories shaped by literary artists. The biblical writers are selective in their details and purposeful in their arrangement of subject matter.

Stories, as previously indicated, are the chosen vessels for much of the biblical writers' precious content. They use the basic devices of storytellers, which this chapter surveys.

While the Bible is more than literature, it is at least literature.[9] C. S. Lewis maintains this balanced perspective:

> Those who talk of reading the Bible "as literature" sometimes mean, I think, reading it without attending to the main thing it is about; like reading Burke with no interest in politics, or reading the *Aeneid* with no interest in Rome. That seems to me to be nonsense. But there is a saner sense in which the Bible, since it is after all literature, cannot properly be read except as literature; and the different parts of it as the different sorts of literature they are.[10]

Biblical writers use stories to teach indirectly and subtly. Like most good artists, they prefer oblique hints over explicit statements. And they reward attentive readers.

3. Biblical narrative is His story.

Above and beyond their role as stories, however, biblical narratives are theological history. They instruct concerning the chief character, namely God, and his dealings with humanity. Frederick Buechner puts it this way:

> The Bible is God's book. It is as unimaginable without him as Moby Dick would be without the great white whale, yet like the great white whale, God is scarcely to be seen. ... God is not to be seen in this book that is his except as he is reflected in the faces and lives of people who have encountered him .... But he can be *heard*.[11]

A literary approach: Definition and a distinction

1. Definition

Through his insightful 1981 book, *The Art of Biblical Narrative*, Robert Alter greatly stimulated interest in literary aspects of Bible study.[12] Alter defines literary analysis as "minutely discriminating attention to the artful use of language, to the shifting play of ideas, conventions, tone, sound, imagery, syntax, narrative viewpoint, compositional units, and much else."[13]

In traditional Old Testament studies of the last two centuries, however, literary analysis, or literary criticism, has primarily meant *source criticism*, the process of detecting hypothetical documents woven together to form the biblical text. The basic hypothesis for the composition of the Pentateuch, and much of the Old Testament, identifies documents J, E, D, and P.[14]

Designating a close reading of a biblical text as a literary approach (rather than literary analysis or literary criticism) avoids possible confusion with source criticism.[15] A *literary approach* pays attention to a text's form and style, as well as content, as indicators of meaning.

2. A distinction

Alter argues for an aesthetic literary approach that allows "for the exercise of pleasurable invention for its own sake." Yet examining the Bible as *art for its own sake* blurs the division between sacred and secular literature.[16]

C. S. Lewis warns that an aesthetic emphasis loses sight of the Bible's unique, sacred nature. It is

> through and through, a sacred book. Most of its component parts were written, and all of them were brought together, for a purely religious purpose .... It is ... not only a sacred book but a book so remorsely and continuously sacred that it does not invite, it excludes or repels, the merely aesthetic approach.[17]

A mere aesthetic focus, however, is not an inherent feature of a literary approach.[18] A literary approach can heighten understanding, as well as appreciation, of the Bible's unique message. Accordingly, the exegetical literary approach advocated here clarifies biblical narrative's moral-theological meaning.

Practical benefits of a literary approach

A literary approach to narrative yields practical benefits in bibliology, comparative literature, exegesis, and exposition.

While source criticism remains alive, its health is deteriorating. Current biblical scholarship is reassessing source criticism's "assured results," partly due to literary studies of the Bible.[19] By concentrating on the form of biblical texts, a literary approach often identifies unifying patterns that challenge traditional source criticism.

Additionally, comparing biblical narratives with other literary works showcases similarities and contrasts. Significantly, a literary approach often emphasizes the Bible's distinctive features, particularly when compared to literature of the ancient world. In sheer amount and certain literary features, biblical Hebrew narratives stand apart from ancient literatures dominated by epics and royal annals.[20]

The greatest benefit of a literary approach, however, is heightened understanding of the biblical text. Many fine literary studies provide insights into biblical narratives[21] and exegesis prospers by implementing the concepts of a literary approach (such as sketched in this chapter).

Lastly, a literary approach links the minister to his audience. People naturally read biblical narratives as great stories. Highlights from a literary approach will be common to readers' intuition or easily demonstrated from the text, usually without recourse to any specialized jargon.[22]

Biblical Hebrew Narrative Devices

The basic devices of scenes, point of view, characterization, dialogue and narration, plot, and stylistic features like repetition aid exegesis.[23]

Scenes and point of view

The most distinctive feature of narrative is the presenting mode of scenes.[24] *Scenes* describe the actions of particular characters in a given setting.

Kaiser summarizes the significance of scenes in the interpretive process:

> The interpreter must identify each of these scenes, much as one would break up a long prose passage into paragraphs. It is helpful to draft a summary statement for each scene ... focus[ing] on the actions, words, or depictions in the scene, keeping in mind the direction the author seems to be following in the whole sequence of scenes. If the author's point in a

given narrative is at first unclear, we can profit by focusing for the moment on God's presence, actions, and comments in each scene where they are relevant.[25]

Mentally restaging the narrative as a play broken down into scenes clarifies understanding. Who are the characters on stage? What are they doing? What are the essential background props (objects in the story that form the scenery)? What is the setting (time and place)?

Related to the scene is the point of view. Scenes are filtered through different perspectives. If your restaged play were videotaped, where would the camcorder focus and from what position would it film?

Often, the biblical narrator holds the camcorder[26] and provides the best guide to a narrative's message. Abraham and Isaac sweated out the so-called sacrifice of Isaac (Gn 22), yet the narrator states up-front that God was testing Abraham's faith (Gn 22:1).

Stories may also be told from a character's point of view. Indicators of a biblical character's point of view include direct speech, dialogue, inner monologue, and the presentative particle *hinneh*, "Look!"[27] An expositor can often step into the sandals of such a character to vividly recreate the narrative. When the character is a prophet or hero of faith, that point of view directs interpretation.

Characterization

1. General considerations of biblical characterization

Characterization refers to how individuals are represented in stories. The realistic portrayal of individuals explains some of biblical narrative's appeal.[28]

Homeric literature tends to represent characters by means of a fixed epithet describing a single quality ("fleet-footed Achilles"). The Bible, on the other hand, has a dynamic conception of individuals as unpredictable and often impenetrable. These differing methods of characterization have been called, respectively, "flat" and "round."[29]

Readers sometimes receive inside information about complex biblical individuals from the narrator, who occupies something of an "omniscient" position. In fact, the biblical narrator typically holds the divine perspective.

However, the biblical narrator exercises his "divine right" only sparingly. Usually he prefers to let the story "speak for itself" and leaves many specifics ambiguous. Alter calls this feature of biblical narrative "the art of reticence."

2. A scale of character-revealing means[30]

Narrator omniscience and reticence in biblical characterization call for careful evaluation of characters' behavior and motives. The following scale helps the minister know when to "pound the pulpit." The higher up the scale, the greater the assurance regarding a character's motives and morals. Toward the bottom of the scale, the exegete must make a case for a specific interpretation (largely from contextual clues) and allow for complex or even inscrutable human behavior.

Transparent/Explicit	- | -	narrator's statement
Relative certainty	- | -	inward speech (summarized or quoted) and prayer
Weighing of claims	- | -	direct speech by a character or by others about him
Opaque/Inference	- | -	actions/appearance/ gestures/posture/attire

Transparent/Explicit. When the narrator overcomes his reticence, evaluations of a character's actions and motives are trustworthy. Assuredly, Noah was righteous (Gn 6:8) and the Sodomites were wicked (Gn 13:13). Sometimes the narrator indicates a character's emotions: Sarah was afraid (Gn 18:15); David was angry (2 S 6:8). At other times, the narrator even draws back the veil in heaven: "God heard their groaning and remembered his covenant" (Ex 3:24).

Relative certainty. A character's inward speech and prayer affords the reader a relatively high degree of certainty; at least it reflects that person's thoughts. A fearful Abraham lied about Sarah ("There is surely no fear of God in this place, and they will kill me because of my wife" [Gn 20:11].). Initially murderous Saul said to himself, "I will not raise a hand against David. Let the Philistines do that" (1 S 18:17). Jonah tells God (and us) he fled rather than go to Nineveh as an instrument of God's mercy (Jon 4:1).

Weighing of claims. Statements by or about a character must be evaluated. The serpent alleged an outright lie, contradicting God's word, "You will not surely die" (Gn 3:4). Abraham deceptively proclaimed a half-truth, "Sarah is my sister" (Gn 20:2). Shimei improperly castigated David, "The LORD has repaid you" (2 S 16:8); but Shimei was ironically partly correct and partly wrong. (David's sin with Bathsheba brought the disciplinary action yet God wasn't taking away the kingdom.) It is difficult to say whether Abimelech honestly claimed, "I do not know who has done this deed" (Gn 21:25).

Opaque/Inference. Non-verbal behavior, while a powerful means of communication, is subject to varied interpretations. Likewise, unraveling narrative actions can be a challenge. For example, interpreters propose different motivations for Cain's bringing crops as an offering (Gn 4:3) and Bathsheba's sleeping with David (2 S 11:4). Although contextual features often provide interpretive clues, biblical writers sometimes show little interest in modern interpreters' questions. When the narrative itself is noncommittal, the interpreter should avoid rushing to judge biblical individuals.

Dialogue[31]

Alter considers dialogue "the key to the essential" in biblical narrative. He describes the Bible's preferred style as "narration-through-dialogue."

Watch for contrastive dialogue that differentiates between characters. The interchange between Potiphar's wife and Joseph displays, in brief, the opposite paths of pagan wickedness and reverent, faithful righteousness. In just two Hebrew words, Potiphar's lustful wife demands Joseph sleep with her (Gn 39:7). Joseph, in contrast, responds with an ethical treatise and catalog of God's provision:

> "With me in charge," he told her, "my master does not concern himself with anything in the house; everything he owns he has entrusted to my care. No one is greater in this house than I am. My master has withheld nothing from me except you, because you are his wife. How then could I do such a wicked thing and sin against God?" (Gn 39:8 NIV)

Initial dialogue also demands attentiveness. "In most instances, the initial words spoken by a personage will be revelatory, perhaps more in manner than in matter."[32] The serpent initially impugned God's goodness by questioning and distorting His word, "*Indeed*, did God say, 'You must not eat from any tree in the garden?'" (Gn 3:1).

Narration

Besides the biblical narrator's importance for point of view and characterization, four major types of narration deserve attention.[33]

Narration proper typically provides a chronicle or a summarizing overview (like long sections in Kings). Less well-recognized are three other types of narration: essential data, expository data, and dialogue-bound narration.

Essential data refers to actions necessary for the unfolding plot. Such details (frequently conveyed through *waw* consecutives) often would be inadequately conveyed in dialogue.

Expository data communicates additional information not strictly part of the story action. Information may appear in "pretemporal verses" that stand before the time of the story, such as the naming of characters. Sometimes expository data explicitly reports attitudes or bits of physical detail; the Bible's sparsity of character-descriptive detail marks such expository data as noteworthy.[34] Joseph's story receives this backdrop: "Israel loved Joseph more than any of his other sons" (Gn 37:3). In another narrative, David is called a "pretty boy" just as he confronts Goliath (1 S 17:42).

Dialogue-bound narration is the verbatim mirroring, subverting, or focussing in narration of statements made elsewhere in direct speech. Close repetition shows emphasis or confirmation, while subverting indicates dissonance. Summaries of speech rapidly advance the narrative, avoid excessive repetition, or devalue the content. On the other hand, a lack of speech — a particular character's silence where speech would be expected (such as Jacob's silence after hearing of his daughter's rape; Gn 34:5) — can foreshadow ominous events.

Plot

Plot is the interaction between characters and their circumstances directed toward an end.[35] Different literary critics propose various elements form a typical plot, but all proposals elaborate on Aristotle's notion that a story has a beginning, middle, and end.[36] Most critics also agree that the middle of a story involves an element of crisis or conflict.

Longacre's description of a typical plot serves as an interpretive template for biblical narrative:[37]

1.	Exposition	'Lay something out'
2.	Inciting Moment	'Get something going'
3.	Developing Conflict	'Keep the heat on'
4.	Climax	'Knot it all up proper'
5.	Denouement	'Loosen it'
6.	Final Suspense	'Keep untangling'
7.	Conclusion	'Wrap it up'

Seeing these seven plot elements in Genesis 3, for example, shows the narrative flow and correlates the "exegetically awkward" final section (3:20-24). Respectively, the seven elements surface in Genesis 2—3:1; 3:2-7; 3:8-13; 3:14-19; 3:20-21; 3:22-23; and 3:24.

A supplemental form of biblical Hebrew plot analysis traces the verb sequencing. Typically, a *waw* consecutive plus preterite [WP] advances the main storyline, while *waw* disjunctive clauses [DW] represent a break or a sidebar of contrastive, circumstantial, or background information.[38]

For biblical Hebrew narrative, tracing the verb sequencing (mentally or visually) is usually quicker and more productive than forms of textual diagramming. A simple schematic of the verb sequencing in Genesis 4:1-5 shows how the narrative advances rapidly after being marked as a new episode and then slows to portray the contrasts between Cain and Abel:[39]

1		[DW]	(introductory) Now the man lay with Eve
		[WP]	and she conceived
		[WP]	and she gave birth
		[WP]	and she said
			(direct discourse [perfect tense])
2		[WP]	and she again gave birth
		[WP]	and *Abel* became a shepherd
		[DW]	(contrastive) but *Cain* became a farmer
3	[WP]	[WP]	(temporal clause plus …) *Cain* brought
4		[DW]	(contrastive) but *Abel* brought
		[WP]	and the LORD had favor on *Abel*
5		[DW]	(contrastive) but not on *Cain*
		[WP]	and Cain was very angry about this
		[WP]	and he sulked

Repetition

Style refers to choices of expression or the way a communicator puts things.[40] The most common stylistic feature in biblical Hebrew narrative — repetition, in various forms — repays close observation.[41] Alter shows that repetition functions on different levels, from a single word to a package of typical actions.[42] After an overview of various forms of repetition, several specific forms (those without listed examples) receive elaboration.

1. A scale of repetitive focusing devices

Type-scene	- -	a crucial episode in a hero's life, with a fixed sequence of motifs
Sequence of Actions	- -	frequently three consecutive repetitions, or "three plus one," concluding with a climax or reversal (Nm 22:21-35; 2 K 1:9-15)
Theme	- -	an idea that is part of the value-system of the narrative (the Abrahamic covenant and reversal of primogeniture in Gn)
Motif	- -	a concrete image, quality, action, or object acquires symbolic meaning or unifies the narrative (stones for Jacob; dreams for Joseph; water for Moses; fire for Elijah)
Phrase	- -	a phrase is expanded or modified
Word-play	- -	a word-root, its semantic range, synonyms, antonyms, or puns

2. Word-play

All biblical Hebrew literature delights in word-play.[43] *Word-play* relates similar sounds or meanings of words, or both at the same time. The sounds of words may be similar (*paronomasia*), or identical (*homonymy*). Words repeat with the same meaning, or with different meanings (*polysemy*), or a single word can imply two meanings at once (deliberate ambiguity or *double entendre*).

Biblical Hebrew narrative especially employs two particular forms of word-play. One is the well-known naming phenomenon. Old Testament persons and places receive names based on etymologies or, more often, popular etymologies with similarities in sound and meaning. Such names typically provide clues to a narrative's main themes.[44]

Another common biblical narrative feature is the leading word or *leitwort*. A particular word-root, its semantic range, synonyms, antonyms, or puns echo throughout a text, often signaling central concerns or themes. In 1 Samuel 15, the repetition of "listen" emphasizes Saul's unworthiness, since Israel's king should obey God rather than men:

> [Saul says, "I *listened* to the people's voice" (v. 24).] This loaded verb, whose sense extends from hearing to obedience, resonates ... as a command ("Now therefore *listen* to the voce of the Lord"); as a call to battle ("Saul *summoned* the people"); as a sarcastic show of innocence ("What then is this bleating ... which I *hear*?"); as a direct accusation ("Why then didst thou not *listen* to the voice of the Lord?'"); as a self-justifying denial (I did *listen* to the voice of the Lord"); and as a doctrinal priority (Is the Lord as pleased with burnt offerings and sacrifice as with *listening* to the voice of the Lord?"). So its new appearance, in the context of *vox populi*, galvanizes in retrospect a whole chain of meaning: it infringes the command, confirms the accusation, denies the denial, reverses the scale of priorities.[45]

3. Phrasal repetition

Phrases repeat in various ways to reveal characters, themes, or actions. Incremental repetition, or progressive elaboration, builds to a climax and often reveals character. Nathan calculatingly stirs David against Adonijah through repetition and elaboration of Bathsheba's account (1 K 1:11-27).

The substitution, suppression, or addition of a single phrase, or a strategic change in order modifies initial perceptions. The angel's announcement of Samson's birth as a deliverer and Nazirite from birth (Jg 13:5) sounds promising; yet in relaying this announcement, Samson's mother portentously adds "until the day of his death" (Jg 13:7).

Understatement or dissonance often foreshadows a coming event. In 2 Samuel 3:21-23, three repetitions emphasize that Abner "went in peace" from David's presence. Joab, however, questions whether Abner "went (away) indeed" (2 S 3:24). This foreshadows Joab's own non-peaceable intention, as he deceitfully retrieves and murders Abner.

4. Type-scenes[46]

A *type-scene* is a recurrent narrative episode at crucial junctures in heroes' lives. Type-scenes form a specific kind of *convention*, or set of tacit agreements between an artist and audience about the ordering of a work which enables communication. American audiences know to expect a shootout in westerns, but they appreciate modifications of the high-noon setting and the good-guy-in-white motif.

Biblical type-scenes include the annunciation of a hero's birth to a barren mother, an encounter with the future betrothed at a well, an epiphany in the field, an initiatory trial, danger in the desert, discovery of a well or other source of sustenance, and the testament of a dying hero. Comparing and contrasting elements in particular type-scenes with "the norm" clarifies a text's message.

Recurrence of the basic pattern often attaches the particular event to a larger pattern of historical and theological meaning, such as a further outworking of the original covenant. Innovation, allusion, transformation, or omission of a type-scene diverges from the expected pattern to convey meaning about the events, characters, or themes of the narrative.

The book of Ruth, for example, modifies the type-scene of encountering the future betrothed at a well on foreign soil.

The heroine (!) comes to Judah, meets Boaz in a field where he commands his young men (counterparts of the traditional maidens) to draw her water, and shares a simple meal (rather than a feast) with her future spouse. These events help Naomi and the readers recognize God's providence and covenant-keeping faithfulness in Ruth's life. Ruth acts as a female "patriarch" through whom the promised line comes.

5. Chiasmus

Chiasmus arranges corresponding elements in an inverted X-pattern and involves repetition.[47] Augmenting a chiasmus with a central element forms a concentric structure and focuses on the centered element. Chiastic patterns showcase textual unity.

One example, Daniel 2—7, clarifies that text's focus on divine providence in the midst of chaotic times:[48]

A   Daniel 2   Four Gentile world empires

    B   Daniel 3   Gentile persecution of Israel

        C   Daniel 4   Divine providence over Gentiles

        C'   Daniel 5   Divine providence over Gentiles

    B'   Daniel 6   Gentile persecution of Israel

A'   Daniel 7   Four Gentile world empires

A Checklist for Narrative:
Keys to Interpretation[49]

1. *Scenes and point of view*: Identify the separate scenes with their characters, setting, and scenery. Determine the different points of view expressed, particularly the narrator's or key characters'.

2. *Characters*: Use the scale of character-revealing means to evaluate motives and actions.

3. *Dialogue and narration*: Listen closely to initial or contrastive dialogue. Also, does the absence of any expected response indicate discontinuity? Does the narration provide a summary or evaluation, or give data essential or extraneous to the plot? In verbatim repetition, watch for small alterations, reversals of order, elaborations or deletions that reveal character or plot.

4. *Plot*: Can you spot at least a beginning, a crisis, and an end? Can you follow the verb sequencing?

5. *Repetitions*: Look for repeated words, phrases, themes, or actions. Does the story represent a type-scene and how does that type-scene compare to the norm? Is there a major structuring repetition, like chiasmus?

Common Errors in Handling Biblical Hebrew Narrative

Seven common practices should be avoided: allegorizing, typologizing, exemplifying, redefining, psychologizing, decontextualizing, and decapitating biblical Hebrew narratives.[50]

Allegorizing

Allegories indeed are always most easy. But it requires a great deal of study and labour, to master the literal sense of the sacred books.[51]

Allegorizing seeks hidden spiritual meaning beyond the historical and literary meaning of the text.[52] Usually such allegories involve several arbitrary points of correspondence.

As an example, Origen proposes that Pharaoh represents the devil, and the male and female Hebrew children respectively represent humanity's rational and animal faculties (Ex 1:22—2:10). Accordingly, the Exodus narrative shows that the devil seeks to destroy rationality and preserve carnal propensities.[53]

While easily created to impress the naive, allegories usually break down at particular points. Invariably, allegorizing belittles the plain meaning of Scripture.[54]

Typologizing

Typology is the study of divinely ordained foreshadowings of future events or aspects of salvation history through persons, events, objects, or institutions. Both the Old and New Testament legitimate a proper typology.[55]

Jesus compares the salvation brought by His crucifixion with the physical deliverance of Israelites who looked in faith on the metal serpent (Jn 3:14-15). Again in the New Testament, Paul presents Christ as a second Adam (Rm 5:12-19).

Even within the Old Testament, typology compares Abraham's sojourn in Egypt with that of the Israelites. Moses' deliverance from water by an ark reflects Noah's. Similarly, the tabernacle was a type for Solomon's temple.

On the other hand, wholesale typologizing apart from specific contextual validation or subsequent revelation distorts a narrative's primary message. Some want to call the raven Noah sent from the ark a type of humanity content with a world under judgment (Gn 8:6). Besides lacking external support, this misses a major point of the flood narrative — rebellious humanity was catastrophically judged while righteous Noah and his family were saved![56]

Although the tabernacle patterns the way to God through Christ, not every splinter need fester a great theological truth.

Exemplifying

Since narratives incarnate truth, popular Bible study method recommends finding examples within the narratives. ("What example is there for me to emulate or avoid?") But easy or unwarranted exemplifying tempts Bible students and ministers.

Impenetrable characterizations and narrator reticence may complicate the process of determining appropriate examples within biblical narratives. Problematically, narratives may simply describe actions or events without endorsing them. Additionally, biblical narratives may contain values not apparent on first reading. (Chapter 8 discusses the related topic of bridging the culture gap.)

One story demonstrates the need to carefully interpret biblical examples. Moses' killing of an Egyptian — often viewed as a negative example — actually marks him as God's deliverer of the oppressed Israelites (Ex 2:11-15). Notice the repetitions of "Hebrew" and "his own people" in this account. To the question "Who made you ruler and judge over us?" (Ex 2:14), Exodus answers, "The LORD appointed Moses." The New Testament concurs with this interpretation by portraying Moses as a type of Jesus: "Moses thought that his own people would realize that God was using him to rescue them, but they did not" (Ac 7:25).

Appropriate exemplary lessons must cohere with the text's main message and the values endorsed within the text. Otherwise authority rests in the interpreter rather than in the text.

Redefining

In another misguided attempt to make biblical Hebrew narratives more "relevant," some interpreters redefine specific terms. Since oil sometimes symbolically represents the Holy Spirit, redefiners assert that Elisha's multiplying the widow's oil shows the need for an increase of the Spirit (2 K 4:1-7). Apart from the questionable pneumatology, such eisegesis detracts from prominent themes in 2 Kings, namely, the LORD's provision (contrary to supposed provision from the pagan fertility deity Baal) and the authentication of His prophets.

Psychologizing

All truth is indeed God's truth and psychological principles derived from general revelation may enlighten biblical revelation. Too often, however, biblical texts become mere springboards for the latest trend in psychology.

Twenty-five years ago, biblical narratives supposedly reflected behavioral psychology principles. Today, family systems principles supposedly emerge, especially principles of dysfunctional families.[57]

For example, psychologizers maintain that biblical narratives demonstrate *generational sin*, the idea that children invariably repeat the parent's sins. Psychologizers support this idea of generational sin by reference to the fathers' sin being "visited" (the King James rendering) upon later generations (Ex 20:5; Ex 34:7; Nm 14:18; Dt 5:9).[58] This phrase, however, emphasizes God's longsuffering mercy in withholding judgment — even for generations. Similarly, Genesis 15:14-16 predicts God would wait for generations to judge the Egyptians and Canaanites. While the power of parental example is undeniable, these commonly-cited passages do not teach generational sin.

Although well-established psychological principles certainly operate in biblical characters' lives, avoid "using" biblical texts with little regard for their real message.

Decontextualizing

In a sense, all the previous errors are specific forms of decontextualizing. Basically, *decontextualizing* means ignoring the historical or literary context of a text. "Any text out of context is a pretext" remains the most potent interpretive guideline.

Decapitating

Attempting to supply an interpretive safeguard otherwise sound exegetes suggest, "Biblical narrative is not didactic."[59] Certainly narrative differs from more propositionally-oriented genres like legal or epistolary literature.

But *biblical narrative teaches*. The Apostle Paul affirms all Scripture is profitable for doctrine and instruction (2 Tm 3:15-16).

Narrative teaches differently than other genres. Frequently, narrative teaches subtly and indirectly through actions and events. At other times, narrative teaches directly, through narrator or character statements or through repetition. But biblical narrative teaches.

A related, and equally misguided, interpretive safeguard insists that all teaching must come from more directly propositional statements elsewhere in the Bible. Narrative is relegated to a mere supporting or illustrative role, as if ancient Israelites sat around campfires saying, "Great story. Someday perhaps someone will come along to explain it."

Even with the best intentions, disallowing its didactic function effectively decapitates biblical narrative and renders it lifeless. This leaves the biblical landscape littered with narrative corpses.

Be aware of the nature of narrative and use narrative devices as interpretive aids. But by all means discover and profit from biblical Hebrew narrative's teaching.

Action Points

1. Evaluate the three proposed aspects of the nature of biblical narrative (history, story, and His story). Which causes you the most difficulty personally? Would you jettison any proposed aspect, and if so, why? Can you suggest another crucial aspect?

2. Assess the value of a literary approach for your own exegetical method. (You might compare the exegetical worksheet in Chapter 2.) Justify why and where you include or exclude it.

3. Give an example of one of the seven common errors regarding biblical narratives. What other errors in the handling of narratives have you observed?

4. Pick a biblical Hebrew narrative text and identify some of the narrative devices there.

5. Review some of the grammatical concepts in the Appendix by studying some specific texts.[60] (For example, can you find three definite articles in Genesis 1:9 and all three types of *waw* in Genesis 2:25? What type of infinitive and volitive appear in Genesis 2:18 and what are their functions? In Genesis 2:24, what is the function of the imperfect tense and all the subsequent *waw* consecutive plus perfect tense forms? *Therefore*, in the last verse, who is the speaker [compare BDB 487B 3f]? Note 60 supplies answers.)

6. Scan (for possible purchase) Leland Ryken and Tremper Longman, III, eds., *A Complete Literary Guide to the Bible* (Grand Rapids: Zondervan, 1993).

7. Read some literary studies of biblical Hebrew narratives. (Begin with those listed in Note 21.)

8. Study a series of narratives as preparation for a preaching series. (The stories of Abraham, Moses, Joshua, the judges, David, and Jonah yield lively and life-changing preaching.)

Notes

1. William W. Klein, Craig L. Blomberg, and Robert L. Hubbard, Jr., *Introduction to Biblical Interpretation* (Dallas: Word, 1993), 261. Graesser estimates seventy-seven percent of the entire Bible is narrative (Walter C. Kaiser, Jr., "The Use of Biblical Narrative in Expository Preaching," *Asbury Seminarian* 34 [3, 1979]: 15, 25). Chapter 7 discusses another broad Old Testament genre, poetry, which overlaps wisdom and prophecy. For legal literature and genre-based interpretive approaches, see Klein, Blomberg, and Hubbard, 259-322; or Walter C. Kaiser, Jr. and Moises Silva, *An Introduction to Biblical Hermeneutics* (Grand Rapids: Zondervan, 1994), 69-158.

2. This definition fits biblical narrative especially if God is seen as the focal character. For other "narrative" genres and implications for interpretation, see Klein, Blomberg, and Hubbard, 259-74; and Leland Ryken, *The Literature of the Bible* (Grand Rapids: Zondervan, 1974).

3. This summarizes Thiselton's four functions of narrative (Anthony C. Thiselton, *New Horizons in Hermeneutics* [Grand Rapids: Zondervan, HarperCollins, 1992], 566-75), particularly his last one ("overlap with self-involving speech acts in which illocutions become operative"). Thiselton makes great contributions in the area of hermeneutics, but his book is not easy reading.

4. Hans W. Frei, *The Eclipse of Biblical Narrative* (New Haven: Yale University, 1974). Kaiser provides a critical evaluation of this book's hermeneutical theory (Kaiser and Silva, 82-83).

5. See "Narrative Theology" in Donald K. McKim, *The Bible in Theology and Preaching* (Nashville: Abingdon, 1994), 125-33.

6. For narrative preaching, start with Bryan Chapell, *Using Illustrations to Preach with Power* (Grand Rapids: Zondervan, 1992), 190-204; and Bruce C. Salmon, *Storytelling in Preaching* (Nashville: Broadman, 1988).

7. McMinn presents a concise practical strategy for narrative counseling (Mark R. McMinn "The Power of a Picture," *Christian Counseling Today* 2:1 [1994]: 42-43).

8. Sidney Greidanus, cited in Kaiser and Silva, 80.

9. The oft-cited evaluation of literary critic Northrop Frye suggests the Bible "is as literary as it can well be without actually being literature" (Northrop Frye, *The Great Code* [New York: Harcourt Brace Jovanovich, 1982], 62). Frye refuses to describe the Bible as literature because he accepts modern literary criticism's denial of true referential meaning in literature. See further Tremper

Longman, III, *Literary Approaches to Biblical Interpretation* (Grand Rapids: Zondervan, 1987), 54-58; or Kaiser and Silva, 82-83.

10. Ronald Barclay Allen, *Praise!* (Nashville: Thomas Nelson, 1980), 23-24.

11. Leland Ryken and Tremper Longman, III, eds., *A Complete Literary Guide to the Bible* (Grand Rapids: Zondervan, 1993), 42-43. Roland Frye likewise comments, "The characterization of God may indeed be said to be the central literary concern of the Bible, and it is pursued from beginning to end, for the principal character, or actor, or protagonist of the Bible is God. Not even the most seemingly insignificant action in the Bible can be understood apart from the emerging characterization of the deity. With this great protagonist and his designs, all other characters and events interact, as history becomes the great arena for God's characteristic and characterizing actions" (Ryken and Longman, *Literary Guide*, 36).

12. Robert Alter, *The Art of Biblical Narrative* (New York: Basic Books, 1981). This chapter's title purposely resembles Alter's book title, as it draws heavily from this influential work. Useful surveys of the history of literary approaches to the Bible include Alter, *Art*, 3-22; Longman, *Literary Approaches*, 13-45; Ryken and Longman, *Literary Guide*, 49-68; and David Norton, *A History of the Bible as Literature* (New York: Cambridge University, 1993).

13. Alter, *Art*, 12.

14. Old Testament introductions discuss the documentary hypothesis. Richard Elliot Friedman, *Who Wrote the Bible?* (New York: Summit Books, Simon & Schuster, 1987) gives a popular modern introduction to this hypothesis. Norman Habel, *Literary Criticism of the Old Testament* (Philadelphia: Fortress, 1971) sketches source critical method. Campbell presents the sources as identified by Martin Noth (Antony F. Campbell, *The Study Companion to Old Testament Literature* [Wilmington, DE: Glazier, 1989]). Tigay seeks to locate the source critical hypothesis within ancient Near Eastern compositional practices (Jeffrey H. Tigay, ed., *Empirical Models of Biblical Criticism*. [Philadelphia: University of Pennsylvania, 1985]. For a history of research, see R. J. Thompson, *Moses and the Law in a Century of Criticism Since Graf* (Leiden: Brill, 1970). A readable evangelical evaluation of source criticism is found in Roland K. Harrison, Bruce K. Waltke, Donald Guthrie, and Gordon D. Fee, *Biblical Criticism* (Grand Rapids: Zondervan, 1978). Garrett

proposes a conservative form of source criticism not based on hypothetical documents that prohibit Mosaic authorship of the Pentateuch (Duane A. Garrett, *Rethinking Genesis* [Grand Rapids: Baker, 1991]).

15.   Longman argues for retaining the literary criticism label in this sense "in spite of ambiguity and possible confusion;" but he somewhat inconsistently uses the term "literary approaches" in the title and throughout his book (Longman, *Literary Approaches*, 8).

16.   Alter, *Art*, 46. Alter denies that his approach minimizes the sacred character of biblical literature.

17.   Cited in Ryken and Longman, *Literary Guide*, 34.

18.   Ryken and Longman, *Literary Guide*, shows a literary approach in service of understanding — as well as appreciation of — biblical literature. It was produced in response to Robert Alter and Frank Kermode, eds., *The Literary Guide to the Bible* (Cambridge, MA: Belknap, Harvard University, 1987), largely to better integrate literary and biblical studies (10).

19.   On the paradigm shift, see Rolf Rendtorff, *The Problem of the Process of Transmission in the Pentateuch* (Sheffield: JSOT, 1990); Joseph Blenkinsopp, *The Pentateuch* (New York: Doubleday, 1992), Chapter 1; and Mark G. Brett, *Biblical Criticism in Crisis?* (Cambridge: Cambridge University, 1991). Critiques of source criticism founded on literary patterning include Umberto Cassuto, *The Documentary Hypothesis and the Composition of the Pentateuch*, 3d ed. (Jerusalem: Magnes, 1983); and Isaac M. Kikawada and Arthur Quinn, *Before Abraham Was* (Nashville: Abingdon, 1989).

20.   Alter discusses the uniqueness of biblical narrative compared to ancient Near Eastern literature, although he tends to downplay the historical aspect of biblical narrative (*Art*, 23-46).

21.   Prime literary studies of biblical narratives can be found in Alter, *Art*; Ryken and Longman, *Literary Guide*; Alter and Kermode, *Literary Guide*; Adele Berlin, *Poetics and Interpretation of Biblical Narrative* (Sheffield: Almond, 1983); Jonathan Magonet, *Form and Meaning: Studies on Literary Techniques in the Book of Jonah* (Sheffield: Almond, 1983); V. Philips Long, *The Reign and Rejection of King Saul* (Atlanta: Scholars, 1989); Edwin M. Good, *Irony in the Old Testament*, repr. of London, 1965 ed. (Sheffield: Almond, 1981); Kenneth R. R. Gros Louis, ed., *Literary Interpretations of Biblical Narratives* (Nashville: Abingdon, 1974); Herbert Chanan Brichto, *Toward a Grammar of Biblical Poetics* (New York: Oxford University, 1992); and

Shimon Bar-Efrat, *Narrative Art in the Bible* (Sheffield: Almond, 1989).

22.   This list concentrates on four practical benefits of a literary approach for conservative ministers. Compare other lists by Mark Allan Powell, *What Is Narrative Criticism?* (Minneapolis: Fortress, 1990), 85-91; and Longman, *Literary Approaches*, 58-62.

23.   "Literary critic John Sider has written that 'what biblical scholars need to hear most from literary critics is that old-fashioned concepts of plot, character, setting, point of view and diction may be more useful than more glamorous and sophisticated theories'" (Ryken and Longman, *Literary Guide*, 23). The works listed in Note 21 provide many examples of the usefulness of such narrative devices for exegesis.

24.   This may be the reason Kaiser calls the scene "the most important feature of the narrative" (Kaiser and Silva, 71).

25.   Kaiser and Silva, 71.

26.   Berlin, *Poetics*, 43.

27.   Berlin, *Poetics*, 43-82 insightfully discusses multiple points of view, although she shares modern skepticism about the historicity and referentiality of biblical narratives. For uses of the particle *hinneh*, see Berlin, *Poetics*, 91-95.

28.   On biblical characterization, see Alter, *Art*, 114-30; and Berlin, *Poetics*, 23--42.

29.   Berlin, *Poetics*, 23. She adds a third character type, the "functionary" who is simply an agent.

30.   Alter, *Art*, 116-17.

31.   Alter has a fine discussion of the importance of dialogue in biblical narrative (*Art*, 63-87), although his proposal that "in the biblical view words underlie reality" strikes some as a suspect literary extrapolation (69-70).

32.   Alter, *Art*, 74.

33.   These functions of narration are found in Alter, *Art*, 75-81.

34.   Longman, *Literary Approaches*, 89.

35.   Kaiser and Silva, 82-83.

36.   Longman, *Literary Approaches*, 93.

37.   David Allan Dawson, *Text Linguistics and Biblical Hebrew* (Sheffield: Sheffield Academic, 1994), 105. The visually oriented should see Longman's chart of plot elements, *Literary Approaches*, 92.

38.   The appendix discusses these forms. For a provocative general guide to Hebrew verb forms in narratives, see Longacre's verb-

rank cline (Dawson, *Text Linguistics*, 115; verb forms in other genres are also discussed, 115-16).

39.   Francis I. Andersen, *The Sentence in Biblical Hebrew* (The Hague/Paris: Mouton, 1974), 136-37 was a stimulus for this schematic on Genesis 4:1-5.

40.   Compare Leach's definition of style (Longman, *Literary Approaches*, 95).

41.   Irony, another stylistic feature in biblical Hebrew narrative, is less common than repetition. Chapter 5, Note 14 briefly discusses irony.

42.   Alter's excellent treatment of repetition forms the basis of this section (Alter, *Art*, 88-113).

43.   Word-play is discussed by Robert B. Chisholm, Jr. "Wordplay in the Eighth-Century Prophets," *Bibliotheca Sacra* 144 (1987): 44-45; J. M. Sasson, "Wordplay in the Old Testament" in *The Interpreter's Dictionary of the Bible: Supplementary Volume*, ed. Keith Crim (Nashville: Abingdon, 1976), 968-70; Luis Alonso-Schökel, *A Manual of Hebrew Poetics* (Rome: Biblical Institute, 1988), 29-33; and Geoffrey N. Leech, *A Linguistic Guide to English Poetry* (Harlow: Longmans, Green & Co., 1969), 209-12.

44.   For example, the name Noah sounds like and draws attention to prominent themes in the flood account, namely, comfort (Gn 5:29; 6:6-7) and rest (Gn 8:4,9; compare 9:20-22); the Israelites would learn that God comforts the righteous in judgment and provides them the rest of divine service. An informative work on naming and popular etymologies in the Hebrew Bible is James Barr, "The Symbolism of Names in the Old Testament," *Bulletin of the John Rylands Library* 52 (1969): 11-29.

45.   Meir Sternberg, "The Bible's Art of Persuasion," in *Beyond Form Criticism*, ed. Paul R. House (Winona Lake, IN: Eisenbrauns, 1992), 269. Sasson calls the plays upon Noah's name in Genesis 6—9 a *leitmotif* ("Wordplay," 970).

46.   Alter gives a fine presentation of biblical type-scenes (Alter, *Art*, 47-62). A similar, though less productive, literary approach to narrative forms identifies archetypes (Ryken and Longman, *Literary Guide*, 36).

47.   Read more about chiasmus in Chapter 7. Unfortunately, some thematic chiasms exist more in the interpreter's mind than in the text itself.

48.   Kaiser and Silva, 76. For other examples of chiasmus in biblical narrative, see Andersen, *Sentence*, Chapter 9; Y. T. Radday, "Chiasm in Biblical Narrative," *Beth Mikra* 20-21 (1964): 48-72,

and "Chiasm in Samuel," *Linguistica Biblica* 9/10 (1971): 21-31; Gordon J. Wenham, "The Coherence of the Flood Narrative," *Vetus Testamentum* 28 (1978): 336-48; and Isaac M. Kikawada, "The Shape of Genesis 11:1-9," in *Rhetorical Criticism*, ed. J. J. Jackson and Martin Kessler (Pittsburgh: Pickwick, 1974), 18-32.

49. Other checklists for narrative are given by Alter, *Art*, 178-89; and Powell, *Narrative Criticism*, 103-105.

50. Two of these seven errors are listed among Fee and Stuart's eight "most common errors" (Gordon D. Fee and Douglas Stuart, *How to Read the Bible for All Its Worth* [Grand Rapids: Zondervan, 1982], 91-93).

51. Brother Bernard Lamy, cited in R. H. Bowers, *The Legend of Jonah* (The Hague: Nijhoff, 1971), 5.

52. A. T. Hanson says allegorizing interprets "a text in a sense which completely ignores its original meaning, or in a sense whose connection with its original meaning is purely arbitrary" (Walter C. Kaiser, Jr., *The Uses of the Old Testament in the New* [Chicago: Moody, 1985], 213). Both Kaiser (*Uses*, 105) and Goldingay (John Goldingay, *Approaches to Old Testament Interpretation*, rev. ed. [Downers Grove: InterVarsity, 1990], 106-107) suggest allegories focus on words while types focus on events, but this seems a questionable distinction.

53. Walter C. Kaiser, Jr., *Toward an Exegetical Theology* (Grand Rapids: Baker, 1981), 199.

54. Paul admits to allegorizing the births of Abraham's two sons (Gl 3:24) to illustrate the contrast between law and grace (Gl 3:21:-31). Yet the New Testament never advocates allegorizing as the normal way to interpret biblical texts. The Old Testament contains a few allegories (such as Ezk 17; 23), but that hardly justifies treating narrative texts allegorically. See Luther's and Calvin's negative evaluation of allegorizing in Kaiser, *Exegetical Theology*, 60-61.

55. Besides discussions in hermeneutics textbooks, Kaiser helpfully treats typology (*Uses*, 101-44. One particularly atrocious example of typologizing is critiqued on page 105.). Books on typology include Patrick Fairbairn, *The Typology of Scripture*, repr. of 1857 ed. (Grand Rapids: Zondervan, n.d.); and Leonhard Goppelt, *The Typological Interpretation of the Old Testament in the New* (Grand Rapids: Eerdmans, 1982). Articles on typology include Donald K. Campbell, "The Interpretation of Types," *Bibliotheca Sacra* 112 (1955): 248-55; Walther Eichrodt, "Is Typological Exegesis an Appropriate Method?" in *Essays on Old Testament Hermeneutics*, ed. Claus Westermann (Richmond:

John Knox, 1963), 224-45; Gerhard von Rad, "Typological Interpretation of the Old Testament," in *Essays on Old Testament Hermeneutics*, ed. Claus Westermann (Richmond: John Knox, 1963), 17-39; Robert H. Gundry, "Typology as a Means of Interpretation," *Journal of the Evangelical Theological Society* 12 (1969): 233-40; Horace D. Hummel, "The Old Testament Basis of Typological Interpretation," *Biblical Research* 9 (1964): 38-50; John H. Stek, "Biblical Typology Yesterday and Today," *Calvin Theological Journal* 5 (1970): 133-62; and David L. Baker, "Typology and the Christian Use of the Old Testament," *Scottish Journal of Theology* 29 (1976): 137-57.

56.   Actually, the Greek text of Genesis 8:7 says that the raven "did not return" to the ark. The Hebrew text says that the raven went out from the ark "going out and returning." This could mean that the raven kept returning to the ark, yet Noah did not bring it inside. (Note the other repetitions for "return" in the context, specifically regarding the dove.) Plotwise, Noah's fruitless experiment with the raven delays the relief experienced after the three-fold experiment with the dove. Also, the raven's status as an unclean animal (Lv 11:15) may factor as a sub-theme.

57.   For a mixed bag of appropriate interpretation, illustrative use of the Bible, and psychologizing, see Dave Carder, Earl Heslin, John Townsend, Henry Cloud, and Alice Brawand, *Secrets of Your Family Tree* (Chicago: Moody, 1991).

58.   Generational sin in these texts hangs on understanding "visit" as "transmit." Perhaps a word study is appropriate?

59.   Students typically interpret Fee and Stuart's first two principles for interpreting narratives to mean narratives do not teach. Students therefore ignore Fee and Stuart's ninth principle, "Narratives may teach either explicitly (by clearly stating something) or implicitly (by clearly implying something without actually stating it)" (Fee and Stuart, *How to Read*, 83-84).

60.   Genesis 2:25 contains, in order, a *waw* consecutive plus preterite (definite past function), a conjunctive, and a disjunctive (contrastive). Genesis 2:18 contains an infinitive construct (substantival use as the subject of that clause) and a cohortative (of God's intention). All the verb forms in Genesis 2:24 have a habitual function and the narrator (not Adam) is the speaker.

Chapter 7

The Artistry of Biblical Hebrew: Poetry

Objectives: After reading this chapter, you should be able to:
1. Identify most biblical texts as poetry or prose.
2. Discuss key biblical Hebrew poetic devices and implications for interpretation.
3. Classify many poetic lines according to the type of semantic parallelism.
4. Explain several interpretive approaches to the Psalms.
5. Use a basic form critical approach to Psalms.

> *The psalmist and proverbial Seer,*
> *and all the prophets' sons of song,*
> *Make all things precious, all things clear,*
> *and bear the brilliant word along.*
> —Christopher Smart, from "Taste"

To some people, poetry seems imprecise and artificial. Imagine their dismay at finding poetry in the Bible, particularly when God himself speaks![1] Yet as much as one-third of the Old Testament (many well-loved portions) is poetry.[2]

While poetry proliferates in the poetic and prophetic books,[3] it appears throughout the Old Testament. Kaiser suggests, "In fact, only seven books in the Old Testament are without any poetry: Leviticus, Ruth, Ezra, Nehemiah, Esther, Haggai, and Malachi."[4] Even among those seven books, selections may arguably be poetic.[5]

Most readers recognize a difference between, say, Psalms and genealogies in Genesis. Yet what is poetry?[6] Specifically, what characterizes biblical poetry? Further, does poetry affect exegesis?

This chapter addresses these questions. Additionally, it provides an exegetical orientation to the well-loved Psalms.

A Poem by Any Other Name: Orientation to Biblical Hebrew Poetry

The nature of poetry

> Just as the miraculous participates in history with the mundane and also transcends it, so poetry participates in language with prose, but also transcends it.[7]

Poetry is measured, or highly regulated, writing which targets emotional response through form and meaning. It is language "in its best dress." In poetry, the form itself attracts as much attention as the content.

Although poetic fashions and their appeal vary across time and cultures, "language in lines" constitutes the fabric of poetry.[8] Correspondences guide the reading of poetry as a series of related segments, or poetic lines; whereas the sentence is the basic unit in narrative. Accordingly, English readers readily recognize texts segmented by end-rhyme as poetic.

Poetic segmentation, or regulation, characteristically depends upon brevity of expression. To that end, poetry employs abundant imagery and figures of speech. Such terseness sometimes heightens ambiguity, or rather, increases the possibility of multiple meanings.[9]

Additionally, correspondences between poetic lines frequently prohibit a strictly sequential reading. Narrative tends to advance in straightforward fashion, one thought or event after another, leading readers to trace the narrative thread. In contrast, poetry is more repetitive and cyclical, leading readers to re-trace the poetic chainlinks.[10]

Feel the difference in the poetic account of Sisera's death at the hand of Jael.[11] The narrative reads simply, "She drove the peg through his temple into the ground, and he died" (Jg 4:21). Compare the poetic version:

> She struck Sisera, she crushed his head.
> > She shattered and pierced his temple.
> At her feet he sank.
> > He fell; there he lay.
> At her feet he sank, he fell.
> > Where he sank, there he fell—dead (Jg 5:26-27, NIV).

Poetry also tends to be emotive. By recreating experiences, the poet both displays emotion and draws the reader into emotional involvement. In the poem of Sisera's death, the gory details and the slow-motion and replay effects celebrate victory over a hated enemy. As another example of poetry's emotive character, contrast the prose account (2 Kings 24—25) with the extended agonizing over Jerusalem's fall in Lamentations.

Controversy about biblical poetry

The Masoretes apparently considered only three books (Job, Psalms, Proverbs) poetic, as shown by a distinct accentual system.[12]

A modern scholar, James Kugel, attacks any differentiation between poetry and prose in the Bible. In an influential 1981 book, Kugel describes both the label and concept of poetry as foreign impositions on the Bible.[13]

However, most recognize a continuum of style in biblical texts, ranging from prose to poetry. This view is linked to a *preference model* of interpretation.[14] Accordingly, a predominance of poetic devices leads an interpreter to "prefer" reading a text as poetry, as the next diagram shows. (The subsequent treatment singles out two items marked with *.)

A Preference Model of Biblical Hebrew Genre Interpretation

Poetry

Prose

Distinctive *Structures*
(parallelism,* strophes or stanzas,
acrostics, inclusio, chiasmus,
specific syntax)
Distinctive *Words*
(word pairs, many figures of
speech, specific vocabulary)
Distinctive *Sounds*
(many word-plays, alliteration,
assonance, consonance, rhythm*)

Of course, a few texts may have some, but not extensive, poetic features. These texts could form an intermediate category of poetic prose.[15] Other texts may contain a mix, with poetic passages inset within narrative (Gn 3:14-19), or vice-versa (Am 7:10-15).[16]

Still, "If something walks like a duck, and quacks like a duck, it may be a duck." So many scholars think a text that looks like poetry and sounds like poetry may be poetry. More significantly, the devices that distinguish biblical Hebrew poetry influence interpretation.

Biblical Hebrew Poetic Devices

Biblical Hebrew poetry contains distinctive structures, words, and sounds. The premier structuring device, parallelism, deserves extended consideration first. Discussion of other poetic devices concludes with the vexed question of rhythm in biblical Hebrew.

Parallelism

1. The nature of parallelism

The primary device in biblical Hebrew poetry is parallelism.[17] In the eighteenth century, Lowth broadcast the structural phenomenon of biblical parallelism.[18] His definition still holds up:

> The correspondence of one Verse, or Line, with another, I call Parallelism. When a proposition is delivered, and a second is subjoined to it, or drawn under it, equivalent, or contrasted with it, in Sense; or similar to it in the form of Grammatical Construction; these I call Parallel Lines; and the words or phrases answering one to another in the corresponding Lines Parallel Terms.[19]

Parallelism is the balance between poetic lines — in language, sound, or structure, or some combination of such correspondences simultaneously.[20] Parallelism resembles binocular vision or stereophonic sound, since the parallel lines combine to convey meaning.

For example, hear the echoes as David prays to experience forgiveness:

> "Thoroughly wash me from my iniquity;
> and cleanse me from my sin" (Ps 51:4).

The earlier example of poetry in Judges 4:21 also shows parallelism. (See more examples in a following chart, "Types of Semantic Parallelism.")

Parallelism operates on different textual levels. *Normal parallelism* operates between adjacent, linked poetic lines. Typically biblical parallelism manifests itself in a poetic couplet or *bicolon*. Parallelism may also exist between two couplets or bicola (in a quatrain or *tetracolon*; Ps 114:1-2), or even in a triplet of poetic lines, a *tricolon* (Ps 24:7, 9).[21] These poetic units, then, serve as the building blocks of Hebrew poetry:

A-colon + B-colon	=	bicolon (couplet) + bicolon	=	tetracolon (quatrain)

Parallel terms sometimes exist within a poetic line, or colon, forming *internal parallelism*.[22] An example is, "Incline your ear and hear the words of the wise" (Pr 22:17, A-colon).

Another level of parallelism appears over stretches of text. *External parallelism* refers to parallelism outside the primary poetic units, whether near (adjacent) or distant (farther away). Proverbs 2:16-18 parallels 2:13-15, showing the protective benefits of wisdom in delivering a young man from both evil men and adulterous women.

As Lowth's definition notes, parallelism is a "many splendored thing." Popularly regarded simply as thought-balance, parallelism is multi-faceted. It operates in different realms — the realms of grammar and sound as well as semantics.

Yet semantic parallelism deals most directly with meaning and appears even in translation. C. S. Lewis comments:

> It is (according to one's point of view) either a wonderful piece of luck or a wise provision of God's, that poetry which was to be turned into all languages should have as its chief formal

characteristic one that does not disappear (as mere metre does) in translation.[23]

Analyzing semantic parallelism provides immediate benefits to the beginning exegete and to the expositor. It offers a provisional interpretive menu and demands interpretive clarity.

2. Types of semantic parallelism

Since Lowth, interpreters have focused on the thought-relations between the parallel lines in biblical poetry. For a general introduction refer to the next chart, "Types of Semantic Parallelism."[24]

In connection with types of semantic parallelism, controversy rages over the precise nature of parallelism itself. Kugel and like-minded scholars insist the parallel line (the B-colon)[25] always advances semantically beyond the first line (the A-colon). Thus, according to the labels used in the next chart, all biblical parallelism is essentially synthetic; no synonymous parallelism occurs.[26]

On the other side of the debate, scholars think parallelism creates a system of interplay between the parallel lines. Such interplay may include grammar and sounds as well as semantics. The system of parallelism directs the reader to view both parallel lines in light of one another.[27] The various elements work in concert to create a sense of repetition and interdependency between the lines.

At issue is whether the interpreter should emphasize subtle semantic differences in corresponding parallel terms. More likely, the systemic pressure of other correspondences in parallel lines sometimes pulls parallel terms together as synonyms. As noted in Chapter 4, absolute synonyms do not exist in any language, yet functional synonyms are common. Likewise, some biblical parallelism seems to function synonymously.[28]

Through continuing analysis and interpretation, the exegete chooses sides in the controversy over the nature of biblical parallelism and the meaning of specific texts.

Types of Semantic Parallelism[29]
(Try the acronym C.A.S.E.S. as a memory aid.)

Type	Description	Examples (English vv.)
1. Synonymous:[30]	strengthens the thought by repetition	
synonymous or quasi-synonymous	corresponding terms or ideas are equivalent or similar	"He does not treat us according to our sins; and He does not repay us according to our iniquities." (Ps 103:10)
complementary	corresponding terms form a related pair	"Day after day they spout speech; Night after night they display knowledge." (Ps 19:2)
numerical[31]	a number corresponds to the next higher number (x // x+1)	"See: Three things are not satisfied; Four things do not say, "Enough!"" (Pr 30:15)
2. Antithetic[32]	contrasts thoughts by opposition	"The memory of the righteous is blessed; but the name of the wicked is rotten." (Pr 10:7)
3. Synthetic:	advances the thought	
addition	adds another thought	"His soul will dwell in prosperity; and his seed will inherit the land." (Ps 25:13)
concatenation	develops a sequence (cause-effect; purpose or result)	"I will teach transgressors Your ways; and sinners will return to You." (Ps 51:13)
extension	extends a concept or theme element	"In the way of sinners he does not stand; and in the seat of scoffers he does not sit." (Ps 1:1)
comparison	makes an analogy or evaluation	"Better a little with the fear of the LORD, than great wealth with turmoil." (Pr 15:17)
completion[33]	completes the thought	"The horse and its rider — He has hurled into the sea!" (Ex 15:21)
explanation	gives a reason	"Sing to the LORD, for He is highly exalted." (Ex 15:21)
4. Climactic[34] (Step)	builds on a repeated word or phrase	"Ascribe to the LORD, mighty ones; ascribe to the LORD glory and strength." (Ps 29:1)
5. Emblematic[35]	illustrates a complete thought by a figure in the parallel line	"As a deer pants for streams of water, so my soul pants for you, O God." (Ps 42:1)

3.   Variations in parallelism

Rarely do parallel lines precisely balance correspondences between all the terms. Indeed, absolute parallelism would be merely verbatim repetition. The artistry of biblical Hebrew poetry exhibits manifold variety along with the repetition of many correspondences.[36]

Such variations have led to analyzing semantic parallelism by degrees. *Inexact parallelism* describes instances of corresponding terms without precise semantic matching.

Proverbs 9:10, displayed next, contains inexact parallelism. No separate matching term for "beginning" appears in the B-colon. Instead, the single term "understanding" corresponds with the dual term "beginning of wisdom." The customary notation of individual terms by lower-case letters, corresponding terms by the same letter and an apostrophe (pronounced as a "prime"), and compound terms with a number equal to the parts, shows this inexact parallelism:

beginning-of wisdom	(is)	the-fear-of	the-LORD
a2		b	c

and-knowledge-of	the-Holy-One	(is)	understanding
b'	c'		a'

Incomplete parallelism describes instances of matching semantics between cola, yet without precise term-for-term correspondences.[37] Amos 8:10 shows incomplete parallelism; no explicit B-colon term corresponds to "I-will-turn."

I-will-turn		your-feasts	to-mourning
a		b	c

[a]	and-all-of	your-songs	to-lamenting
	d	b'	c'

"I-will-turn" can further be described as having a *double-duty* function; it effectively operates in the B-colon as well.[38] The additional term "all-of" keeps the B-colon length comparable to the A-colon (even minus a corresponding A-colon term). Therefore, *compensation*[39] describes this poetic process and such an additional term serves as a *ballast variant*.[40]

Even with these refinements, a purely semantic analysis of Hebrew parallelism often falls short of describing the artistic turns.[41] Nevertheless, such an initial approach heightens appreciation and understanding of biblical poetry.

4 . Parallelism and interpretation

Referring primarily to parallelism, Gray notes, "Failure to perceive what are the formal elements in Hebrew poetry has, in the past, frequently led to misinterpretation of Scripture."[42]

Earlier interpreters identified "the one who dwells in heaven" (Ps 2:4) as a particular bird, rather than the Lord, as the parallelism clarifies.[43] Rabbis mistook Lamech's comment "I have killed a man for wounding me, a young man for injuring me" (Gn 4:23); they identified Cain and Tubal-Cain as two murder victims, rather than a single John Doe victim. Recognizing parallelism guards against such misinterpretations.

However, recognizing parallelism does not assure interpretive agreement on the relation between specific parallel lines, as the controversy over the nature of parallelism shows. Kugel and Alter, convinced that the B-colon always shows an advance, offer finely nuanced readings of many parallel lines; other interpreters read some parallel lines as basically synonymous. Even so, semantic parallelism guides the interpretation of biblical Hebrew poetry.

Other poetic devices

Parallelism is the crown jewel of biblical Hebrew poetry, but other adornments set Hebrew poetry apart from prose.

1.   Other distinctive structures

The syntax of biblical Hebrew poetry often varies from prose, so that recent studies emphasize syntactic features as poetic criteria.[44] One acknowledged criterion is the limited use of so-called prose particles (the definite article, the definite direct object marker, and the relative pronoun).[45] Distinctive word order,[46] unusual forms and constructions,[47] and abundant ellipsis in poetry may color interpretation.

Double-duty dependency, mentioned previously in regard to parallelism, is one form of elliptical structure common to biblical Hebrew poetry. *Ellipsis* is the purposeful omission of words needed to complete a meaning or a grammatical construction; such omitted words are implied and recoverable from the context. Ellipsis contributes to the poetry's generally comparable short line lengths.

Clearly, recognizing ellipses and properly "filling in the blanks" affects interpretation. Later editions and recent translations correct the King James rendering of Psalm 9:18 [19 Hebrew] by including the important negative in the B-colon:

> For the needy shall not always be forgotten;
> And the hope of the lowly shall *[not]* perish forever.[48]

Another structuring device common in poetry is *chiasmus*, or inverted parallelism between corresponding terms. Connecting the corresponding parallel terms between horizontally paired lines results in the shape of the Greek letter *chi* (an X), as in an ab // b'a' pattern. (Try this on the earlier diagrammed example of Proverbs 9:10.)

Sometimes chiasmus is augmented, forming a *concentric structure* with corresponding terms inversely repeated on both sides of a central point.[49] This produces an abc // c'b'a' pattern. Psalm 19:1, in the Hebrew order, is concentric and emphasizes creation as God's glorious work:

| The-heavens | declare | the-glory-of God |
| a | b | c |

| and-the-work-of His hands | proclaims | The-sky |
| c' | b' | a' |

Chiasmus, like pulling the strands on a corset, tightens the binding between parts. Besides providing variety, chiastic structures can heighten a particular focus, stress emphasis (especially contrast), alter word order, unite a complete poem,[50] indicate closure, and segment larger sections of texts.[51]

The boundaries of poetic units are also often indicated by inclusio, otherwise known as ring-composition, envelope-structure, or book-ending. *Inclusio* describes a repetition or return, at the end of the textual unit, to the same word/phrase/idea(s) used at its beginning. For instance, Psalm 1 begins and ends with reference to "the wicked;" and the repetition of "by the abundance of force" at the beginning and end of Psalm 33:16-17 indicates a tetracolon.

Chiasmus and inclusio sometimes mark out poetic paragraphs, or *strophes*, and larger sections (*stanzas*). In biblical Hebrew, such sections reflect artistic license:

> In some poems, a repeated *refrain* occurs, which marks off sections or stanzas of the poem. In some poems these units are of approximately equal length, in others they are not. Then there are poems, which naturally divide into verse paragraphs of approximately equal length, though there are no formal indications of this division in the text. At the same time, there are many poems in which such paragraphs are very unequal in length, and still others where the lines of demarcation are difficult to determine, if they exist at all.[52]

Another obvious poetic structure is the alphabetic *acrostic*, where each unit begins with a successive letter of the alphabet. Few translations consistently approximate acrostics, although the following example from Psalm 37 provides their flavor:

> Agree not to fret yourself because of the wicked ...
> Be confident in the LORD, and do good...
> Commit your way to the LORD...
> Do not worry about the the LORD's deeds...[53]

The two best-known biblical acrostics are Psalm 119 and Proverbs 31:10-31; the other acrostics are Psalm 9-10 (?); 25; 34; 37; 111; 112; 145; Lamentations 1—4; and Nahum 1:2-8. Biblical poets manipulate even the rigid acrostic structure by varying the length and shape of the strophes, and occasionally the sequence of letters.[54]

Poetic structuring devices like chiasmus, inclusio, and acrostics typically mark text boundaries, affect word choice and meaning, and direct attention to particular themes.

2. *Distinctive words*

In conjunction with semantic parallelism, many word pairs mark the presence of biblical Hebrew poetry.[55] *Word pairs* are recurrently associated terms, like "father" and "mother," "heaven" and "earth," "gold" and "silver," and "Israel" and "Jacob."

Also, poetry often uses specialized vocabulary. Rare words and archaic forms can serve poetic purposes, such as heightened style, deliberate ambiguity, word-play, or rhythm. Recent grammars, in particular, comment on words that appear predominantly in biblical poetry.[56]

Furthermore, poetry typically abounds with figures of speech. So much so that some scholars consider figurative language *the* mark of poetry.[57]

As with parallelism, the sustained use of distinctive words and other poetic devices identifies a text as poetry. Consequently, poetic words attract attention and influence interpretation by: 1) demanding an overall interpretive strategy appropriate to the text's poetic nature; 2) offering additional semantic possibilities (see Chapter 5 regarding figures of speech); 3) tempering semantic distinctions (in word pairs or archaic words); or 4) establishing the syntax or even the textual wording (particularly in the case of special endings affecting word divisions).

3. Distinctive sounds

Biblical Hebrew poetry resonates with sound effects.[58] Hearing such sounds, often irreproducible in translation, requires sensitivity on the part of the Hebrew reader.

Besides heightening appreciation for the biblical poets' artistry, listening to sound-plays can direct attention to a poetic text's meaning. Sound-plays often enhance word-plays,[59] parallelism, and chiastic structures, or help mark boundaries in texts. Prophetic judgment oracles delight in sound-plays to emphasize God's appropriate justice; one example, Isaiah 10:29-32, follows shortly.

Consonance, repetition of consonant sounds, is rather frequent, partly due to Hebrew's triconsonantal root system. *Alliteration*, repetition of an initial consonant or syllable, also occurs. *Assonance*, repetition of vowel sounds, is less frequent and less certain, because Hebrew lost vocalic case endings early and added vowel signs relatively late.

Onomatopoeia reproduces the sound of the very thing named or described. Even as the English word "bottle" may recall the sound of pouring liquid from a container, the Hebrew word is *baqbuq*.[60] Similarly, imitative sounds may describe actions in texts. Widely accepted examples, in simplified transliteration, include:

a bird's chirping (Is 10:14):	*upotseh peh umetsaptsayp*
burning straw crackling (Is 5:24):	*lakayn ke'ehkol qash leshon aysh*

As a rule, biblical Hebrew exhibits little *rhyme*, or repetition of syllable sounds, especially the end-rhyme familiar to readers of English poetry. However, *weak rhyme*, the repetition of similar-sounding grammatical endings, can contribute to poetic style. A simplified transliteration shows such weak rhyme in the first three verses of the well-known Psalm 23: *adonay roee ... yarbeetsaynee ... al-may ... yenachalaynee nafshee ... yanchaynee bemagelay ....*

Determine whether sound repetitions are purposeful by considering: 1) the frequency of the repetitions; 2) the relation of the sound-plays to the message; and, 3) the availability of other options to the Hebrew poet.

Attempting to mimic Hebrew sound-plays in translation, while challenging, helps English readers feel the poetic message. Such a free translation accompanies the simplified transliteration of sound-play and word-play in Isaiah 10:29-32:

aberu mabarah	"They pass over the pass."
charedah haramah	"Ramah rumbles."
tsahalee qolayk bat-galeem	"Cry 'Bitter gall,' daughter of Gallim!"
nadedah madmaynah	"Madmenah flees like madmen."

Rhythm is an additional sound effect, deserving separate treatment.

4. Distinctive rhythm

There was a young poet named Dan,
Whose poetry never would scan.
When told this was so,
He said, "Yes, I know.
It's because I try to put every possible syllable into the last line I can."

Many readers perceive structured sound patterns in poetry, and much biblical Hebrew poetry has distinctive rhythm.[61] (Psalms, after all, are music — minus the accompaniment.) Such rhythm results from the generally short and balanced parallel lines.[62] Little agreement exists, however, about meter or the proper measuring system for biblical Hebrew poetry.

Ross represents the prevailing attitude toward this disputed characteristic:

> Hebrew poetry certainly has meter and rhythm, but it is not possible as yet to identify and determine that meter with any degree of certainty. Most commentators are satisfied to count the number of accented Hebrew words or word units in a line as the basis of their poetical analysis.[63]

Manifest variety suggests rhythmic parallelism, rather than meter, distinguishes biblical Hebrew poetry. "*Rhythm* implies discernible patterns, used with fluidity and flexibility throughout a poem; *metre* implies a system imposed upon the poem from outside."[64]

One recurrent pattern, three stresses paralleled by two stresses, often appears in funeral dirges and laments:

> With regard to the rhythm, commonly designated *kinah* [*qinah*], Budde stipulated that normally the first unit consists of three words or stresses, and the second of two. Variations are possible, but the division is never equal: if the first element has only two words, these are heavier than the corresponding pair.[65]

In general, however, Hebrew poets avoid fixed patterns. Even if viewed through the microscope of a particular metrical system, variety is evident. Sometimes varied rhythm serves identifiable purposes such as pacing or closure.

Further, even these brief comments caution against using a metrical theory to propose changes in the wording of the biblical text, as commonly practiced by text critical scholars of earlier generations.[66] Freedman elaborates:

The chief danger in invoking the formula *metri causa* lies in the necessarily circular reasoning which is used to support proposed emendations. Since there are no external criteria for determining the meter, it must be derived or calculated from the existing text. Then the same text is corrected or improved on the basis of the meter which was derived from it.[67]

Biblical Hebrew poetry — with its distinctive structures, words, and sounds — challenges the exegete's observational and interpretive skills. The following checklist summarizes the keys to unlock this treasure of biblical revelation. Then the next section peeks into the storehouse of the Psalms.

A Checklist for Poetry: Keys to Interpretation

1. *Parallelism*: Starting with the normal parallelism in the poetic unit (typically a bicolon), analyze the type of semantic parallelism. Then look for internal or external semantic parallelism and correspondences in grammar and sound.

2. *Other poetic structures*: Look for any ellipsis, inclusio, chiasmus, acrostic, refrain, strophe, or stanza. Consider how the poetic structure impacts word choice and arrangement.

3. *Figures of speech*: Identify, classify and interpret any figures. (Review Chapter 5 or use the charts on the major figures of speech; and check Bullinger's indexes.)

4. *Repetitions, word-plays, and sound-plays*: Scan the Interlinear for repeated or similar words. Commentaries will point to many of these. Time and interest permitting, read aloud the Hebrew or chart repeated words or sounds.

Searching the Psalms

Psalms have greatly impacted history, as evident in the life of our Lord, Jewish and Christian corporate worship, and private devotional piety. Psalms is the most frequently quoted book in the New Testament and probably the most frequently read Old Testament book. As a prime collection of biblical Hebrew poetry, Psalms merit some additional consideration here.

Approaches to Psalms

Songs composed and collected over time comprise the book of Psalms. Biblical scholars' concerns also shift with the passing of time. Therefore, different approaches have been used in the study of Psalms.

Basic issues like identifying the psalmists, their historical setting, their role in ancient Israel, and the content of their songs stimulated these approaches, which are summarized in the following chart, "Approaches to Psalms."

The history of Psalms research prompts two suggestions: 1) An eclectic approach respects the individuality of each psalm and represents "the best of all possible worlds" for studying Psalms. 2) A modified form critical approach — sifting speculations about original settings — effectively coaxes a great deal out of many psalms.

Forms of Psalms[68]

Most people have little trouble distinguishing a cry for help from a presidential citation of honor, or distinguishing rap music from country Western. These are samples of different forms with recognizable features. Psalms likewise come in recognizable forms, although the forms are not as rigid as an Elizabethan sonnet or a Japanese *haiku*.

Whereas form criticism offers tenuous reconstructions of ancient songs' original settings, recognizing similarities among psalms provides practical interpretive help. Psalms with the same form share common features derived from the psychology of prayer and worship. At the same time, psalms that appear identical to the casual observer manifest incredible individual variety, like snowflakes.[69]

Petition, thanksgiving, and praise characterized the worship led by the Levitical singers in the Jerusalem temple (1 Chronicles 16:4). Songs of petition, or *pleas*, are cries for help commonly referred to as laments.[70] Songs that publicly thank God, acknowledging His work on behalf of the offerer, voice *declarative praise*. Hymns generally extolling God's attributes and actions constitute *descriptive praise*.

Either an individual or the Israelite nation might offer a psalm. The individual pleas and individual declarative praise psalms often contain elements not found in their national counterparts. Thus five basic psalm forms typically contain ordered elements of prayer or praise, as shown on the chart, "Forms of Psalms."

A number of psalms do not show the common patterns that constitute distinct forms. A few *mixed forms* contain elements seen in several of the basic forms. *Songs of trust* expand the confession of trust element found in some of the basic forms. The remainder of the psalms have some teaching function and may be broadly labeled didactic.

Didactic psalms include wisdom psalms, salvation history psalms that review God's work with Israel, royal songs that focus on the king, songs of prophetic exhortation, and liturgies for festivals and temple entrance or songs of blessing.[71] Such content designations provide less exegetical help than the five basic forms.[72]

Identifying a psalm by form describes its basic character and more. The form offers an interpretive grid for tracing thematic development and understanding specific parts, like enigmatic verb forms. Particular variations from the common formal elements often signal a psalm's unique message. (Variations also create disagreement over some psalms' forms.) Action Point five challenges you to explore the value of this analysis of psalms by form.

The forms of psalms are vessels holding poetic riches and the treasury of Psalms invites readers to share its wealth.

Approaches to Psalms

Approach	Focus	Description	Proponents	Evaluation
Traditional-historical	Life of the psalmist	Reconstruct the historical event	older commentaries (Delitzsch, Perowne)	Subjective if no history is stated
Literary-analytical historical	Event in Maccabean era	Discover the politics/persons of that time	older "JEDP" practitioners (Duhm, Briggs)	The Dead Sea Scrolls dealt a "death blow;" a few holdouts
Form critical	Life situation	Reconstruct the setting of the psalm; identify form	many (Gunkel, Westermann)	Forms are not rigid; settings may be subjective
Cultic	Worship setting	Find worship act(s) or feast(s) in the psalm	Mowinckel, Weiser, Kraus	Can be subjective, and read in Ancient Near Eastern rituals
Eschatological-Messianic	Life of Christ	Find Christ exclusively	patristics, older commentaries	Can be eisegesis or allegorizing
Canonical	*Book* reflects David/Israel's life	Fit each psalm within the book	some moderns (following Childs)	Can ignore Psalms' history of collection or unique psalms
Eclectic	Varies	Each psalm controls approach	many conservatives	The "best of all worlds"

Forms of Psalms

National Plea (Lament)	Individual Plea (Lament)
ntroductory plea ("O God;" report of former deliverances) ament (complaint: foes, we, You) Confession of trust lea (Hear! Save! Judge! Because ...) ow of praise Ps 14, 44, 53, 58, 60, 74, 79, 80, 83, 85, 90, 106, 108, 123, 125, 126, 129, 137	1. Introductory plea ("O God") 2. Lament (complaint: foes, I, You) 3. Confession of trust 4. Plea (Hear! Save! Judge! Because ...) 5. Affirmation of answer 6. Vow of praise [7. Report of deliverance = "heard" plea] Ps 3, 4, 5, 6, 7, 9-10, 12, 13, 17, 22, 25, 26, 27:7-14, 28, 31, 35, 36, 38, 39, 40:12-18, 41, 42-43, 51, 54, 55, 56, 57, 59, 61, 64, 69, 70, 71, 77, 84, 86, 88, 94, 102, 109, [120], 130, 139, 140, 141, 142, 143
National Declarative Praise[73]	*Individual Declarative Praise*
ntroductory praise eflection on past need eport of deliverance Ps 65, 107, 124	1. Introductory praise (includes proclamation of intent to praise) 2. Reflection on past need 3. Report of deliverance 4. Conclusion (renewed vow of praise, testimony, or instruction) Ps 18, 30, 32, 34, 40:1-11, 63, 66:13-20, 73, 92, 116, 118, 138
Descriptive Praise (Hymns)	*Other Types*
all to praise (or focus on majesty) ause for praise oncluding praise (and/or instruction) s 8, 19:1-6, 29, 33, 66:1-12, 67, 95, 100, 103, 104, 105, 111, 113, 117, 35, 136, 145, 146, 147, 148, 149, 150 plus songs of Zion Ps 46, 48, 76, 87; and songs of the LORD's kingship Ps 47, 93, 96, 97, 98, 99)	Mixed forms Ps 89, 115, 120, 144 Songs of trust Ps 11, 16, 23, 27:1-6, 62 Didactic psalms wisdom psalms Ps 1, 37, 49, 52, 112, 127; (plus torah songs Ps 19:7-14, 119) salvation history psalms Ps 78, 114 royal songs Ps 2, 20, 21, 45, 72, 101, 110 prophetic exhortation Ps 75, 81, 82, 91 liturgies Ps 15, 24, 50, 68, 121, 122, 128, 131, 132, 133, 134

Action Points

1. List what you consider the primary characteristics of poetry in general and biblical Hebrew poetry specifically. How do these characteristics impact interpretation?

2. Practice classifying parallelism by semantic type in Psalm 22:4, Proverbs 10:1, Deuteronomy 32:2, Psalm 103:13, and Proverbs 23:9.[74] Although these are English Bible references, the Hebrew text itself may be clearer. (See the answers in Note 74.)

3. Identify some variations in semantic parallelism by labeling Psalm 3:1 and Proverbs 19:4 as incomplete or inexact parallelism or both.[75] (Compare the answers in Note 75.)

4. Review the major figures of speech presented in charts in Chapter 5.

5. Using the chart on "Forms of Psalms," pick one psalm from each of the five basic forms and trace the elements of prayer and praise. Can you find the pattern and does it help you think your way through the psalm? Do you disagree with any of the proposed classifications?

6. Read more about biblical Hebrew poetry. (Begin with some of the references in Note 31.)

7. Read more about different approaches to Psalms in S. E. Gillingham, *The Poems and Psalms of the Hebrew Bible* (Oxford: Oxford University, 1994), 173-89.

8. Read more about forms of Psalms. (Start with the references in Note 68.)

Notes

1. See Hans Kosmala, "Form and Structure in Ancient Hebrew Poetry," *Vetus Testamentum* 14 (1964): 423. 1 Chronicles 25 explicitly connects the temple singers with prophecy and may serve as a corrective to depreciating Old Testament poetry. Positively, Freedman likens poetry to God's thunderbolts hurled from heaven (David Noel Freedman, "Pottery, Poetry, and Prophecy" in *The Bible in its Literary Milieu*, ed. John Maier and Vincent Tollers (Grand Rapids: Eerdmans, 1979), 98.

2. Walter C. Kaiser, Jr., *Toward an Exegetical Theology* (Grand Rapids: Baker, 1981), 228.

3. "Prophets such as Amos and Isaiah borrowed from the proverbial poetry and rhetorical sayings of wisdom; they used secular songs (Isa. 22:13); they appropriated funeral laments — over nations, if not over individuals (Amos 5; Isa. 14, 23; Ezek. 27, 28, 32); they used love songs to depict the depth of Yahweh's love for Israel (Hos. 2, 6; Isa. 5; Jer. 3; Isa. 49, 51, 54); they took up oracles of blessing and cursing (Num. 22—4); and they utilized war poetry in order to dramatize the coming judgement on Israel before the other nations (Amos 3, 6, 9; Isa. 5, 10, 28; Jer. 4, 5, 6). In addition, the prophets used a good deal of liturgical poetry from the cult, sometimes in short poetic fragments, and at other times in longer, sustained verse" (S. E. Gillingham, *The Poems and Psalms of the Hebrew Bible* [Oxford: Oxford University, 1994], 122). On the connection between poetry and prophecy, see Freedman, "Pottery," 93-98; or Robert Lowth, *Lectures on the Sacred Poetry of the Hebrews*, repr. of 1787 ed. (Hildesheim: Georg Olms, 1969), 2:2-59.

4. Kaiser, *Exegetical Theology*, 228.

5. Leviticus is typically considered the most prosaic Old Testament book, yet even it contains some poetic passages. Murray H. Lichtenstein ("Biblical Poetry" in *Back to the Sources*, ed. Barry W. Holtz [New York: Summit Books, 1984], 105) cites Leviticus 10:3:
    "Through My intimates is My holiness to be made manifest,
    Before all the people is My glory to be perceived."

6. Often "beauty is in the eye of the beholder" when it comes to evaluating poetry as good or bad. Analyzing biblical poetry according to its actual form is more productive exegetically than applying personal or cultural aesthetic criteria.

7. Freedman, "Pottery," 92.

8. Walter Theophilus Woldemar Cloete, *Versification and Syntax in Jeremiah 2—25* (Atlanta: Scholars, 1989), 5-6. Visual

representation of poetry in lines, however, is more of a modern phenomenon and inconsistently used even today. As in other ancient texts, the Dead Sea Scrolls, Cairo Genizah manuscripts, and the Aleppo and Leningrad manuscripts contain isolated poetic passages graphically arranged in lines. Examples are shown by James L. Kugel, *The Idea of Biblical Poetry* (New Haven: Yale University, 1981), 119-27; see also Michael P. O'Connor, *Hebrew Verse Structure* (Winona Lake, IN: Eisenbrauns, 1980), 29-32. Such graphical arrangements do not consistently correspond to the poetry and sometimes ornamentally represent a particular theme.

9. Multiple meanings differ from indeterminate meaning, or even conflicting meanings such as advocated by deconstructionists. The context often clarifies the intentionality of multiple meanings or disambiguates between possible meanings. On ambiguity, see Cloete, 109-15; William Empson, *Seven Types of Ambiguity* (Cleveland: World, 1955); James G. Williams, "The Power of Form," *Semeia* 17 (1980): 35-58; and S. Wittig, "A Theory of Multiple Meanings." *Semeia* 9 (1977): 75-103.

10. Jakobson thinks "the essence of poetic artifice consists in recurrent returns" and notes the etymology of prose, "straight forward" contrasts with verse, "return" (Roman Jakobson, "Grammatical Parallelism and Its Russian Facet" *Language* 42 [1966]: 399).

11. Lichtenstein, "Biblical Poetry," 105-27 also compares Judges 4 and 5 in some detail.

12. Chapter 3, Note 25 provides bibliography on biblical Hebrew accents. Two accent signs worth learning, *athnach* and *oleh we yored*, show how the Masoretes divided the poetic lines. Comparing these divisions with BHS highlights interpretive options.

13. Kugel, *Idea*; O'Connor, *Hebrew Verse Structure*, 101-103. Georgiades argues similarly regarding Greek literature, but few want to jettison the term and concept of poetry altogether (Duane L. Christensen, "Narrative Poetics and the Interpretation of the Book of Jonah," in *Directions in Biblical Hebrew Poetry*, ed. Elaine R. Follis [Sheffield: Journal for Study of the Old Testament, 1987], 29).

14. Background and a demonstration of the preference model is given by Dennis Pardee, "Structure and Meaning in Hebrew Poetry" in *Sopher Mahir*, ed. Edward M. Cook (Winona Lake, IN: Eisenbrauns, 1990), 239-80. The preference model says the text itself indicates its own genre and recommends an appropriate

reading strategy, rather than suggesting that interpretation is left to individual reader's preferences (as in reader-oriented criticism).

15. Burden refers to an area of overlap, with "borderline cases" (J. J. Burden, "Poetic Texts," in *Words from Afar*, ed. Ferdinand E. Deist and Willem S. Vorster [Cape Town: Tafelberg Publishers, 1986], 59). According to Cooper, Saadia Gaon described this middle ground about A.D. 915 (Alan Mitchell Cooper, "Biblical Poetics," Ph.D. dissertation [Yale University, 1976], 150). De Moor discusses the existence of this middle ground (Johannes C. de Moor, "The Poetry of the Book of Ruth," *Orientalia* 53 (1984): 262-72). Suggested cases include Joshua 23 (William T. Koopmans, "The Poetic Prose of Joshua 23," in *The Structural Analysis of Biblical and Canaanite Poetry*, ed. Willem Van der Meer and Johannes C. de Moor [Sheffield, England: Sheffield Academic, 1988], 83-118), Ruth (Jacob M. Myers, *The Linguistic and Literary Form of the Book of Ruth* [Leiden: Brill, 1955]), Ecclesiastes (Burden), and Jonah (Christensen). However, lacking consensus on the nature of poetry, scholars differ in their assessments and variously consider these texts poetry or prose instead.

16. Gather a convenient list of such inset poems from Theodore H. Robinson, *Poetry of the Old Testament* (London, Duckworth, 1947), 47-66.

17. G. M. Hopkins is often cited: "The artificial part of poetry, perhaps we shall be right to say all artifice, reduces itself to the principle of parallelism. The structure of poetry is that of continuous parallelism, ranging from the technical so-called Parallelisms of Hebrew poetry and the antiphons of Church music to the intricacy of Greek or Italian or English verse."

18. Lowth was, in effect, a popularizer rather than the first to recognize biblical parallelism (Adele Berlin, *The Dynamics of Biblical Parallelism* [Bloomington: Indiana University, 1985], 1; Brian Hepworth, *Robert Lowth* [Boston: Twayne, 1978]). Kugel discusses many predecessors in this area (*Idea*, 204-86).

19. Lowth, *Isaiah*, 1778; cited by Berlin, *Dynamics*, 1.

20. Lichtenstein "Biblical Poetry," 15.

21. Mowinckel finds few tricola in biblical Hebrew, but the general consensus accepts many more (Sigmund Mowinckel, *Real and Apparent Tricola in Hebrew Psalm Poetry* [Oslo: Norske Videnskaps Akademie Oslo, 1957]).

22. Van der Lugt apparently coined "internal and external parallelism" (Marjo C. A. Korpel, and Johannes C. de Moor, "Fundamentals of Ugaritic and Hebrew Poetry," in Van der Meer

       and de Moor, *Structural Analysis*, 17). For internal parallelism, see Wilfred G. E. Watson, "Internal or Half-Line Parallelism in Classical Hebrew Again," *Vetus Testamentum* 39 (1 1989): 44-66.

23.   C. S. Lewis, *Reflections on the Psalms* (New York: Harcourt, Brace, Jovanovich, 1958), 4-5.

24.   Other systems of analyzing semantic parallelism show similarities. Gillingham's alternate classification of semantic parallelism as interchangeable (A = B), qualification (A > B), and expansion (A < B) overlaps the traditional system (*Poems and Psalms*, 78-88); as does Bratcher and Reyburn's static, dynamic, and non-parallel (Robert G. Bratcher and William D. Reyburn, *A Handbook on Psalms* [New York: United Bible Societies, 1991], 4-9). The same is true of Geller's six types: synonym, list, antonym, merism, identity, and metaphor (Stephen A. Geller, *Parallelism in Early Biblical Poetry* [Missoula, MT: Scholars, 1979]). For greater precision in analyzing biblical parallelism, semantic or otherwise, read some of the following: Berlin, *Dynamics*; Gillingham, *Poems and Psalms*; Watson, *Classical Hebrew Poetry*; George Buchanan Gray, *The Forms of Hebrew Poetry*, repr. of 1915 ed. (New York: KTAV, 1972); Robert Alter, *The Art of Biblical Poetry* (New York: Basic Books, 1985); Kugel, *Idea*; Alonso-Schökel, *Manual*; Geller, *Parallelism*; Pardee, *Ugaritic and Hebrew Poetic Parallelism*; Lowth, *Lectures*; and Newman and Popper, *Studies*. Useful surveys of the history of research on parallelism are Cloete, *Versification*, 1-98; and the annotated bibliographies on Hebrew poetry by Erhard S. Gerstenberger, "The Lyrical Literature," in *The Hebrew Bible and Its Modern Interpreters*, ed. Douglas A. Knight and Gene M. Tucker (Chico, CA: Scholars/Fortress, 1985), 409-44; and Nahum M. Waldman, "Rhetoric and Poetry" in *The Recent Study of Hebrew* (Winona Lake: Eisenbrauns and Hebrew Union College, 1989), 71-78.

25.   The current scholarly labels used here safeguard discussions in a terminological minefield, despite Alter's humorous critique: "the older scholarly label 'hemistich' and the current 'colon' (plural 'cola') both have misleading links with Greek versification, the latter term also inadvertently calling up associations of intestinal organs or soft drinks" (Alter, *Art*, 9). Alter proposes replacing "verset" for colon and "line" for bicola and tricola; however, the additional confusion in Alter's labels explains their failure to supplant the traditional ones.

26. John Gammie, "Alter Vs. Kugel," *Bible Review* (February 1989): 25-33. A helpful introductory survey of the major recent approaches to biblical poetry is William D. Reyburn, "Poetic Parallelism," in *Issues in Bible Translation*, ed. Philip C. Stine (New York: United Bible Societies, 1988), 81-112.

27. Jakobson, "Grammatical Parallelism;" Segert, "Parallelism;" Samuel R. Levin, *Linguistic Structures in Poetry* (The Hague: Mouton, 1962), 31-50; and J. L. Foster, *Thought Couplets and Clause Sequences in a Literary Text: The Maxims of Ptah-hotep* (Toronto: Society for the Study of Egyptian Antiquities Publications, 1977).

28. Even Alter describes Genesis 4:23 in terms of synonymous parallelism (*Art*, 7); yet he sees a dynamic advance in the common pattern of general terms in the A-colon and literary terms in the B-colon. Alter also implies Genesis 4:23, as a formulaic ancient Near Eastern convention, is not representative of biblical parallelism (*Art*, 12).

29. Compare the chart in John H. Walton, *Chronological and Background Charts of the Old Testament* (Grand Rapids: Zondervan, 1978), 75. A basic introduction to semantic parallelism is William E. Mouser, Jr., *Walking in Wisdom* (Downers Grove, IL: InterVarsity, 1983), 25-79.

30. *Thetic parallelism* may be a better label than synonymous, describing parallel lines running in the same direction. Besides corresponding to the other labels of antithetic and synthetic, thetic incorporates synonymous, complementary, and numerical parallelism, as well as parallel lines not containing actual synonyms, like Jeremiah 13:23 (Stanislav Segert, "Parallelism in Ugaritic Poetry," *Journal of the American Oriental Society* 103 [1983]: 295-306; Luis Alonso-Schökel, *A Manual of Hebrew Poetics* [Rome: Biblical Institute, 1988], 72).

31. Numerical parallelism appears as 1 // 2 (Dt 32:30; Jg 5:30; Jb 33:14, 40:5; Ps 62:11; Jr 3:14); 2 // 3 (Jb 33:29; Hs 6:2); 3 // 4 (Pr 30:15, 18, 21, 29; Am 1:6, 9, 11, 13; 2:1, 4, 6); 6 // 7 (Jb 5:19; Pr 6:16); and 1,000 // 10,0000 (Dt 32:30; 1 S 18:7, 21:11, 29:5; Ps 91:7). See further Wilfred G. E. Watson, *Classical Hebrew Poetry* (Sheffield: JSOT, 1984), 144-49; John J. Davis, "The Rhetorical Use of Numbers in the Old Testament," *Grace Journal* 8:3 (1967): 40-48; W. M. W. Roth, *Numerical Sayings in the Old Testament* (Leiden: Brill, 1965); and Menahem Haran, "Biblical Studies: The Literary Applications of the Numerical Sequence x/x+1 and Their Connections with the Patterns of Parallelism," *Tarbiz* 39

(1969/70): 109-136 or "The Graded Numerical Sequence and the Phenomenon of 'Automatism' in Biblical Poetry" in *Congress Volume, Uppsala 1971*, ed. G. W. Anderson (Leiden: Brill, 1972), 238-67.

32.   Greater precision results from distinguishing contraries from contradictories (Alonso-Schökel, *Manual*, 85-91; Jean Calloud, "A Few Comments on Structural Semiotics" in *Beyond Form Criticism*, ed. Paul R. House [Winona Lake, IN: Eisenbrauns, 1992], 130-33). Krasovec deals specifically with antithesis, although he omits Proverbs as "neither stimulating nor rewarding," and Ec, SS, Dn, and the Minor Prophets as having few examples; yet he appends "a comprehensive list" of antithetic units in the Hebrew Bible (Joze Krasovec, *Antithetic Structure in Biblical Hebrew Poetry* [Leiden: Brill, 1984]).

33.   Often called *formal parallelism*, due to the absence of close semantic correspondences between the poetic lines, this moniker may apply to other varieties of synthetic parallelism. Gray declares this is not parallelism at all (*Forms*, 49-50) and Segert refers to non-parallel bicola ("Parallelism," 300-301). Pardee would call it *positional parallelism*, poetic merely by placement between two identifiable bicola (Dennis Pardee, *Ugaritic and Hebrew Poetic Parallelism* [Leiden: Brill, 1988], 181; Lewis I. Newman and William Popper, *Studies in Biblical Parallelism* [Berkeley, CA: University of California, 1918, 1923], 381, 385).

34.   Climactic is apparently Alex Gordon's label (Alex R. Gordon, *The Poetry and Wisdom of the Old Testament* [Edinburgh: T. & T. Clark, 1913], 11-12).

35.   Theodore Robinson proposed the emblematic label (*Poetry*, 22-24).

36.   C. S. Lewis supports the suggestion that "the same in the other" is the very principle of art (*Reflections*, 4).

37.   Incomplete parallelism is Gray's label (*Forms*, 49).

38.   Double-duty dependency is "a form of reciprocal binding relationship between a word(s) and another group of words, or an adjacent or nearby clause" in which "the binding element performs a dual function — not always identical" (Don Parker, "Syntactic and Poetic Structures in Proverbs 10:1—22:16," Ph.D. dissertation, [UCLA, 1992], 21). Dahood, if not the originator, popularized this label.

39.   Compensation is Gray's label (*Forms*, 74).

40.   Ballast variant is Gordon's label (Cyrus H. Gordon, *Ugaritic Textbook* [Rome: Biblical Institute, 1965], 135-37). Alter

objects to this designation as reducing the value of the poetic term (*Art*, 9).

41.   Collins is representative in his critique: "First of all, when we come to look closely at the various attempts to follow out the semantic analysis in detail we find a startling lack of agreement as to the essentials of the system. Each successive attempt produces its own list ...in a way that can only be described as subjective. This is to be expected when one tries to reduce all the fine shades of meaning that a poet can work into his lines to arbitrary general categories where nuances must inevitably be obscured. Secondly, in classifying lines according to semantic content we are often led to ignore the more basic structural patterns a poet is using" (Terence Collins, *Line Forms in Hebrew Poetry* [Rome: Biblical Institute, 1978], 92-93).

42.   Gray, *Forms*, 3.

43.   Lewis, *Reflections*, 3.

44.   The distinctive syntax of poetry is emphasized by O'Connor; Collins; Geller; Stanley Gevirtz, *Patterns in the Early Poetry of Israel*, 2d ed. (Chicago: University of Chicago, 1973); Theodore Alexander Hildebrandt, "Proverbial Poetry," Th.D. dissertation (Grace Theological Seminary, 1985); Parker; Raphael Sappan, *The Typical Features of the Syntax of Biblical Poetry in Its Classical Period [Hebrew, with English summary]* (Jerusalem: Kiryat Sefer, 1981); and Mitchell Dahood, *Psalms III [101-150]* (Garden City, NY: Doubleday, 1970), 364-444.

45.   The Appendix includes the forms of these prose particles. The old standard reference grammar observes their frequent absence from poetic texts (GKC #2q), but Freedman ("Pottery," 79-80) and others have recently emphasized it.

46.   For example, contrary to the common generalization for Hebrew word order, my dissertation research establishes subject-verb word order as normative for the bulk of Proverbs. Chiastic structures also factor into word order generalizations.

47.   Poetic forms and syntax receive brief, scattered treatment in the standard reference grammar, GKC (#2s,r; #87n; #90f, g, l, m; #91b; #102b, c; #103f, k, o; #114m1, r1; #117a, b, z, ll; #118r; #120h; #124b, g; #125g; #126h; #132c; #141d; #144p; #150h; #152a, t, u; #155b, n; #165b); GKC takes insufficient account of poetry's effect on word order, however. An important feature for interpreting biblical Hebrew poetry is that seeming imperfect verb forms are actually preterites without *waw* consecutive (Moshe Held, "The *YQTL-QTL [QTL-YQTL]* Sequence of Identical Verbs in Biblical Hebrew and in Ugaritic," in *Studies*

and Essays in Honor of Abraham A. Neuman, ed. M. Ben-Horin, B. D. Weinryb, and S. Zeitlin [Leiden: Brill for Dropsie College, 1962], 281-90). See the Appendix for verb tenses.

48.   Hildebrandt cites this example from Hemmingsen ("Proverbial Poetry," 331).

49.   Alonso-Schökel, *Manual*, 192. *Mixed chiasm* labels chiastic structures formed from separate realms, such as semantics on one "branch of the X" and syntax or sound on the other branch. The previous chapter displayed one concentric structure governing an entire narrative (Dn 2—7). Poetry, however, uses such structures for basic units as well as entire poems. The example of Psalm 19:1 is adapted from Magonet (Jonathan Magonet, *A Rabbi Réads the Psalms* [London: SCM, 1993], 89), who proposes concentric structures govern all of Psalm 145, 92, and 25 (34-51, 73-75).

50.   Alden's series on chiastic structuring in Psalms is provocative (Robert L. Alden, "Chiastic Psalms," *Journal of the Evangelical Theological Society* 17 [1974]: 11-28; 19 [1976]: 191-200; 21 [1978]: 199-210).

51.   Anthony R. Ceresko, "The Function of Chiasmus in Hebrew Poetry," *CBQ* 40 (1978):1-10; Nels W. Lund, *Chiasmus in the New Testament*, repr. of 1942 ed. (Peabody, MA: Hendrickson, 1992); John W. Welch, ed., *Chiasmus in Antiquity* (Hildesheim: Gerstenberg, 1981); and Francis I. Andersen, *The Sentence in Biblical Hebrew* (The Hague: Mouton, 1974), 119-40. Classifications of chiasmus include Watson, *Classical Hebrew Poetry*, 202-204; O'Connor, *Hebrew Verse Structure*, 391-95; and Parker, "Syntactic and Poetic Structures," 33-35.

52.   Freedman summarizes and concurs with Gray in the "Prolegomenon" to Gray, *Forms*, xxi. Watson, *Classical Hebrew Poetry*, 160-200 discusses poetic sections.

53.   Gillingham, *Poems and Psalms*, 196-97, citing Hempel. Roland Knox's translation produces English acrostics (*The Holy Bible* [Kansas City: Sheed & Ward, 1956]).

54.   Watson, *Classical Hebrew Poetry*, 192-200 describes these acrostics. The acrostics in Lamentations 2, 3, and 4 reverse *'ayin* and *peh*, reflecting an attested older order of the Semitic alphabet. Useful articles on acrostics include John F. Brug, "Biblical Acrostics and Their Relationship to Other Ancient Near Eastern Acrostics" in *The Bible in the Light of Cuneiform Literature*, ed. William W. Hallo, Bruce William Jones, and Gerald L. Mattingly (Lewiston, PA: Mellen, 1990), 283-304; and David

Noel Freedman, "Acrostic Poems in the Hebrew Bible: Alphabetic and Otherwise" *CBQ* 48 (1986): 408-31.

55.   Ginsberg, Cassuto, Melamed, and Dahood pioneered study on word pairs. A valuable collection of biblical and Ugaritic word pairs is Loren R. Fisher, ed., *Ras Shamra Parallels: Volumes I and II* (Rome: Biblical Institute, 1972, 1975) and Stan Rummel, ed., *Ras Shamra Parallels: Volume III* (Rome: Biblical Institute, 1981). Watters considers word pairs a primary criterion for identifying poetry (William R. Watters, *Formula Criticism and the Poetry of the Old Testament* [Berlin: de Gruyter, 1976]). Formerly designated "fixed pairs," both the order of the words' usage and their textual proximity are somewhat flexible. Summaries of the history of research are Watters, 20-38; Robert G. Boling, "'Synonymous' Parallelism in the Psalms," *Journal of Semitic Studies* 5 (1960): 223; and Perry B. Yoder, "Biblical Hebrew," in *Versification*, ed. William K. Wimsatt (New York: Modern Language Association/New York University, 1972), 62n10. Semantic relationships between words in pairs are explored by Berlin, 65-88; O'Connor, *Hebrew Verse Structure*, 97-111; Watson, *Classical Hebrew Poetry*, 130-35; Geller, *Parallelism*, 31-41; and Segert, "Parallelism," 302-304.

56.   Chapter 10 briefly discusses about two dozen biblical Hebrew grammars. A few examples of rarer wordforms and uses found in biblical Hebrew poetry include vocative *lamed*, alternative forms of pronouns, and lengthened prepositions and verbs.

57.   Leland Ryken, "The Bible as Literature: Part 3," *Bibliotheca Sacra* 147 (1990): 259-69.

58.   Perhaps the best brief treatment of sound-plays in biblical Hebrew is Alonso-Schökel, *Manual*, 20-33.

59.   Chapter 6 includes a discussion of types of word-plays.

60.   Leo I. Weinstock, "Sound and Meaning in Biblical Hebrew," *Journal of Semitic Studies* 28 (1983): 49-62 examines semantic fields and concludes onomatopoeia exists, but is limited in biblical Hebrew. His fields could be expanded and others added to yield a higher percentage.

61.   Allen notes that the Church of Scotland has rhymed and metered versions of the Psalms in her hymnbooks (Ronald Barclay Allen, *Praise* [Nashville: Nelson, 1980], 22), even as selected English rhymed versions exist. *The Psalms: An Inclusive Language Version Based on the Grail Translation from the Hebrew* (Chicago: GIA, 1993) attempts to preserve the measured character of parallelism in translation.

62.   Gordon, *Ugaritic Textbook*, 132.

63.   John F. Walvoord and Roy B. Zuck, eds., *The Bible Knowledge Commentary: Old Testament* (Wheaton, IL: Victor Books, Scripture, 1985), 780. The *Word Biblical Commentary* volumes on Psalms clearly show such counts, or scansion. Alternate proposed metrical systems include syllable counting (or vocable or consonant-counts) and alternating stresses. Surveys of research include O'Connor, *Hebrew Verse Structure*, 34-39; Cooper, 19-34; and Watters, 14n39, 99-100n20.

64.   Gillingham, *Poems and Psalms*, 68.

65.   In the Prolegomenon to Gray, *Forms*, xi. Psalm 23:5-6 uses *qinah* meter, showing it is not exclusive to laments.

66.   Gray, *Forms*, 225

67.   Freedman in the Prolegomenon to Gray, *Forms*, xxxix.

68.   Helpful books on Psalms form criticism include conservatives William H. Bellinger, Jr., *Psalms* (Peabody, MA: Hendrickson, 1990); and Ronald Barclay Allen, *Praise!* (Nashville: Thomas Nelson, 1980). Readable books by non-conservative scholars include Bernhard W. Anderson, *Out of the Depths*, rev. ed. (Philadelphia: Westminster, 1983); Claus Westermann, *Praise and Lament in the Psalms*, repr. of 1965 ed. (Atlanta: John Knox, 1981) or *The Living Psalms* (Grand Rapids: Eerdmans, 1967); Sigmund Mowinckel, *The Psalms in Israel's Worship* (Sheffield: JSOT, 1992); Hermann Gunkel, *The Psalms* (Philadelphia: Fortress, 1967); and Klaus Seybold, *Introducing the Psalms* (Edinburgh: T. & T. Clark, 1990).

69.   This snowflake simile appears in Allen, *Praise!* 26. Westermann uses another analogy from nature: "the forms share in that diversity which marks all living things. As in the natural world we can recognize the species, which yet preserves the distinctiveness of its individual members, so the single psalms belong to categories which can be shaped in a boundless variety of ways, none of which is ever quite the same" (Westermann, *Living Psalms*, 10).

70.   "Lament" is a lamentable, negative-sounding label for psalms characterized more specifically by prayer and often including praise. Furthermore, "prayer" is often a technical term used of these psalms (Leslie C. Allen, *Psalms 101—150* [Waco: Word, 1983], 9) and "how long?" occurs commonly, suggesting the appropriate label "plea."

71.   Sabourin's label is enlarged here by the inclusion of royal songs (Marvin E. Tate, *Psalms 51—100* [Waco: Word, 1990], 257).

72.   Often differences in psalm classifications are attributable to confusing, or variously emphasizing, content or function over

form. Other common classifications are penitential psalms (6, 32, 38, 51, 102, 130, 134); psalms of innocence (7, 17, 26; and perhaps 35, 57, 69, 94, 109, 139); hallelujah psalms (104-106, 111-116, 135, 146-150) and pilgrim psalms (120-135 especially). The first two groups are more content specific subgroups of pleas, although some interpreters also stress related cultic functions and a few propose distinctive forms. The last two groups stress content and/or function over form.

73. Crüsemann argues for deleting this rarely exampled form altogether (Allen, *Psalms 101—150*, 188).

74. The answers for Action Point #2 are: climatic, antithetic, synonymous, emblematic, and synthetic; that is, matching the suggested acronym C.A.S.E.S.

75. The answers for Action Point #3 are: synonymous, incomplete and inexact; antithetic, incomplete and inexact. For such relaxed parallelism (Segert's label), analyzing the nature of specific correspondences — in semantics, grammar, and sound — provides more help than the mere labels "inexact" or "incomplete."

Chapter 8

From Text to Life: Bridging the Culture Gap

Objectives: After reading this chapter, you should be able to:
1. Assess the relationship between the Testaments.
2. Identify three theological systems that differ on the relation between Israel and the Church.
3. Evaluate several positions on determining the normativeness of the Bible.
4. Use three basic processes to bridge the culture gap.
5. Suggest several criteria for determining the degree of applicability of biblical texts.

One of the *B.C.* cartoons gives an ant's answer to his son's question, "What is culture, Daddy?": "It's something you ain't never gonna get, cause your old lady and me never got none."

Culture refers to learned behavior patterns characteristic of a given society's members and transmitted to a succeeding generation.[1] Biblical revelation is "culture-conditioned" in having come primarily to and through Israelites, in specific historical settings quite diverse from our own. Recognizing this culture gap — variously called *historical consciousness* or *distanciation* — clarifies the exegetical task.

Establishing what the text *meant* to its original readers is only a portion of exegesis. To apply the Bible, modern readers must also grapple with what the text *means* for people today. Application is *here and now*, although mediated by way of *there and then*. As Karl Barth said, "The Christian must always read with the Bible in one hand and the morning paper in the other."

The Apostle Paul repeatedly affirmed the Old Testament's relevancy (2 Tm 3:15-16; Rm 15:4; 1 Cr 10:6). Clearly generations beyond the original readers benefited from portions of the Old Testament (Dt 6:7-25, 31:9-13; 2 K 22—23; Nh 7:73—8:18).[2]

But just how are culturally-limited particulars distinguished from transcultural principles? How are ancient cultural forms separated from normative principles to determine God's Word for today?

The difficulty manifests itself in certain denominational distinctives (such as sabbath-keeping or foot washing), and varied applications of controversial texts (like the infamous "head covering" of 1 Cr 11). Also, modern cultural contextualizations like liberation theology and so-called biblical feminism highlight the importance of appropriately bridging the culture gap.

In particular, missionaries sense the culture gap. When translating the Bible, they apply *dynamic equivalence translation theory* — seeking comparative translational "equivalents" in culturally specific terms. The interaction of missionaries with other cultures prompts a call for the *globalization of hermeneutics* (asking new questions of the Bible and proposing new answers based on different interpretive communities).

Although a culture gap exists between our own culture and the New Testament, the gap often widens with Old Testament texts. Further, a person's viewpoint on the relationship between the Old and New Testaments, and between Israel and the Church, typically shapes the bridges constructed over the culture gap.

This chapter surveys these theological pylons, describes three bridge-building processes, and offers some practical planks to use in bridging the culture gap.

The Relationship between the Old and New Testament

Use of the Old Testament in ministry depends largely on how it relates to the Christian message. Indeed, many acknowledge that the relationship between the Testaments forms *the* key issue in hermeneutics and theology.[3] An intertwined issue is the nature of the relationship between Israel and the Church.

The spectrum of viewpoints[4]

Obviously, individuals and denominations hold different viewpoints about the relation of the Old Testament to the New. These viewpoints cover a spectrum producing the least to the highest degree of relevance for the Old Testament. Without claiming comprehensiveness, and allowing for overlapping elements of truth in different viewpoints, the following sketch sets out major options and serves as a self-diagnostic aid.

The Spectrum of Viewpoints on the Theological Relationship
of the Old Testament [OT] to the New Testament [NT]

unessential	- | -	The OT is obsolete, non-Christian background (Marcion; Bultmann). Result: No use for the OT.
initial	- | -	The OT precedes as historical preparation for the NT (progressive revelation), or as spiritual preparation (OT = law; NT = grace). Result: The OT is inferior, with limited usefulness.
integral	- | -	The OT is part of a unified "salvation history" actualized in the NT (promise-fulfillment schemes; von Rad's "descendants"). Result: The OT can be tacked on the NT, with questionable usefulness.
foundational	- | -	The OT is indispensable and formative, yet distinct, containing continuities and discontinuities with the NT message (John Bright). Result: The OT's own message must be sifted through the NT.
equal	- | -	The OT is totally on a par with the NT, with the same theology (many Calvinists, like W. Vischer). Result: Both testaments are equally scripture and Christ is seen throughout both.
cardinal	- | -	The OT is the primary testament and the NT is its interpretive glossary (some Calvinists, like A. A. van Ruler). Result: The OT message is central; Christ is God's "emergency measure" when all other means to establish God's kingdom failed.

The "foundational" viewpoint

A building needs a foundation to shape and support the superstructure. The foundation is indispensable and often constructed out of similar materials as the rest of the building. Still, the foundation is not the superstructure; nor does the superstructure alone comprise the building. This limited analogy suggests the complex relationship of the Old Testament to the New Testament.

The foundational viewpoint accords the Old Testament full status as divine revelation. At the same time, the foundational viewpoint recognizes continuities and discontinuities with the New Testament.

Continuities between the Testaments include elements suggested by the other viewpoints: promise and fulfillment, typology, salvation history, a Christocentric emphasis, and sin and grace. However, the New Testament also manifests discontinuities with the Old, as in the case of the Levitical sacrifices.

The writer to the Hebrews put the relation between former and later revelation this way: "In the past God spoke to our forefathers through the prophets at many times and in various ways, but in these last days he has spoken to us by his Son ..." (Hb 1:1-2, NIV). Both testaments contain a message from God; but the distinctive New Testament message demands Christians hear the Old Testament differently than the original recipients.[5]

Also, the wording of Hebrews 1:1-2 suggests several supplemental analogies (besides the analogy of a foundation and superstructure forming a building). The New Testament acts as a respondent and moderator for the Old Testament's presentation. The New Testament does not act as a narcissist who cannot bear to listen to another, nor as a ventriloquist imposing its voice on the Old Testament.

In brief, a foundational viewpoint finds Old Testament texts have varying degrees of applicability as Christians bridge the culture gap.

The relationship between Israel and the Church

Tied to the relationship between the Testaments is the relationship between biblical Israel and the Church (and Mosaic law and grace). Is that relationship one of continuity or discontinuity, or both at the same time?

Covenantism, or covenant theology, sees history and the Bible as governed by two related covenants of works and grace, established in the Garden of Eden and serving as the basis of all later biblical covenants.[6] Covenantism emphasizes continuity between Israel and the Church, variously suggesting that the Church is spiritual Israel or the replacement for biblical Israel.

Dispensationalism thinks that history is God's administration and the Administrator has imposed different programs and means of operation at various times. Accordingly, the dispensation of the Mosaic law differs from the Church age and both differ from a predicted future dispensation. Traditional dispensationalism completely distinguishes biblical Israel from the Church in God's program,[7] while progressive dispensationalism finds more continuities in God's peoples and program.[8]

Walter Kaiser promotes a middle ground between dispensationalism and covenantism. Epangelicalism, or *promise theology*, emphasizes the promise made to the patriarchs, continually fulfilled in the Old Testament, climactically fulfilled in Christ's two advents, and eternally operative.[9] This theological system downplays discontinuities between the Testaments.[10]

Whatever the theological system, the church's relation to biblical Israel radically influences the interpretation and the degree of applicability of many Old Testament texts.

Two Contrasting Positions on Determining Normativeness

Exegetes content with their viewpoint of the relation between the testaments (and between Israel and the Church) need one more theological and hermeneutical pylon to bridge the culture gap. While this book assumes scripture's inherent authority, that very assumption raises the issue of the criteria for normativeness of particular details. (*Normative* describes timeless, authoritative teaching everyone in every culture should directly apply to life.) Two polar positions clarify this issue.[11]

Position #1:
Only Scripture can limit a biblical teaching.[12]

This position considers every scriptural teaching normative unless scripture restricts itself. The Bible may limit its own teaching by: indicating a clearly cultural custom or cultural reasoning, referring to specific individuals, simply describing rather than prescribing behavior, or providing additional revelation.

Such a position maintains a high view of the Bible and warns against cultural relativism. The Bible critiques and shapes culture rather than the other way around.

However, this position may not adequately account for differences between biblical and modern cultures. It may also beg the question of identifying cultural elements in the Bible. ("There are no cultural elements other than what the Bible identifies.")

At any rate, this position expects a lot from the Bible, including its every limitation. Everything is normative unless tagged, "P.S.: Only for this and not succeeding generations and cultures."

Such a position poses some practical problems. Few Christians today insist on obeying the often repeated command to "greet one another with a kiss" (Rm 16:16; 1 Cr 16:20; 2 Cr 13:12; 1 Th 5:26; 1 Pt 5:14). Most consider an enthusiastic comment, a warm smile, or a handshake appropriate Christian greetings in an American culture saturated with promiscuity and homosexuality.

Position #2:
Culture typically limits a biblical teaching.[13]

According to this position, the meaning of all language is culture-related (including the language of revelation); and all biblical texts are *occasional texts* that address specific historical situations. Application should not impose culturally specific forms of revelation. So neither normativeness nor explicit revelational limitations on cultural factors should be expected.

Such a position stresses the part background information can play in interpretation and recognizes some biblical forms in themselves may be irrelevant to contemporary cultures. For example, the custom of Levirate marriage required a brother-in-law to propagate children with his brother's widow (Dt 25:5-10). Tribal, agrarian inheritance laws involving the promised land necessitated this now outdated practice.

On the other hand, the position that culture limits biblical teaching fails to adequately acknowledge the generally normative character of biblical revelation. Christ and the Apostles often settled issues with, "It is written."

In practice, this position elevates contemporary cultural biases over biblical teaching. For example, advocates insist any biblical teaching on differing male and female roles in marriage and ministry must be either patriarchal or occasional.

Bridging the Culture Gap

A proposal

The two polar positions on normativeness present two dangers, comparable to denying either the humanity or deity of the incarnate Word. One danger lies in imagining that all of the Bible propounds timeless propositional truth apart from any historical conditioning. The other peril reduces divine revelation to merely cultural status.[14]

At the risk of alienating all sides, a mediating position proposes both scripture and culture may limit a biblical teaching. This position emphasizes scripture's generally normative character, yet recognizes that the culture gap requires evaluation of both the Bible's teaching and ancient and modern cultures.

As Paul says, scripture is "useful for doctrine, for reproof, for correction, for instruction in righteousness" (2 Tm 3:16). Even the Old Testament teaches a great deal, particularly regarding the character of God and humanity, creation, moral issues, or instruction echoed in the New Testament. Yet that instruction sometimes comes wrapped in the trappings of ancient cultures.

Bridge-building processes

Evaluation of biblical texts' normative character typically involves the related processes of differentiation, principlization, and particularization to bridge the culture gap.

Differentiation identifies ancient cultural specifics and acknowledges their foreignness to a contemporary culture. "The beginning of wisdom in biblical study is the realization that the Bible is an exotic book about which modern readers understand very little."[15] The greater the cultural differentiation in a biblical text the greater the need to principlize.

Principlization seeks the timeless universal truth underlying a specific text. Principlization finds support in the generalizing practice observable within the Old Testament itself. The law is summarized in the ten commandments (Ex 20:1-17), eleven principles (Ps 15), six commands (Is 33:15), three commands (Mc 6:8), two commands (Is 56:1) and one statement (Hb 2:4; Am 5:4; Lv 19:2).[16] After principlization, application de-generalizes principles into contemporary particulars.

Particularization identifies comparable contemporary cultural specifics or circumstances addressed by a biblical principle. What particulars or circumstances do we share in common with the writers, recipients, or objects of biblical revelation? James 2:2-7 particularizes Leviticus 19:15 ("Do

not show partiality.") by applying it to prejudice in early
church worship.[17]

Consider these three processes in regard to the Old
Testament law against coveting: "You shall not covet your
neighbor's house; you shall not covet your neighbor's wife
or his male servant or his female servant or his ox or his
donkey or anything that belongs to your neighbor" (Ex
20:17, NAS).[18] Differentiation recognizes that coveting
someone else's slaves, oxen, and donkeys are not temptations in modern urban America. Principlization points out
that coveting is wrong, whatever the object of desire. (Note
the phrase, "anything that belongs to your neighbor.")
Particularization warns against allowing another's car,
computer, or bank account to corrupt our perspective of
people and possessions.

Paul uses similar processes in applying Old Testament
passages. From the law about feeding oxen, he principlizes
that laborers ought to share in the produce and applies this to
supporting gospel ministers (1 Cr 9:8-12).[19] Paul makes the
same application from provisions for Old Testament Levitical
ministers (1 Cr 9:13-14). From the distributed sufficiency of
the manna given to wandering Israelites, wealthier Christians
learn to aid poorer believers; then Paul applies this principle
to the Corinthians' donation for the poor Jerusalem saints (2
Cr 8:1-15).

Using these bridge-building processes for any biblical
text, however, requires validation from scriptural and/or
cultural evidence. Apart from such supportive evidence,
cultural relativity tends to reign over biblical authority.

General criteria for normativeness
(versus cultural specificity)

The preceding discussion focuses on some theological
pylons (essential theory) and three processes for bridging the
culture gap. Now is the time to offer some practical planks
for placement in culture gap bridges.

1. Scriptural factors

In many respects, Scripture is its own interpreter.

1) Does the literary genre impact application? Much in narrative is descriptive without being *prescriptive* (affirming behavior as binding on the reader).[20] Poetry, as Chapters 5 and 7 indicate, contains many non-literal elements. Psalms were often sung within the context of Israelite temple worship. Wisdom literature, especially Proverbs, contains many generalized statements. Prophetic and legal literature are closely bound to the Mosaic covenant made with biblical Israel.

2) Does the literary or historical context limit the recipient or the application? God's pronouncement "You have not spoken of me what is right" (Jb 42:7, 8) provides a strong literary clue for interpreting and applying the speeches of Job's comforters. The historical context features prominently in Paul's advocation of celibacy: It was "because of the [then] present crisis" (1 Cr 7:26). Far from being a general directive, celibacy formed only one element of his call for contentment in the Corinthians' circumstances.

In particular, what argumentation does the biblical writer marshall to support his teaching? The biblical injunction to "work with your hands" (1 Th 4:11-12) does not require manual labor as the only legitimate vocation; some form of gainful employment, however, reflects well on the gospel across cultures ("win the respect of outsiders" and do "not be dependent on anybody"). Paul's arguments from the Trinity (1 Cr 11:3), creation (1 Cr 11:8-9), angelology (1 Cr 11:10), nature (1 Cr 11:14), and early church consensus (1 Cr 11:16) suggest not everything in the controversial head-covering passage relates specifically to a Corinthian situation.

3) Does subsequent revelation limit the recipient or application? Dietary laws are no longer directly in force (Mk 7:13; Ac 10:15; 1 Tm 4:3-5), nor circumcision as a legal requirement (Gl 2:11-21), nor the ceremonial and sacrificial laws, according to Hebrews.

4) Does the specific teaching conflict with other scriptural teaching? Certainly Israelites did not understand the commandment against killing (Ex 20:13) as forbidding warfare or governmental capital punishment (Gn 9:6; Rm 13:4). While tolerated, polygamy was not approved (Dt 17:17) or advocated (Mt 19:4-6; 1 Tm 3:2).[21]

2. Cultural factors

Ancient and modern cultural factors may influence normativity.

1) Is the situation addressed by the teaching (or its supporting argumentation) in existence today? Few today advocate Levirate marriage and primogeniture (the firstborn gets special inheritance rights). Rarely do modern Christians confront the social dilemma of eating meat sacrificed to idols (1 Cr 8).

Such cases call for principlization. Additionally, the history of interpretation warns against a reverse form of normative application: In 1728, Scotland outlawed potatoes because the Bible does not mention them!

2) Does the ancient cultural form of the teaching find similar expression today? While few modern cultures practice monarchy, Christians can still pray for authorities (1 Tm 2:2). Admonitions regarding slaves' behavior toward owners and vice-versa find application in labor relations. Some biblical prescriptions of wine justify using available medical treatments (1 Tm 5:23; Pr 31:6-7).

3) Do contemporary cultural issues modify application? Although total alcoholic abstinence is difficult to defend scripturally, epidemic alcoholism and the law of love might commend it (Rm 14; 1 Cr 8). To prosper his ministry among the contentious Corinthians, Paul forfeited his right to financial support (1 Cr 9:14-23); yet he accepted support from the Philippians (Pp 4:10-18).

3. Spiritual factors

In reality, individuals play a role in determining normativity.

1) *Maturity* promotes discernment and obedience in matters of faith and practice (Hb 5:13-14); yet even mature believers disagree about interpretations and applications of biblical texts.[22]

2) *Teachability* includes engaging in "dialogue" with other interpreters (past and present) and being open to their insights and teaching gifts in the body of Christ.

3) *Humility* recognizes no interpretive criteria guarantee unanimity and allows individuals their own responsible decisions (Rm 14:1-12), while concentrating on essentials (Rm 14:17, 19).

4) *Charity* sometimes yields our Christian liberty regarding "correct" applications (Rm 14:13-21) and always accepts others as worthwhile individuals, even when we disagree with their views.

Those who would use biblical Hebrew in ministry can not avoid the challenging work of bridging the culture gap.

> The interpreter must bridge the gulf of explaining the cultural elements that are present in the text of Scripture, acknowledge his or her own cultural baggage as an interpreter, and then transcend both in order to communicate the original message of Scripture into the culture of the contemporary audience.[23]

Action Points

1.   Identify your viewpoint of the relationship between the Old and New Testament. (Refer to the "Spectrum" chart.)

2.   Classify the following biblical issues as strictly cultural, partly cultural, or transcultural: footwashing as a church ordinance (Jn 13:14-15); prohibition of single-fabric garments (Dt 22:11); sabbath-keeping (Saturday or Sunday? What is the sabbath in Hb 4:9-11? Why is this the only one of the ten commandments not repeated in the New Testament?); tithing (Ml 3:10; What is "the storehouse?"); anointing the sick with oil (Jm 5:14; Lk 10:34); singleness as a liability (Gn 2:18) or a benefit (1 Cr 7:31-32); manifold procreation (Gn 1:28; Ps 127:3-5); the danger of idolatry (1 Jn 5:21); prohibition of divorce and remarriage (Dt 24:1-4; Ml 3:16; Mt 19:1-12; 1 Cr 7:10-16). Try this with a group of people to surface different ideas and clarify your own.

"Yesterday" (strictly cultural)	"Yesterday and Today" (partly cultural)	"Always" (transcultural)
|	|	|

3.   Principlize and particularize any issues in Action Point two *not* considered transcultural.

4.   List what you consider the two or three most important criteria for determining the normative aspects of a biblical text.

5.   Read more about the relationship between the Testaments. (Start with the references in Note 4.)

6.   Read more about the theological systems of covenantism, dispensationalism, and epangelicalism. (Begin with the references in Notes 6-8.)

7.   Read more about bridging the culture gap. Start with William W. Klein, Craig L. Blomberg, and Robert L. Hubbard Jr., *Introduction to Biblical Interpretation* (Dallas: Word, 1993), 401-26; Walter C. Kaiser, Jr., and Moisés Silva, *An Introduction to Biblical Hermeneutics* (Grand Rapids: Zondervan, 1994), 172-

90; and Grant R. Osborne, *The Hermeneutical Spiral* (Downers Grove, IL: InterVarsity, 1991), 318-38.

Notes

1.   For similar and expanded definitions of culture, see J. Robertson McQuilkin, "Limits of Cultural Interpretation," *Journal of the Evangelical Theological Society* 21 (1980): 113; and Walter C. Kaiser, Jr., and Moisés Silva, *An Introduction to Biblical Hermeneutics* (Grand Rapids: Zondervan, 1994), 174.

2.   William W. Klein, Craig L. Blomberg, and Robert L. Hubbard Jr., *Introduction to Biblical Interpretation* (Dallas: Word, 1993), 402.

3.   See especially Walter C. Kaiser, Jr., *Toward Rediscovering the Old Testament* (Grand Rapids: Zondervan, 1987), 13-32.

4.   Two helpful treatments on the relationship between the Testaments are John Bright, *The Authority of the Old Testament*, repr. of Abingdon, 1967 ed. (Grand Rapids: Baker, 1975), 184-209; and David L. Baker, *Two Testaments, One Bible*, rev. ed. (Downers Grove, IL: InterVarsity, 1992). The "spectrum of viewpoints" draws heavily from these works. See also Walter C. Kaiser, Jr., *Toward an Old Testament Theology* (Grand Rapids: Zondervan, 1978), 265-68; and John S. Feinberg, ed., *Continuity and Discontinuity* (Westchester, IL: Crossway, 1988).

5.   For a sampling of how a foundational viewpoint treats varied types of Old Testament texts, see Bright, *Authority*, 213-51.

6.   Introductions to covenantism and its view of the relation between Israel and the Church include William Hendricksen, *The Covenant of Grace* (Grand Rapids: Baker, 1978); William E. Cox, *Amillennialism Today* (Nutley, NJ: Presbyterian and Reformed, 1966); and Charles D. Provan, *The Church is Israel Now* (Vallecito, CA: Ross House, 1987). Readable critiques from a dispensational view are Richard P. Belcher, *A Comparison of Dispensationalism and Covenant Theology* (Columbia, SC: Richbarry, 1986); and Renald E. Showers, *There Really Is a Difference! A Comparison of Covenant and Dispensational Theology* (Bellmawr, NJ: Friends of Israel Gospel Ministry, 1990).

7.   A clear presentation of traditional dispensationalism is Charles Caldwell Ryrie, *Dispensationalism*, rev. ed. (Chicago: Moody, 1995). For more on the history of this theological system, see Larry V. Crutchfield, *The Origins of Dispensationalism* (Lanham, MD: University Press of America, 1992). Critiques of dispensationalism include John H. Gerstner, *Wrongly Dividing the Word of Truth* (Brentwood, TN: Wolgemuth & Hyatt, 1991); and Vern Sheridan Poythress, *Understanding Dispensationalists* (Grand Rapids: Zondervan, 1987).

8. Progressive dispensationalism is represented by Craig Blaising and Darrell L. Bock, *Progressive Dispensationalism* (Wheaton, IL: BridgePoint, 1993); Robert L. Saucy, *The Case for Progressive Dispensationalism* (Grand Rapids: Zondervan, 1993); and Craig Blaising and Darrell L. Bock, eds., *Dispensationalism, Israel, and the Church* (Grand Rapids: Zondervan, HarperCollins, 1992).

9. Kaiser presents promise theology in *Old Testament Theology*, especially 33-35, 264-65.

10. Kaiser's later writing reveals latent features of promise theology which dispensationalists find less than promising. An implicit critique of dispensationalism is *Toward Old Testament Ethics* (Grand Rapids: Zondervan, 1983), 307-14.

11. Something close to these polar positions on determining scriptural normativeness were espoused at the International Council on Biblical Inerrancy, Chicago, 1982.

12. Judicious spokespersons for this view are J. Robertson McQuilkin, "Problems of Normativeness in Scripture," and George W. Knight, "A Response to Problems of Normativeness in Scripture," papers presented at the International Council on Biblical Inerrancy, Chicago, 1982.

13. Although not clearly in the "culture typically limits Scripture" camp, Alan F. Johnson leans this direction in his critique of McQuilkin ("A Response to Problems of Normativeness in Scripture," paper presented at the International Council on Biblical Inerrancy, Chicago, 1982).

14. "Too often, I fear, we either have had, in fact, a docetic Bible, which somehow sees timeless truths apart from the historically conditioned texts, or we have collapsed or reduced the divine initiative and revelation into only cultural phenomena" (David M. Scholer, "Issues in Biblical Interpretation," *Evangelical Quarterly* 88 [1988]: 19).

15. Carmi's preface, citing Greenberg (T. Carmi, ed., *The Penguin Book of Hebrew Verse* [New York: Viking, 1981], 10).

16. Kaiser and Silva, 276.

17. A number of commentators consider the letter of James essentially a particularization of Leviticus 19:12-18 because of frequent citations or allusions (Kaiser and Silva, 278).

18. On the debate over the tenth commandment prohibiting coveting as an attitude rather than an action, see Kaiser, *Ethics*, 7-8, 235-39.

19. Kaiser finds a different principle in these passages, namely, giving promotes gentle concern. He highlights concern for others in the Old Testament context (Kaiser, *Rediscovering*, 174).

20. Greidanus chronicles the exemplary preaching controversy in the Netherlands during the 1930's and early 1940's. The debate centered on the proper treatment of historical texts. Exemplary preaching often draws shallow applications from the historical subject matter within narratives rather than from the text's theological intent. Greidanus himself basically advocates the theologically-oriented redemptive-historical approach (Sidney Greidanus, *Sola Scriptura* [Toronto: Wedge, 1970]).

21. Kaiser labors strenuously to show polygamy was rare in ancient Israel (*Ethics*, 92-92, 182-90).

22. On limits in the Spirit's work in believers, see Roy B. Zuck, "The Role of the Holy Spirit in Hermeneutics," *Bibliotheca Sacra* 141 (1984): 120-130. William W. Klein, Craig L. Blomberg, and Robert L. Hubbard Jr., *Introduction to Biblical Interpretation*, 425-26 summarize Zuck's article.

23. Kaiser and Silva, 173-74.

Chapter 9

From Text to Life:
Bridging the Communication Gap

Objectives: After reading this chapter, you should be able to:
1. Trace the steps for moving from text to preaching.
2. Distinguish a textual idea from a sermon idea.
3. Develop a sermon idea by means of three "worlds," three roles, and three questions.
4. Preach purposefully.
5. Package a sermon according to the Whiting Method.

What are essentials in good preaching?[1] In terms of method, how does the biblical text relate to life and exegesis relate to expository preaching?

If communicating a text's significance is the goal,[2] how do you reach that goal while being true to the text? Further, how can you package and deliver your message to impact others?

Whereas the culture gap requires a standing broad jump, the communication gap demands a running jump. Although this is not a textbook on *homiletics* (the science and art of preaching),[3] the preaching application is a primary use of biblical Hebrew texts. Leaving all discussion of preaching to the homiletics teachers only perpetuates the misconception that biblical Hebrew is useless.

On the other hand, homiletics teachers often focus on matters of delivery and style, while assuming biblical language teachers cover all the interpretive issues (hermeneutics). Students, sadly, miss out on both ends.

Consequently, this chapter surveys the preaching process, presenting some guidelines and one practical approach to packaging a sermon.

Overview: The Process of Moving from Text to Life[4]

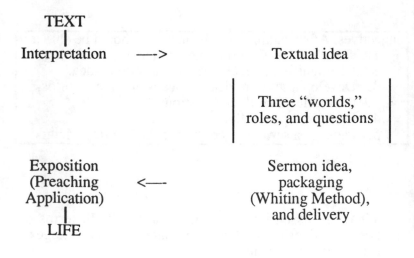

TEXT
|
Interpretation   —->   Textual idea

                                               Three "worlds,"
                                               roles, and questions

Exposition   Sermon idea,
(Preaching   <—-   packaging
Application)   (Whiting Method),
| and delivery
LIFE

Distinguishing the Textual Idea from the Sermon Idea

An important distinction

This book offers a broad view of exegesis. Application — what the text *means*, or signifies — is part of the process. Yet interpretation — what the text *meant* — may be distinguished.[5]

Unfortunately, preachers sometimes limit exegesis to interpretation and limit the sermon to that original meaning.[6] In its worst form, that type of preaching presents the Bible as an ancient document and fails to connect with a modern audience.

Hayes and Holiday agree with this assessment, using different terms:

> In employing the Bible in preaching, the biblical text is a central ingredient and for this reason exegesis is a fundamental prerequisite. Yet it is just as important to remember that exegesis and proclamation are distinct activities. The transition from text to sermon is a natural transition, but it is a transition nevertheless. It is as much of a mistake to assume that proclamation consists of doing exegesis as it is to assume that exegesis is essentially a form of preaching. Both exegesis and preaching may inform each other but they should not be merged into a single, undifferentiated activity.[7]

Definitions

The *textual idea* is a concise, complete interpretive sentence stating what the text meant to its original audience. The textual idea should inform any sermon. Otherwise, the text resembles the national anthem at a sporting event — heard only at the start and bearing little relation to the main event. By anchoring your message to the biblical text you share God's authority.[8]

While the preceding chapters contributed toward digging out textual ideas, these often differ from sermon ideas. A *sermon idea* states the text's significance for your audience in a concise, complete sentence. In journalistic terms, it represents the preacher's angle. A sermon idea weds a biblical truth with an appropriate response.[9]

A honed sermon idea makes a sermon "sing and sting." It enables people to both understand and act upon your message.

Chemist George Schweitzer suggests the aim of all science is to put everything into one formula. He also affirms that Einstein is revered "because he put more formula into one formula than any other scientist."[10] In the science of preaching, the sermon idea is the formula of the sermon's essence.

While developing sermon ideas is both a science and an art, the following suggestions provide some guidance. The challenging work of forming a sermon idea repays the preacher by greatly easing the remainder of sermon preparation and facilitating sermon delivery.

Developing Your Message

Sometimes direct, apparent correlations with the original audience permit using the textual idea as your sermon idea (with the sermon outline closely following the textual outline). For example, New Testament epistles originally intended for a Christian audience frequently permit this strategy.

Often, however, the textual idea will need some restatement, especially when preaching from the Old Testament. Such reshaping into a sermon idea acknowledges a different speaker and different audience.

Reshape the textual idea into your sermon idea by considering three "worlds," three roles, and three questions. Roughly, each triad corresponds, respectively, to a focus on the recipients, the messenger, and the message.[11] For any given exposition, analyzing one of these aspects of communication should provide a clue to developing your message.

A sub-theme of the textual idea may legitimately develop into a sermon idea. However, inform your audience when you do this, why you are doing it, and how your sub-theme derives from the text's overall meaning. In toning down or modifying dominant themes within the text, the expositor is like an orchestra conductor interpreting a musical piece for a particular occasion.[12]

The three "worlds" (recipient analysis)[13]

A precise sermon idea reflects both the contents of your text and the needs of your audience. Consider similarities and differences between the ancient world (the world of the biblical text), the modern world (contemporary society), and the particular world (your specific audience).

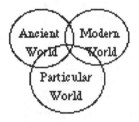

The biblical text and books on biblical backgrounds portray *the ancient world* of the Bible. Although determining the precise original social setting may be difficult (if the text is not explicit), such information colors interpretation and exposition.

Chapter 8 dealt with some effects of differences between the biblical world and the modern world. Differences abound: Imagine a confused, time-traveling Abraham in the midst of Los Angeles![14] Yet significant correspondences with the modern world exist, particularly in the nature of God and humanity.

Additionally, the dynamic expositor exegetes *the modern world* of contemporary culture. "A sermon ought to have heaven for its father and the earth for its mother."[15]

In what way does the biblical text address modern worldviews, issues, situations, and struggles? Keeping current with modern media, arts, and literature prevents sterile, monastic sermons.

In a related vein, analysis of the modern world may also affect the selection of a preaching text. Luther admonished, "If you preach the gospel in all aspects with the exception of the issues which deal specifically with your time, you are not preaching the gospel at all."

Last, but not least, enter *the particular world* of your audience. The Apostle Paul modified his presentation at Athens (Ac 17:16-34) from that at Antioch (Ac 13:13-44). An effective preacher knows his audience like a good shepherd knows his sheep.

What do you know about your listeners' background, capabilities, vocations, preferences, prejudices, relationships, interests, experiences, needs, and struggles? For life-changing exposition, Tim Timmons recommends preachers live, think (in terms of shared reading), play, and counsel with those in their care.[16]

Preachers need to avoid neglecting people for their study, as much as neglecting their study for people.[17] Adams makes this point with a hunting metaphor: "All the other work you do will be in vain if you are aiming at shadows in the underbrush rather than real live animals."[18]

Considering how the biblical text addresses your listeners, as well as the biblical world and a modern setting, can help shape your sermon idea.[19]

The three roles (ministry analysis)[20]

God's ministers in the Old Testament performed three general functions, or forms of ministry. *Prophet*, *priest*, and *sage* (wisdom teacher) constitute three roles, or models for ministry.[21]

In broad terms, the prophet challenged his audience's actions or outlook, the priest supported, and the sage instructed. The prophet offered hope for the future, the priest celebrated God's past workings, and the sage analyzed the present. Sages targeted selected individuals, priests ministered to the community of the elect, and prophets addressed a diverse audience.

Additional general characteristics of these roles, and possible parallels with other communication analyses, appear in the following chart.

	Prophet	*Priest*	*Wisdom Teacher*
Rhetorical Function[22]	judicial: judge a past situation	epideictic: celebrate or condemn, while seeking assent to values	deliberative: advise for potential near-situation
Religious Experience[23]	theological truth	sacred memory	worldview
Method	rebuke	ritual	reason
Goal	challenge	worship	education
Purpose (Cicero[24])	persuade	delight	instruct
Style (Augustine[25])	majestic	temperate	calm
Audience Size (Church growth[26])	congregation (c. 20-200)	celebration (mid-to-large)	cell or class (about 10)

Identifying the primary original ministry role in a text serves as a guide to appropriate modern use.[27] Present needs, however, may direct a focus on a sub-function of the text.

In light of your interpretation, the text's original function, and the needs of your audience, will you primarily act as a prophet, priest, or sage? Visualizing yourself in one of these three roles might help shape a functional sermon idea.

The three questions (message analysis)[28]

Craft a textual idea into a sermon idea by asking — and answering — three developmental questions. Often a sermon idea involves a combination of these questions, but usually one will stand out.

1. "What does that mean?"

Explain it. Is the biblical author explaining an idea? Does your audience need a similar explanation?

Does the biblical author assume things your audience might not know? If your audience heard the textual idea in raw form, would they immediately ask for additional explanation?

2. "Is that really true?"

Prove it. Is the biblical author substantiating the truth of his idea? How does he prove it?

Do your listeners readily believe the textual idea? What kind of evidence or argument would they need to accept it as valid?

3. "So what?"

Apply it. Why did the biblical author advance this idea? How is the biblical situation similar or dissimilar to ours?

What difference does it make? In what particular life situations today does this idea help? If you acted on the biblical truth, how would your thinking and life change?

One of these three questions, roles, and worlds should reveal a sermon idea lurking within a textual idea.

Deciding on Your Purpose[29]

Crafting your purpose

Your purpose is what you want to accomplish in your audience. According to David Mains, an experienced pastor and radio preacher, "The major component necessary for better preaching ... is the imperative — the call for specific action arising from the sermon text."[30] How are people's lives to change as a result of your message?

Unger warns: "Teaching, no matter how biblical in content, accurate in interpretation, or coordinated in its presentation, is not expository preaching, if it does not bring the Word of God down to the plane where men live and, with the unction and power of the Holy Spirit, challenge them with its claims."[31]

Craft your purpose in an infinitival phrase, such as "to motivate involvement in the church's community life." Although publicly stating your purpose is unnecessary, a clear purpose focuses your message preparation.

As one pundit said, "If you aim at nothing, you're sure to hit it." A purpose guides selection and organization in shaping a sermon. Purposeful preaching aids audience attention and, ultimately, achieves true audience participation, as the sermon reaches its target.

Choosing your purpose[32]

Select your purpose by asking, "What was the purpose of the text? Why did God make this a part of His revelation?"

Your purpose should be in line with the biblical author's purpose. In the case of a sub-theme, your purpose should be appropriate in light of the audience differential.

Ask, "What does the Holy Spirit want to accomplish through this text in my listener's lives today?"

Packaging Your Message: The Whiting Method[33]

Understanding the textual idea and its significance for the audience, and having a clear purpose, makes a preacher worth listening to. But your reception, and the listeners' response, depends on how you package your message.

One practical approach to sermon packaging incorporates key elements for communicating in a structured fashion. Certainly, preachers develop their own approaches. Different genres of texts[34] and audience attentiveness also demand variety. Yet the Whiting Method provides a useful general approach, especially for beginning preachers.

Summary of the Whiting Method

The Whiting Method includes an *introduction* to a theme; several related *mini-messages* explained, illustrated, and applied;[35] and a powerful *conclusion*.

Overview of the Whiting Method

Introduction
> Whet the appetite
> State the theme

Mini-Message #1: Keynote #1
> Explain
> Illustrate
> Apply
> Restate theme in relation to keynote

Mini-Message #2: Keynote #2 [also any #3/ #4/#5]
> Explain
> Illustrate
> Apply
> Restate theme in relation to keynote

Conclusion
> Summary of the keynotes
> Specific application
> Haymaker illustration
> Closing statement regarding the theme

Elements in the Whiting Method

1. The theme

The sermon *theme* is your polished sermon idea, concisely, appealingly, and (hopefully) memorably phrased. The plan is to burn a single thought into people's hearts, minds, and lives.

The Whiting Method suggests preaching is more like elephant hunting than duck hunting.[36] Shooting a bull elephant with buckshot would only annoy him and prompt him to turn on you.

Fire a clean shot by developing a single sermon theme.

2. The introduction

Too often the phrase "Open your Bible to ..." signals people to close their minds. A good introduction attracts attention, raises a need, creates interest, and orients to your theme.

Admittedly, a congregation is a captive audience. Yet a boring or irrelevant introduction almost ensures their escaping minus your message. If you want listeners to take your message to heart and take it home (apply it to life), you must take hold of their attention.

Chuck Swindoll reveals: "When I begin my sermons I dare the person not to listen to me. Not that I'm that great — it's just that I've got something to say that's too important to ignore." Good introductions make listeners care about your important message.

Other communicators, such as journalists, know the importance of powerful "leads." Galli and Larson, drawing from journalism, suggest effective introductions contain three prongs for capturing listener's attention: a hook, development, and a transition.[37]

The hook could involve humor, tragedy, amazing facts, incongruous beliefs, or the "big three" topics of sex, money, and power. A hook may take the form of an engaging story, a motivating problem, a startling question, an involving mystery, or an unusual statement, list or metaphor.

The second prong is the development of the theme as found in the hook. Aim at the heart and emotions. Take the time to draw in the listeners. Let them recall a similar experience and feel the relevance of your theme.

The final prong, the transition, may be simply the statement of the theme or a lead-in to the first keynote. The transition serves to stir curiosity by a promising prospect.

Optionally, the introduction may include a preview of the keynotes.

3. The keynotes[38]

Keynotes are the main points, or mini-themes, which develop or support your theme. Under other circumstances, keynotes might become full-blown themes for other messages. So keynotes share the characteristics of themes. Specifically, keynotes must be concise statements that lead from biblical truth to response.

4. The explanation process

Your keynote demands a response based on the biblical text's authority. But people can only respond to what they understand and accept.

Explain the text by sharing primarily those exegetical gems that lead to your keynote. What definitions, textual observations, background information, word studies, figures of speech, cross-references, arguments, or examples would be helpful?

The explanation renders a keynote authoritative and convincing by making God's Word understandable. Also, your explanation demonstrates how to mine the Bible for life-changing truth.

5. The illustration process[39]

While powerful quotations, images, or allusions may shed some light, the best illustrations involve narration. Chapell describes them as life-stories that relate theology to experience:

> Illustrations are "life-situation" stories within sermons whose details (whether explicitly told or imaginatively elicited) allow the listeners to identify with an experience that elaborates, develops, and explains scriptural principles. Through the details of the story, the listener is able imaginatively to enter an experience in which a sermonic truth can be observed.[40]

Typically, such audience-involving illustrations are specific rather than general, true rather than hypothetical, personal rather than "canned," and people-oriented rather than thing-oriented. In their development, stories show rather than tell, and appeal emotionally as well as logically. Nevertheless, because stories lend themselves to listeners' interpretations, always indicate the main point of an illustration.

Good illustrations move listeners from the sermon toward response:

> They take it out of the realm of abstraction and anchor it to everyday occurrences, to the things people know.... Illustrations are where the sermon puts on its overalls and goes to work in people's lives. The people in the congregation know in the illustrations whether the sermon is practical or not; if they can see the principles at work in the stories, then they know the principles will work for them.[41]

Illustration sources include illustration collections,[42] pastoral periodicals,[43] devotionally-oriented materials,[44] secular magazines,[45] and life itself.[46] Some filing and retrieval system is essential to long-term ministry.[47]

6. The application process[48]

Will Rogers, after an admiral described the menace of German U-boats during World War I, suggested as a solution: "Just boil the ocean." The admiral stared blankly and then muttered, "How?" Rogers smiled, "I gave you the idea — you work out the details."[49]

Unfortunately, even response-oriented messages can be weak on the details of application. People often need specifics to respond appropriately.

By exploring ways and means to live out God's will, the preacher equips God's people. Rather than taking the place of the Holy Spirit, such suggestions often break ground for His fertile work.

Beware! Application is a dangerous process. Howard Hendricks used to tell seminarians: "It was because of their applications that people killed the prophets!"

The application process requires courage constrained by love and guided by wisdom. Specific applications include the "who, what, where, when, and how." Relevant, realistic application often treats the situations, resources, and instructions for implementation.

Situations are occasions for the timely application of God's timeless truth. Chapell advocates preachers discuss one concrete life situation in detail, and then briefly suggest other situational possibilities.[50] Areas where the Word can again become incarnate include the home, church, business, school, neighborhood, society, the mind, leisure, and sex. The church setting is ripe for application through an altar call, an after-service meeting, follow-up classes, and sponsored groups or activities. Think in terms of relationships with God and others (believers or unbelievers, friends or "enemies," Jews or Gentiles, parent or child, and male or female).

Resources enable people to apply truth. During, before, or after your message, provide helpful resources. You could mention, supply, loan, or sell books, tapes, or other materials related to your theme or keynotes. Recommend "homework" in the form of response cards, Scripture memory, or bulletin inserts. Advertise the availability of pastoral staff, counselors, and mentors, including times, addresses, or phone numbers.

Sometimes, specific instructions are needed to translate willingness into action.

7. The conclusion

Berkley describes the conclusion as "the final push that makes a good sermon great and changes lives."[51] Conversely, a poor conclusion makes a good sermon appear weak and leaves people unmoved.

The haymaker constitutes a key element in a Whiting Method conclusion. The *haymaker*, like a boxer's powerful punch, is your most powerful illustration of your theme.[52] It drives home the theme, aims at your purpose, and serves as the sermon's climax. Realistically speaking, the haymaker may be the one thing listeners recall weeks later.[53]

The haymaker follows a final recommended specific application of your theme. So the haymaker seals a rational decision rather than prompting a merely emotional and fleeting response.

When concluding, avoid imitating an aircraft circling the airport in a holding pattern. Land the plane with a single, concise closing statement.

Sample Sermon Profile: Overcoming Temptation (Gn 3:1-6)

Textual Idea	The entrance of sin into the world resulted through the process of temptation.
Developmental Stages	Commonalities: human nature and the process of temptation; Key question: How does it apply? Key role: wisdom teacher; Sermon idea: a textual sub-theme and a multiple complement idea
Theme	What You Need to Know to Avoid Going with the Flow: Overcome by knowing God's Word, God's character, and your weak spots.
Purpose	to encourage resistance and provide the means
Introduction	Presidential candidate Hart, others brought down by temptation; Mark Antony's tutor: "Oh, Marcus, oh, colossal child! Able to conquer the world, but unable to resist a temptation." Learn to overcome from the first temptation.
Keynote #1	by knowing God's Word (Gn 3:1-3)
	Explain: Temptation begins by questioning (doubting and twisting) God's Word.
	Illustrate: Jesus overcame by it (Mt 4:1-11).
	Apply: Bible study and memory (Ps 119:9-11)
Keynote #2	by knowing God's character (Gn 3:4-5)
	Explain: Temptation includes questioning God's character, His truth and goodness.
	Illustrate: husband sees his wife kissing a stranger leaving his house; all depends on her character
	Apply: focus on God's beneficence in Christ
Keynote #3	by knowing your weak spots (Gn 3:6)
	Explain: Temptation succeeds through the appetites (lust of the eyes and flesh, pride of life).
	Illustrate: military analogy; Luther on age-specific temptations; alcoholic passing by a bar
	Apply: Which area poses your greatest temptation? besetting sin? strategy and resources
Final Application	Resist temptation! Life and death — choose life!
Haymaker	At the North Pole, the ice-battering atomic submarine Thresher exploded, its steel hull crushed by water pressure. Yet small fish survive at the same depth. How? By equalizing the pressure internally. Similarly, we can survive the pressure of temptation, by knowing ....

Delivering Your Message

Discussion to this point has concentrated primarily on *what* you say in a message. Obviously, *how* you say it also affects your reception. Although homiletics textbooks provide more thorough treatments of presentational characteristics, a preacher's delivery includes his style and manner.

Style, technically, refers to word choice.[54] Appropriate grammar, memorable phrasing, and vivid imagery contribute to a positive reception.

Keep technical jargon to a minimum and define any you must use. Avoid throwing around Hebrew, unless the terms are crucial to comprehension or for the appreciation of wordplays. Flaunting foreign languages can be offensive, like a public display of supportive undergarments.

Related to style is the *register*, or level of address, a speaker uses. Speakers range from a formal and eloquent high-style to a more down-to-earth, colloquial-style.

Polish your own style to present in your best fashion. "Faith had better be dressed as best and as skillfully as this world dresses its lies."[55]

In addition, *manner* describes aspects of delivery like energy and conviction, posture and gestures, eye-contact, and voice variety and inflection. Abe Lincoln preferred supercharged sermon delivery: "When I hear a man preach, I like to see him act as if he were fighting bees."

Certainly, few listeners will be more enthusiastic about your message than you. Yet a speaker's manner can degenerate into distracting mannerisms. Somerset Maugham's comments about certain writers fit some preachers:

> Their flashy effects distract the mind. They destroy their persuasiveness; you would not believe a man was very intent on ploughing a furrow if he carried a hoop with him and jumped through it at every other step.[56]

Practicing into a recorder or before a mirror or camcorder can refine sermon delivery. Furthermore, soliciting and accepting feedback from others can lead to marked overall improvement.

Becoming the Message

Especially in the spiritual realm, the messenger is intimately related to the message. Jesus is the Word and Christians serve as "living epistles" (2 Cr 3:2). Hosea lived out his message to Israel by redeeming his errant wife.

A minister's character fosters or hinders acceptance of his message. People want ministers to "walk the talk." Otherwise, they insist, "Who you are speaks so loudly, I can't hear what you're saying."

Clearly the minister who exhibits integrity, holy passion,[57] and compassion gains a better reception.[58] Prayer[59] and sufficient advance preparation promote our transformation into the message we wish to share with others.

In conclusion, if a sermon looms in your future, WRAP it up:

Whiting Method
Rehearse your delivery
Act positively (rest and groom well;
   envision positive results)
Pray throughout

Action Points

1. Outline your own approach to preaching if it differs from that presented in this chapter.

2. For additional input on preaching and identifying ideas in texts, read Haddon Robinson, *Biblical Preaching* (Grand Rapids: Baker, 1980). A companion volume is Donald Weber, *Biblical Sermons: How Twelve Preachers Apply the Principles of Biblical Preaching* (Grand Rapids: Baker, 1989.) Note 4 lists other homiletics textbooks.

3. Practice developing sermon themes. Use the three worlds, roles, and questions on textual ideas. Then polish your sermon ideas into concise, memorable themes. Do they "wed biblical truth with an appropriate response?" Try them on friends and mature believers.

4. Read further on the process of illustrating sermons. (Begin with some of the references in Note 40.)

5. Evaluate some sermons using the evaluation form provided on the next page (or in a similar fashion).

6. After videotaping or audiotaping one of your sermons, have at least one other person evaluate it. (Suggestion: To avoid discouragement and enhance objectivity, refrain from personal evaluation for twenty-four hours after preaching.)

7. Establish some means of receiving regular feedback on your sermons. (Note 21 supplies suggestions. If you use the provided sermon evaluation form, give evaluators a brief description of each listed item.)

8. Schedule at least one Old Testament book on your annual preaching calendar. Perhaps include special occasion messages based on Old Testament texts; standards are Isaiah 7:14, 9:6, Genesis 49:10, and Micah 5:2 for Christmas, Isaiah 53 or Psalm 22 for Easter, 1 Samuel 1-2 for Mother's Day, Nehemiah or Haggai while church-building, and Genesis 12:1-3 or Jonah for a missions conference.

Sermon Evaluation Form

Theme: _____

	Help!	O.K.	Great!
Introduction			
Whets my appetite?	1	2	3
States the theme?	1	2	3
Mini-Message #1: Keynote #1: _____			
Explanation (clear, convincing?)	1	2	3
Illustration (illuminating?)	1	2	3
Application (provocative, realistic?)	1	2	3
Restates theme in relation to keynote (smooth?)	1	2	3
Mini-Message #2: Keynote #2: _____			
Explanation (clear, convincing?)	1	2	3
Illustration (illuminating?)	1	2	3
Application (provocative, realistic?)	1	2	3
Restates theme in relation to keynote (smooth?)	1	2	3
Mini-Message #3: Keynote #3: _____			
Explanation (clear, convincing?)	1	2	3
Illustration (illuminating?)	1	2	3
Application (provocative, realistic?)	1	2	3
Restates theme in relation to keynote (smooth?)	1	2	3
Conclusion			
Summary of the keynotes (clear?)	1	2	3
Specific application (realistic?)	1	2	3
Haymaker illustration (powerful, appropriate?)	1	2	3
Closing statement (lands the plane?)	1	2	3
Overall, I rate the content of this message:	1	2	3

Comments on Delivery ("You Should …)

	Continue	Start	Stop
Language (style) •Correct•Understandable •Vivid•Memorable •Little jargon			
Manner •Posture•Energy •Movements•Voice •Gestures•Eye-contact			

Other comments:

Notes

1. Besides prayer and the Holy Spirit's work; the latter is always perfect and this is not the occasion to preach about the former.

2. Osborne affirms, "The hermeneutical process culminates not in the results of exegesis (centering on the original meaning of the text) but in the homiletical process (centering on the significance of the Word for the life of the Christian today)" (Grant R. Osborne, *The Hermeneutical Spiral* [Downers Grove, IL: Inter-Varsity, 1991], 343).

3. Worthwhile homiletics textbooks include Haddon Robinson, *Biblical Preaching* (Grand Rapids: Baker, 1980); Mark Galli and Craig Brian Larson, *Preaching That Connects* (Grand Rapids: Zondervan, 1994); Bryan Chapell, *Christ-Centered Preaching*, (Grand Rapids: Baker, 1994); Wayne McDill, *The 12 Essential Skills for Great Preaching* (Nashville: Broadman & Holman, 1994); and Sidney Greidanus, *The Modern Preacher and the Ancient Text* (Grand Rapids: Eerdmans, 1988).

4. My thinking on this process was stimulated by James McHann, *Biblical and Theological Communication*, unpublished class notes (Arrowhead Springs, CA: ISOT, n.d.). I taught the Old Testament portion of that course several years.

5. Hirsch made famous the distinction between meaning and significance (Eric D. Hirsch, Jr., *Validity in Interpretation* [New Haven, CT: Yale University, 1967] and *The Aims of Interpretation* [Chicago: University of Chicago, 1976]). Gadamer seems to have originated this distinction (Osborne, 6-7).

6. Richard Mayhue and Robert L. Thomas, eds., *Rediscovering Expository Preaching* (Dallas: Word, 1992) is basically a general introduction to the narrow view of exegesis. It presents exposition as interpretation-plus-illustrations, rather than the application of an authoritative biblical truth to a new situation.

7. John Hayes and Carl R. Holladay, *Biblical Exegesis* (Atlanta: John Knox, 1987), 149.

8. Osborne helpfully suggests the text itself has *implicit* authority, our interpretation has *derived* authority, and preaching has *applied* authority. (Osborne includes preaching under the term "contextualization.") He also notes that our preaching should cohere with our interpretation, which should approximate the text, in turn (Osborne, 8).

9. Chapell, who terms the sermon idea a formal proposition, emphasizes including both principle and response (Chapell, *Christ-Centered Preaching*, 140-41).

10. Fred Smith, "Does Anyone Know What Creative Means?" in *Preaching to Convince*, ed. James Berkley (Waco: Word, 1986), 34. Smith's comment that "Most of us are fortunate to have one good idea out of ten and so we must screen out the nine" (39) also applies to developing sermon ideas.

11. The sermon itself, particularly its form, is part of the "medium," another element of a communication act. Later in this chapter, the Whiting Method offers one means of packaging a sermon. The preacher's character, style, and delivery round out the sermon communication medium.

12. Hayes and Holladay, 152.

13. The idea of different worlds, or horizons, now common in homiletic theory, dates back to Dilthey and has roots in Schleiermacher. Compare the popular work by John R. W. Stott, *Between Two Worlds* (Grand Rapids: Eerdmans, 1982). Kaiser, among others, recognizes *three* worlds, or horizons (Walter C. Kaiser, Jr. and Moisés Silva, *An Introduction to Biblical Hermeneutics* [Grand Rapids: Zondervan, 1994], 189-90).

14. In hermeneutics, *distanciation* describes the recognition of differences between the biblical and modern world.

15. The nineteenth-century German theologian Tholuck, cited to a slightly different end in Berkley, 77.

16. Tim Timmons, "Why Should They Listen to Me?" in Berkley, 18-19.

17. Ben Patterson, "Five Temptations of the Pulpit" in Berkley, 155.

18. Jay E. Adams, *Truth Applied* (Grand Rapids: Zondervan, 1990), 137.

19. Robinson suggests practical ways to learn people's concerns: a monthly discussion group (centered on books, plays, or movies), an *ad hoc* group of specialists, a pre-sermon Bible study on your text, pre-sermon discussion with the church board [or elders, or deacons] or your spouse or a friend or shut-in, and post-sermon question and answer sessions or reaction groups (Haddon Robinson, "Listening to the Listeners," in Berkley, 45-50).

20. Hayes & Holladay, 151-52.

21. The roles of prophet, priest, and sage loosely correspond to the New Testament ministries of evangelist, pastor, and teacher.

22. Osborne, 125-26.

23. McClure suggests four symbolic dimensions of congregational life (John S. McClure, *The Four Codes of Preaching* [Minneapolis, MN: Fortress, 1991). I have subsumed three under his additional term "religious experience."

24. "An eloquent man must speak so as to teach, to delight, and to persuade." — Cicero.

25. Aurelius Augustine, "How to Declare the Gospel," in Berkley, 65-76.

26. William Kruidenier, "Why Some Sermons Work Better than Others," in Berkley, 77-88.

27. The roles of prophet, priest, and wise man somewhat correspond, respectively, to the New Testament spiritual gifts of leadership: prophet, apostle, and pastor-teacher.

28. For an extended discussion of these three functional questions, see Robinson, *Biblical Preaching*, 79-97. These correspond to Adams' three general purposes: to inform, to convince, to motivate (Jay E. Adams, *Preaching with Purpose* [Grand Rapids: Zondervan, 1982], 31).

29. See also Adams, *Purpose*, and Galli and Larson, *Preaching*.

30. David Mains, "Building Bridges to Action," in Berkley, 128. Adams warns a lack of purpose can result in a mere lecture (*Purpose*, 2).

31. Merrill F. Unger, "Expository Preaching," *Bibliotheca Sacra* 111 (1954): 335.

32. Similar suggestions are found in Adams, *Truth Applied*, 54.

33. In personal conversation, Gary Stanley informs me that this method of sermon organization owes its name to a Biola University professor. The basic method, however, dates back at least to Chalmers, who developed a sermon theme "continually recurring throughout ... in argument, illustration, and application" (Adams, *Truth Applied*, 117n1). Teachers at the International School of Theology have slightly adapted the Whiting Method and Stanley, an Associate Professor in homiletics, is currently writing a manuscript on it.

34. For help on preaching different genres or styles of Old Testament texts, consult Greidanus, *The Modern Preacher*; Osborne, *Spiral*; and Walter C. Kaiser, Jr., *Toward an Exegetical Theology* (Grand Rapids: Baker, 1981), 185-231 and *Toward Rediscovering the Old Testament* (Grand Rapids: Zondervan, 1987), 172-83. Also suggestive are John Bright, *The Authority of the Old Testament* (Grand Rapids: Baker, 1975), 213-51; and Walter C. Kaiser, Jr., *The Old Testament in Contemporary Preaching* (Chicago: Moody, 1973), 49-134.

35. Chapell considers this the most common approach, calling it "a generic approach" (*Preaching*, 85-87), and urging customization in proportioning these processes. A similar method is employed

in the *Life Application Bible*; it provides an explanation of the text, a bridge to relevance, and an application.

36. Gary Stanley, untitled forthcoming book on the Whiting Method.

37. Galli and Larson, 36-46.

38. Instead of "principles," the common term in the Whiting Method, "keynotes" describe main points which combine a biblical truth with appropriate response. "Principle" might suggest merely the former and could be confused with the over-lapping process of principlization as discussed in Chapter 8.

39. Find additional help on the illustrating process in Bryan Chapell, *Using Illustrations to Preach with Power* (Grand Rapids: Zonder-van, 1992); Chapell, *Preaching*, 181-90; Mark Littleton, "Raisins in the Oatmeal," in Berkley, 89-100; and Galli and Larson 57-79.

40. Chapell, *Illustrations*, 19-20.

41. Chapell, *Illustrations*, 58, citing Killinger.

42. Serviceable recent illustration collections include Michael P. Green, ed., *Illustrations for Biblical Preaching* (Grand Rapids: Baker, 1989); Michael Hodgin, ed., *1001 Humorous Illustrations* (Grand Rapids: Zondervan, 1994); Craig Brian Larson, *Illustrations for Preaching and Teaching* (Grand Rapids: Baker, 1993); and Paul Lee Tan, *Encyclopedia of 7700 Illustrations* (Rockville, MD: Assurance, 1979). Although pricey, useful electronic collections are available; one product is the Autoillustrator (Dos/Windows/Mac), POB 5056, Greeley, CO 80631. (David Krueger, "Illustration Databases," *Christian Computing Magazine* 6:4 [1994]: 14-19 positively reviews three Dos/Windows products — AutoIllustrator 5.0; Bible Illustrator 1.5; and Infosearch 3.5.) Collections of folktales or myths, children's stories, trivia, and speaker's sourcebooks (or periodicals like *Quote*) provide some useful material.

43. Pastoral periodicals include *Pulpit Digest, Pastoral Resource,* and *Leadership*. Harvest illustrations from Christian magazines like *Christianity Today* and *Moody Monthly*.

44. Devotional guides, such as *Our Daily Bread*, applicationally-oriented study Bibles, and printed sermons by great preachers (like Haddon Robinson, Max Lucado, and Chuck Swindoll) often contain useful illustrations.

45. Secular magazines with life-stories include *Reader's Digest, Time, Newsweek,* and *U.S. News and World Report*.

46. Besides books and periodicals, Davies suggests increasing creativity by observing and evaluating music, nature, art, people

— especially children, cards, posters and emotions (Loma G. Davies, *The Nuts and Bolts Writer's Manual* [Ft. Lauderdale, FL: Cassell, 1991], 8-9).

47. For basic filing systems and tips, see Susan Silver, *Organized to Be the Best!* 2d ed. (Los Angeles: Adams-Hall, 1991). Suggestions for filing preaching illustrations are given in Chapell, *Illustrations*, 178-86; and Leslie B. Flynn, *Come Alive with Illustrations* (Grand Rapids: Baker, 1988).

48. Treatments of the application process include Chapell, *Preaching*, 199-225; Mains, in Berkley, 123-34; Dave Veerman, *How to Apply the Bible* (Wheaton, IL: Tyndale, 1993); Adams, *Truth Applied*; and Roy B. Zuck, "Application in Biblical Hermeneutics and Exposition," in *Walvoord: A Tribute*, ed. Donald K. Campbell (Chicago: Moody, 1982), 15-38.

49. Smith, in Berkley, 39.

50. Chapell, *Preaching*, 213-16.

51. Berkley, 125.

52. See Galli and Larson, 136, for a fine haymaker used by William Willimon.

53. Chapell's "sermon component retention hierarchy," arranges the most-to-least remembered sermon elements. Adapted slightly to our terminology, it runs: haymaker illustration, introductory illustration, other illustrations, specific applications (particularly if the listener strongly agrees or disagrees), theme, an interesting incidental thought, a keynote, an exegetical concept (*Illustrations*, 151).

54. Augustine warned of "eloquent nonsense" and cited Cicero approvingly: "Although wisdom without eloquence is often of little service, eloquence without wisdom does positive injury and is never of service" (Berkley, 70).

55. Galli and Larson, 146, citing Christian writer Walter Wangerin.

56. Calvin Miller, "Zeal as Art," in Berkley, 63.

57. Someone has said, "If the fire of the gospel is not in your sermons, better to put your sermons in the fire."

58. In Aristotelian terms, *ethos* and *pathos* are factors as much as *logos*.

59. A few of many helpful works on prayer are D. A. Carson, ed., *Teach Us to Pray* (Grand Rapids: Baker, 1990); P. T. Forsyth, *The Soul of Prayer* (Grand Rapids: Eerdmans, 1967); William Law, *A Serious Call to a Devout and Holy Life.*, repr. ed. (Philadelphia: Westminster, 1948); John T. McNeill, ed., *Calvin: Institutes of the Christian Religion in Two Volumes* (Philadelphia: Westminster, 1977), 2:850-920; John White, *Dar-*

ing to Draw Near (Downers Grove, IL: InterVarsity, 1977); Thomas L. Constable, "What Prayer Will and Will Not Change," in *Essays in Honor of J. Dwight Pentecost*, ed. Stanley D. Toussaint and Charles H. Dyer (Chicago: Moody, 1986), 99-113; Roy B. Zuck, "The Role of the Holy Spirit in Hermeneutics," *Bibliotheca Sacra* 141 (1984): 120-130; and Kaiser, *Exegetical Theology*, 235-47. E. M. Bounds wrote several classics on prayer.

Chapter 10

Going Further:
Progressing in Biblical Hebrew

Objectives: After reading this chapter, you should be able to:
1. Determine your target level of biblical Hebrew proficiency.
2. Choose one or more means for continuing education in biblical Hebrew.
3. Evaluate a number of biblical Hebrew resources.

Walking down a New York street, a man stopped to ask a little elderly lady, "How do I get to Carnegie Hall?" She looked up and said, "Practice, young man. Practice."

This book offers a tool-based approach with minimal Hebrew proficiency. Yet regularly employing this approach will sharpen your exegetical skills. Additionally, this approach provides entree to developing greater Hebrew proficiency.

After a description of proficiency levels, this chapter suggests ways to use your biblical Hebrew skills and specific resources for advancing personal study.

How High Is Up? Proficiency Levels[1]

Obviously, some Bible students prefer using English-based tools (particularly concordances and commentaries) with some transliterated Hebrew. This book, however, recommends Christian ministers take a first step in biblical Hebrew.

To that end, the Appendix provides the alphabet and Hebrew basics. Elementary reading proficiency enables using Hebrew-based tools for first-hand study of the Hebrew Bible/Old Testament. Reading level one, or simply R-1, registers this ability.

Some may aspire to higher Hebrew reading proficiency levels. Limited working proficiency allows unassisted reading of uncomplicated texts containing common words and basic sentence patterns. At reading level two, students begin to critically interact with Hebrew-based commentaries and other tools.

To reach R-2 level, you must master some basic grammatical concepts (such as those contained in the Appendix and in beginning Hebrew grammars), and memorize the most common vocabulary. A practically-oriented course of seminary classes can also lift you to this level.

R-3, professional proficiency, means the ability to read all but complicated texts, or rare words, without the aid of a dictionary. Such ability requires extensive vocabulary and knowledge of Hebrew forms. This level has been the aim, although seldom the accomplishment, of traditional seminary studies.

A language reader who has attained full proficiency or fluency, level R-4, has no need of a dictionary. Only the ambitious and dedicated few will devote many years seeking this lofty goal.

"Use It or Lose It"

Possibilities for advancing biblical Hebrew skills are limited solely by your own creativity. The few suggestions given here may provoke such creativity.

Scan the Interlinear as part of your devotional reading, or use the Interlinear as your study Bible. Take the Interlinear (or a copy of the specific biblical text) to scan while listening to sermons.

Teach and preach from the Old Testament regularly. Because of its inherent variety and the change of pace from the New Testament, Old Testament exposition finds a receptive audience.

Consider taking classes to develop your biblical Hebrew skills. Often local seminaries allow visiting students to audit or enroll in classes (for credit or enrichment). Tutors may also be available in your area.

Build your personal library with books based on Hebrew exegesis or collect additional resources for Hebrew exegesis. Some specific resources follow.

Advancing Personal Study

Besides the resources already presented in this book, grammars, reading aids, and vocabulary builders can advance personal study of biblical Hebrew.

In the following descriptions, occasionally parenthetical references provide page numbers in these resources for ready access to some mentioned topics.

Back to school (standard grammars)

Consult beginning grammars for a fully traditional approach to biblical Hebrew.

This section briefly describes both beginning and advanced grammars, in order of recommendation, on a preferred A-list or on a B-list . Clarity, coverage, linguistic approach, level of difficulty, and recency factored in this admittedly subjective ranking.

1. Beginning grammars: A-list

Sawyer, John F. *A Modern Introduction to Biblical Hebrew.* Stocksfield, Northumberland: Oriel, Routledge & Kegan Paul, 1976.
Sawyer employs some modern linguistic concepts and avoids some traditional jargon in a concise, introductory grammar.

Lambdin, Thomas Oden. *Introduction to Biblical Hebrew.* New York: Charles Scribner's Sons, 1971.
Many students in a traditional approach started with this fine introductory grammar. Use the companion volume by Hugh G. M. Williamson, *Annotated Key to Lambdin's Introduction to Biblical Hebrew* (Sheffield: JSOT, Sheffield Academic, 1989). Electronic versions (Dos/Mac) are also available.[2]

Hunter, A. Vanlier. *Biblical Hebrew Workbook.* Lanham, MD: University Press of America, 1988.
This helpful first year grammar, with numerous excellent charts and paradigms, is largely (but not exclusively) inductive in approach. It uses Holladay's lexicon and BHS, while treating Genesis 12 and 22, Deuteronomy 5, and (more briefly) Genesis 1—2:4, Joshua 24, 2 Samuel 11—12, Psalm 51, and Jeremiah 1.

Kelley, Page H. *Biblical Hebrew.* Grand Rapids: Eerdmans, 1992.
Informed by an inductive approach, this introductory grammar presents biblically-based examples from BHS. The companion volume is Timothy Crawford, Page H. Kelley, and Terry Burden, *Handbook to Biblical Hebrew Grammar* (Grand Rapids: Eerdmans, 1994).

Kittel, Bonnie Pedrotti, Vicki Hoffer, and Rebecca Abts
    Wright. *Biblical Hebrew*. New Haven, CT: Yale Uni-
    versity, 1989.
    Visually oriented learners will appreciate some of the
graphical features in this introductory grammar. The second
half of the book contains the following reading selections,
with brief comments: Genesis 22:1-14, 28:10—29:11, 37:1-
24, Exodus 3:1-17, Deuteronomy 6:1-25, 1 Kings 17:1-24,
18:20-46, 19:1-21, Psalm 24, and Psalm 100. A useful
glossary is included (340-90). The book by ben Zvi,
Hancock, and Beinert, mentioned in the next section, is
basically a follow-up volume.

Seow, C. L. *A Grammar for Biblical Hebrew*. Nashville:
    Abingdon, 1987.
    This neatly printed beginning grammar incorporates
more syntax than most grammars and presents exercises
from the biblical text. The terminology often departs from
traditional grammars. For further explanations, an answer
key, and a study guide, see Jeffries M. Hamilton and Jeffrey
S. Rogers, *A Grammar for Biblical Hebrew: Handbook,
Answer Keys, and Study Guide* (Nashville: Abingdon,
1989).

2. *Beginning grammars: B-list*

Weingreen, Jacob. *A Practical Grammar for Classical
    Hebrew*. 2d ed., Oxford: Clarendon, 1959.
    This is an older, classic beginning grammar from a
traditional approach.

Blau, Joshua. *A Grammar of Biblical Hebrew*. Wiesbaden:
    Harrassowitz, 1976.
    This traditional introductory grammar also includes a
summary of syntax, based on Genesis 37—45 and Jonah
(82-115).

Doukhan, Jacques B. *Hebrew for Theologians.* Lanham, MD: University Press of America, 1993.

Combining inductive and deductive approaches, this introductory grammar is still generally traditional. However, Doukhan attempts to set Hebrew within the life and dynamics of Hebrew thinking (including some questionable linguistic theology; xii-xiii, 191-218).

Guided reading selections are Genesis 22, Psalm 23, and Micah 4:1-4.

Greenberg, Moshe. *Introduction to Hebrew.* Englewood Cliffs, NJ: Prentice-Hall, 1965.

This basic, traditional grammar briefly comments on Genesis 37, 42—45 (180-92).

Harris, R. Laird. *Introductory Hebrew Grammar.* Grand Rapids: Eerdmans, 1978.

A conservative Christian wrote this basic, traditional introductory grammar.

Marks, John H. and Virgil M. Rogers. *A Beginner's Handbook to Biblical Hebrew.* New York: Abingdon, 1958.

This traditional grammar places heavy emphasis on verb paradigms. Many of the examples are from Genesis.

Watts, J. W. *A Survey of Syntax in the Hebrew Old Testament.* Grand Rapids: Eerdmans, 1964.

Watts presents a basic survey, but offers a non-traditional perspective on the verbal system.

3. Advanced grammars: A-list

Williams, Ronald J. *Hebrew Syntax.* 2d ed., Toronto: University of Toronto, 1976. [WHS]

Thoughtfully working through the many examples in this survey of intermediate grammar will pay multiple dividends. Recommended in Chapter 3.

Waltke, Bruce K. and M. O'Connor. *An Introduction to Biblical Hebrew Syntax*. Winona Lake, IN: Eisenbrauns, 1991. [IBHS]

Recommended in Chapter 3, this excellent intermediate Hebrew grammar contains a contemporary linguistics perspective and extensive bibliography. A third corrected printing was published in 1991. Rather than attempting to read IBHS straight through, gain a quicker exegetical payoff by first studying noun case functions and nominal clauses (125-72), the verb system (479-95, 502-79), and clauses (632-85).

Kautsch, E., ed. *Gesenius' Hebrew Grammar*. Revised in accordance with the Twenty-Eighth German Edition (1909) by A. E. Cowley. Repr. of 1910, 2d English ed., Oxford: Clarendon, 1976. [GKC]

Despite its age, GKC remains *the standard reference grammar*, as noted in Chapter 3.

Joüon, Paul. *A Grammar of Biblical Hebrew*. Translated and revised by T. Muraoka. 2 vols. Rome: Biblical Institute, 1991.

As mentioned in Chapter 3, biblical Hebrew scholar Francis I. Andersen considers this "the best overall general reference grammar for biblical Hebrew."

Gibson, John C. L. *Davidson's Introductory Hebrew Grammar: Syntax (4th Ed.)*. Edinburgh: T. & T. Clark, 1994.

A well-exampled, concise work, this revision and updating of a classic serves as a useful reference, especially for the analysis of the sentence or clause. Despite the title, it is more for intermediate than beginning study.

Read about the following first: nouns (16-59), verbs (60-121), and clauses (162-88). Make use of the subject and scripture indexes.

4. Advanced grammars: B-list

Andersen, Francis I. *The Sentence in Biblical Hebrew*. The Hague: Mouton, 1974.

Andersen draws on modern linguistics approaches (largely on tagmemics, discourse grammar, and transformational grammar). He provides a technical, excellent clause-level and inter-clausal analysis of biblical Hebrew. Most of his examples are from the Pentateuch and primarily narrative; often the examples come from what Andersen labels as "epic narrative." The display of different ways of saying essentially the same thing forms a major contribution. (Transformational grammar describes these as deep structure relationships realized in a variety of alternative surface structures)

Muraoka, Takamitsu. *Emphatic Words and Structures in Biblical Hebrew*. Leiden: Brill, 1985.

Muraoka presents needed cautions and caveats when referring to "emphasis" in biblical Hebrew texts.

Ewald, Heinrich. *Syntax of the Hebrew Language of the Old Testament*. Repr. of the 3d part of *Ausführliches Lehrbuch der hebräischen Sprache des alten Bundes*, 1870 (Göttingen). 8th ed., Translated by James Kennedy. Edinburgh: T. & T. Clark, 1891.

Müller, August. *Outlines of Hebrew Syntax*. Translated by James Robertson. Glascow: James Maclehose & Sons, 1882.

Both of these older works are still worth scanning for this neglected area.

Affordable personal tutors (biblical Hebrew chrestomathies)

A *chrestomathy* contains reading selections with annotations on specific vocabulary, forms, and constructions. The following list presents some biblical Hebrew chrestomathies in order of generally increasing difficulty.

Of course, Hebrew-based commentaries often perform a similar function.[3] Also, some annotated biblical readings in grammars were noted in the preceding section.

Tregelles, Samuel P. *Hebrew Reading Lessons*. New York: Harper & Brothers, 1876.

Tregelles discusses Genesis 1—4 and Proverbs 8. This work is most helpful for initially reading through the first two chapters of Genesis, and repetitious afterwards. One nice feature is the highlighting of prefixes and suffixes (in outline form) on the actual Hebrew text.

LaSor, William S. *Handbook of Biblical Hebrew*. Grand Rapids: Eerdmans, 1978-79.

This is a good primer from a fully inductive approach to Esther.

Spurrell, George James. *Notes on the Hebrew Text of the Book of Genesis*. 2d, rev. and cor. ed., Oxford: Clarendon, 1896.

Kennedy, Archibald R. S. *The Book of Ruth*. London: SPCK, 1928.

Mansoor, Menahem. *Biblical Hebrew Step-by-Step: Volume 2: Readings from the Book of Genesis*. 3d ed., Grand Rapids: Baker, 1984.

Hammershaimb, Erling. *The Book of Amos*. Translated by J. Sturdy. New York: Schocken, 1970.

Snaith, Norman H. *Notes on the Hebrew Text of Genesis I—VIII*. London: Epworth, 1947.

_____. *Notes on the Hebrew Text of 2 Samuel XVI—XIX*. London: Epworth, 1945.

_____. *Notes on the Hebrew Text of the Book of Jonah*. London: Epworth, 1945.

_____. *Notes on the Hebrew Text of Amos*. London: Epworth, 1945-46.

Consider working through these books or using them in preliminary grammatical analysis for any sermon series on these specific biblical texts.

Ben Zvi, Ehud, Maxine Hancock, and Richard Beinert. *Readings in Biblical Hebrew.* Yale Language Series, New Haven, CT: Yale University, 1993.

A sampling of major styles of biblical Hebrew includes historical, legal, prophetic, wisdom, and psalmic literature. Explanatory notes discuss structure, genre, literary devices, and accents, as well as lexical, grammatical, and text critical features.

Assuming a year of traditional beginning study, this builds mostly on Kittel, Hoffer, and Wright's introductory grammar, yet cross-references other grammars. The sample texts are Exodus 21:28-36, Leviticus 5:20-26, Deuteronomy 24:14-22, 1 Samuel 1:1-28, 2 Kings 14:23-29, Psalm 1, Psalm 15, Psalm 150, Proverbs 3:13-26, 10:1, 16:8, 22:22-23, 24:29, 25:28, Ecclesiastes 1:1-11, Isaiah 49:1-6, Jeremiah 22:1-5, and Ezekiel 37:1-14.

Bitzer, Heinrich, ed. *Light on the Path.* Grand Rapids: Baker, 1982.

Bitzer intend this as a daily devotional aid, with both New Testament Greek and Hebrew Bible passages. The Hebrew is briefly annotated. Note that the annotations do not distinguish "imperfect" from similar forms (preterite, cohortative, jussive).[4] A scripture index is provided. (About one-third of the Old Testament passages come from Psalms.)

Eaton, John H. *First Studies in Biblical Hebrew.* Birmingham: Birmingham University, 1980.

This basically traditional presentation of biblical Hebrew grammar contains a helpful section of linked exercises (65-143). Unfortunately, handprinted Hebrew and transliteration, resort to the King's English in translations, omission of accents, and the unnecessary three declensions of nouns present difficulties. Eaton includes some beginning work with unvocalized Hebrew.

Eaton, John H. *Readings in Biblical Hebrew I*. Birmingham: Birmingham University, 1982.

Eaton, John H. *Readings in Biblical Hebrew II*. Birmingham: Birmingham University, 1978.

These cover a broad selection of biblical readings and include some extra-biblical Hebrew inscriptions.

Muraoka, Takamitsu. *Modern Hebrew for Biblical Scholars*. Sheffield: JSOT, Sheffield Academic, 1982.

So you want to read articles or books in modern Hebrew, increase your language skills for a trip to Israel, or pass a competency exam for a graduate program? With some initial review of biblical Hebrew, this could be your starting point.

Tripping down memory lane (lexical aids)

This book minimizes memorization and emphasizes using helpful tools for study of the Hebrew Bible; Hebrew vocabulary and specific forms may be learned "in route." However, available resources help build biblical Hebrew vocabulary quickly and effectively.

Mitchel, Larry A. *A Student's Vocabulary for Biblical Hebrew and Aramaic*. Grand Rapids: Zondervan, 1984.

Mitchel lists words according to usage frequency in the Hebrew Bible and in manageable bites (20-25 words in each group) for personal study. An electronic version is available (*Memcards: Biblical Hebrew Vocabulary*, 2d ed. [DOS]).

Armstrong, Terry A., Douglas L. Busby, and Cyril F. Carr. *A Reader's Hebrew-English Lexicon of the Old Testament*. 4 vols. Grand Rapids: Zondervan, 1980-88. [ABC]

ABC is comparable to Sakae Kubo, *A Reader's Greek-English Lexicon of the New Testament, and a Beginner's Guide for the Translation of New Testament Greek* (Grand Rapids: Zondervan, 1975). Useful for reading through the Hebrew Bible, ABC provides a translation of infrequently used words. An appendix lists biblical Hebrew words occuring more than fifty times.

ABC follows the order of the Hebrew Bible and supplies the page number for BDB's entry. Word frequency counts help identify both rare words and repeated words in a biblical book.

As We Bid *Adieu*,

During the Civil War, President Lincoln became increasingly frustrated with McClellan's constant training of his troops and lack of action against the enemy. Finally, Lincoln wrote to him, "General, if you're not going to use your army, do you mind if I do?"

While preparation is important, so is engagement. Better to have used Hebrew (via tools) and lost (prestige or a minor point) than never to have used it at all.

Learning to use biblical Hebrew in ministry is like learning to catch a ball. First you start with a big, soft ball thrown slowly in a high arc. Then you graduate to smaller, harder balls. After a while, you can catch a hardball moving about ninety miles an hour. It becomes almost a reflex.

Keep going with biblical Hebrew and you may impress yourself and others. At least you may minister to yourself and others, as you "Do your best to present yourself to God as one approved, a workman who does not need to be ashamed and who correctly handles the word of truth" (2 Tm 2:15, NIV).

Action Points

1. If you have not yet purchased biblical Hebrew tools, re-read Chapter 2 (or scan the summary chart) and determine your initial purchases.
2. Review again the basics of biblical Hebrew from the Appendix.
3. Write down your plan to increase your biblical Hebrew skills in the coming year. You might use biblical Hebrew tools as a devotional aid, work through a grammar or chrestomathy, take a seminary class, preach through a particular Old Testament book, memorize vocabulary, or combine these or other courses of action. Whatever you decide, be specific about times, places, and resources.
4. Which of the resources mentioned in this chapter will you soon purchase?
5. Consider what level of biblical Hebrew proficiency you would like to reach in five years. Sketch a plan for reaching that level.

Notes

1. These proficiency levels are discussed with regard to New Testament Greek by David Alan Black, *Using New Testament Greek in Ministry* (Grand Rapids: Baker, 1993), 28.

2. Bernard Grossfeld created an interactive set of exercises based on Lambdin's grammar (for Macintosh computers). Contact the University of Wisconsin, Milwaukee; POB 413; Milwaukee WI 53201-0413; (414) 229-4313.

3. Although both are technical and critical, the *Anchor Bible* and the *International Critical Commentary* discuss the Hebrew text. So do older commentators like Perowne, Keil and Delitzsch, and Driver, and Jewish commentaries such as the Soncino series. (Refer to Chapter 2 for commentary recommendations.)

4. The Appendix describes these verb formations.

Appendix: Basic 'Brew:

Essential Ingredients to Start "Cooking"

I.	Alphabet, Vowels, and Syllables		238
	A.	Alphabet	
	B.	Vowels	
	C.	Syllables	
II.	Particles		240
	A.	Definite article	
	B.	"Direct object" marker	
	C.	Conjunctions	
	D.	Prepositions	
	E.	Interrogatives	
III.	Nouns		243
	A.	Noun endings	
	B.	Construct state	
	C.	Adjective and participle uses	
	D.	Nominal sentence patterns	
IV.	Verbs		245
	A.	Verb patterns	
	B.	Verb tenses	
	C.	Volitives	
	D.	Verb parsing	
	E.	Verb functions	
	F.	Qal verb profile	
V.	Syntax		253
	A.	Word order	
	B.	Subordinate Clauses	
	C.	Disjunctive Clauses	
VI.	Discourse analysis (supra-syntax)		255

Alphabet, Vowels, and Syllables

The Alphabet

	Name	Letter		Transliteration	Pronunciation
1.	'aleph	א		', ø	[ø] (silent)
2.	beth	בּ		b	[b] as in ball
		ב		b̲, v	[v] as in vote
3.	gimel	גּ		g	[g] as in girl
		ג		g̲, g	[g] as in girl
4.	daleth	דּ		d	[d] as in dog
		ד		d̲, d	[d] as in dog
5.	he'	ה		h	[h/ø] as in hot (or silent)
6.	waw	ו		w, v	[v/ø] as in vote (or silent)
7.	zayin	ז		z	[z] as in zoo
8.	heth	ח		ḥ, 'gh	[k̲] as in Bach
9.	teth	ט		ṭ, t	[t] as in top
10.	yod	י		y	[y/ø] as in yes (or silent)
11.	kaph	כּ		k	[k] as in kit
		כ	ךּ	k̲, 'ch	[k] as in kit
12.	lamed	ל		l	[l] as in lap
13.	mem	מ	ם	m	[m] as in map
14.	nun	נ	ן	n	[n] as in nap
15.	samech	ס		s	[s] as in sat
16.	'ayin	ע		', g̱	['/ø] as in Gaza (or silent)
17.	pe'	פּ		p	[p] as in pay
		פ	ף	p̲, ph	[f] as in *ph*one
18.	tsade	צ	ץ	ṣ, tz	[ts] as in hits
19.	qoph	ק		q, k	[q] as in unique
20.	resh	ר		r	[r] as in rat
21.	sin	שׂ		ś, s	[s] as in sat
22.	shin	שׁ		š, sh (TWOT)	[sh] as in ship
23.	tav	תּ		t	[t] as in stop
		ת		t̲, th	[th] as in that

Four letters tended to become silent (*quiesce*), thus the zero phonetic value [ø] in the chart. They are א, ה, ו, י and came to be used sometimes as vowel markers.

Five letters have distinct (final) forms when written at the end of words.

Six letters, remembered as *begadkephat*, have allophones — a different pronunciation (represented by a dot) depending on whether they precede or follow a vowel. These letters without dots are distinguished in transliteration by underlining; pronunciation distinctions are preserved with *beth*, *pe'*, and sometimes *tav*.

Englishman's distinctive transliterations are listed secondarily in the preceding chart for reference.

Vowels (The letter ב helps locate the vowels' positioning.)

Full Vowels

Short			Long		
בַ	patah	a as in *bad*	בָ / בָה	qames / qames-he	ā as in *father* / āh/à as in *comma*
בֶ	segol	e as in *bed*	בֵ / בֵי	sere / sere-yod	ē as in *they* / ê as in *they*
בִ	hireq	i as in *bid*	בִי	hireq-yod	î as in *machine*
בֻ	qibbus	u as in *put*	בוּ	sureq	û as in *flute*
בָ	qames hatuph	o as in *top*	בֹ / בוֹ	holem / holem-waw	ō as in *hole* / ô as in *hole*

This vowel system contains both the early semi-vowels and Masoretic vowel points. The next chart shows additional reduced vowels (*vocal shewas*) and a silent syllable closing marker (*silent shewa*).

Shewas

Silent		Vocal	
Simple Shewa	untrans-literated	ְ (æ)	[uh] as in America
Compound Shewas	(always vocal and transliterated)	ֲ (ă)	as patah
		ֱ (ĕ)	as segol
		ֳ (ŏ)	as qames-hatuph

Syllables

Syllables begin with a consonant and have only one vowel (rarely, a diphthong/triphthong — usually at the end of a word). Two exceptions are the word-initial conjunction which sometimes appears as וּ , and a *furtive patah* appearing spontaneously between a long vowel and a final guttural letter. Although some Hebrew Bibles place it under the guttural letter, a furtive patah is pronounced before the guttural (in a syllable with two vowels).

Particles

Definite article

There is no separate indefinite article in Hebrew. הַ is prefixed to a noun to make it definite. (A dot is placed in the noun's first letter.) The definite article without the dot (the Interlinear helps here!) appears as: הַ , הֶ , and הָ

    דָּבָר   "(a) word"   »»   הַדָּבָר   "the-word"

"Direct object marker"

Definite direct objects are preceded by the (untranslated) particle אֶת/־אֶת .

Conjunctions

waw

This prefixed conjunction has many functions (such as an adversative or correlative, or for subordination) besides its use as a simple connective ("and"). Primary uses are:

Uses of waw

On a non-verb	*On a finite verb*
Conjunctive Function: joins items in a series Form: same type and level items (words/phrases/clauses)	*Conjunctive* Function: joins actions in a series Form: same tense/mood verbs
Disjunctive Function: marks a break in a sequence Form: initiates a clause	*Consecutive* Function: continues the aspect of the lead verb in a series Form: ·ן + preterite; or simple waw on a perfect tense (and context is determinative)

AKOT does not differentiate *waws* as disjunctive, nor as consecutive when on a perfect tense verb. (For disjunctive *waw* see "Disjunctive clauses." On the preterite and *waw* consecutives see under "Verb tenses.")

כִּי

This "key" multi-functional conjunction commonly introduces indirect discourse ("that"), direct discourse (equivalent to quotation marks), and causal clauses ("because").

Prepositions

Prepositions appear three ways:

1. As a separate word

   אֵצֶל הַנָּהָר   near the-river

2. Joined by a maqqeph (a raised hyphen) to a noun

   עַל־הַדֶּרֶךְ   upon the-road

3. Joined directly to a noun (prefixed, inseparable). When indefinite, the prefixed prepositions have a simple shewa. When directly prefixed to a definite noun (already having the article), the preposition takes the place of the ה while adopting the pointing of the article.

   לְמֶלֶךְ   for-a-king

   הַסֵּפֶר »« בַּסֵּפֶר   (*not* בְּהַסֵּפֶר)
   the-book   in-the-book

Interrogatives

Questions are indicated by the interrogative particle הֲ (distinct from the definite article!), interrogative pronouns (personal = מִי who?" and impersonal = מָה "what?"), interrogative adverbs (אַיֵּה "where?" or לָמָה "why?" or אֵיךְ "how?"), or intonation (validated only from the immediate context for a written text).

Nouns

Noun endings

Hebrew uses distinct suffixes to indicate gender (not necessarily ontological reality) and number for nouns. The same endings appear on adjectives and participles. Those endings are added in the next chart to the Hebrew noun סוּס "horse."

Number	Masculine	Feminine
Singular	no special ending (סוּס) "horse (stallion)"	[also תָ and תְ] הָ (סוּסָה) "horse (mare)"
Plural	ִים (סוּסִים) "horses (stallions)"	וֹת (סוּסוֹת) "horses (mares)"
Dual		ַיִם (סוּסַיִם) "two horses (stallions or mares)"

Construct state

Two or more adjacent nouns may closely unite to form one compound idea. The preceding noun is in the *construct state*, while the second noun (or last in a longer series) is in the *absolute state* (the lexical form). If the absolute noun is definite, then the entire construct chain is definite. (Besides nouns with the article prefixed, proper nouns and nouns with suffixed pronouns are definite.) The construct noun often undergoes a slight change in form. The Interlinear uses a "[noun]-of" translation under the construct noun.

יְהוָה	דְּבַר		
Lord	word-of	»»	"the word of the Lord"
absolute	construct		

Adjective and participle uses

Predicate	Attributive	Substantive
הָאִשָּׁה טוֹבָה "the woman (is) good"	הָאִשָּׁה הַטּוֹבָה "the good woman"	הַטּוֹבָה "the good (woman)"
טוֹבָה אִשָּׁה "a woman (is) good"	אִשָּׁה טוֹבָה "a good woman"	טוֹבָה "a good (woman)"

Attributive and predicate use are marked, respectively, by agreement and lack of agreement in definiteness between the adjective/participle and the noun it modifies. (Note that if neither the adjective/participle and the modified noun are definite, context determines whether the use is attributive or predicate.) For substantive uses, the gender and number of the adjective/participle indicate the appropriate noun form to be supplied in English. (The acronym P.A.S.S.— the last S representing "Simple!" — helps recall these three uses.)

Nominal sentence patterns

Hebrew sentences do not need an expressed verb. Sentences without a verb are called *nominal (or, verbless) sentences*. Common nominal sentence patterns are:

1. Nominal + predicate adjective

טוֹב   הָאִישׁ
good   the-man
"The man (is) good."

2. Nominal + preposition + nominal

הַדֶּרֶךְ   עַל   הָאִישׁ
the-way   upon   the-man
"The man (is) on the road."

3. Nominal + participle (predicate use) + nominal

הָאֲדָמָה	אֶת	שֹׁמֵר	הוּא
the-ground	***	tending	he

"He is tending the ground."

4. Nominal + adjective + מִן + nominal

שְׁלוֹמֹה	מִן	טוֹב	דָּוִד
Solomon	from	good	David

"David (is) better than Solomon."

5. (Particle of existence +) nominal + לְ + nominal

לָאִישׁ	כֶּסֶף	יֵשׁ
to-the-man	money	there-is

"The man has money."

Verbs

Verb patterns

Except for the basic pattern (Qal), the verb pattern names "make" the appropriate form when imposed on most roots (perfect tense 3 m.s.). The patterns (or *stems*) themselves derive their names when imposed on the root פָּעַל "make." Three forms have characteristic doubling of the second root consonant, so the names do not fully represent the actual forms (marked in the next chart with an *).

Pattern	Form	Primary Meanings
Qal	(כָּתַב)	basic, active pattern
Niphal	נִקְעַל	passive, reflexive, or reciprocal of Qal
Piel	*פִּעֵל	intensive, denominative, or transitive of Qal
Pual	*פֻּעַל	passive of Piel
Hiphil	הִקְעִיל	causative, denominative, declarative, ingressive of Qal
Hophal	הָקְעַל	passive of Hiphil
Hithpael	*הִתְפַּעֵל	reflexive, reciprocal, or iterative of Piel

Using שׁבר as a sample, notice representative meanings in the various patterns (perfect tense, 3d masculine singular):

Voice	Simple Patterns	"Doubled" Patterns	Causative Patterns
Active	Qal "he broke"	Piel "he shattered"	Hiphil "he caused to break"
Passive	Niphal "it was broken"	Pual "he was shattered"	Hophal "he was made to break"
Reflexive	Niphal "he broke himself"	Hithpael "he shattered himself"	

Verb tenses

Distinctives (between the two primary tenses)

	Perfect Tense	Imperfect Tense
Conjugation	suffixed	prefixed (some suffixes)
Type of situation	completed	uncompleted
Primary time	past	future

Additionally, a distinct *preterite tense* essentially shares the imperfect form and the nuances of the perfect tense, often as a simple past narrative verb (see further: "Verb functions"). Preterites typically appear with a *waw* consecutive prefixed, and continue the aspect of the lead verb in a series. By analogy, a *waw* consecutive prefixed to a perfect tense verb can continue the nuance of the lead verb in a series (generally an imperfect tense verb).

Volitives

Volitive		Command	Translation	Form (compare the imperfect)
Cohortative	(1st)	indirect	*Let me/us (do)*	often lengthens
Imperative	(2d)	direct	*(Do!)*	may lengthen
Jussive	(3d)	indirect	*Let him/her/ them (do)*	often shortens
	(2d)	negative	*(Don't!)*	

אַל plus second person *jussive* is normally used for immediate, negative commands, or "sometimes to express the conviction that something cannot or should not happen" (GKC #109e). לֹא plus second person *imperfect* is normally used for general, non-specific prohibitions. The imperative is *never* used for negative commands.

Verb parsing

Finite Verbs (inflected for person, gender, and number)

Pattern	Tense or Mood	Person	Gender	#
Qal	Tenses	1st/2d/3d	M/F/C	S/P
Niphal	Perfect			
Piel	Imperfect			
Pual	Preterite			
Hiphil	Moods (volitives)			
Hophal	Cohortative	[=1st]		
Hithpael	Imperative	[=2d]		
(=Q-Ht)	Jussive	[=3d/2d]		

Parsing: root, verbal pattern, tense/mood, person, gender, number. Example: √ כתב Qal perfect 3 m.s.

Verbals (participles and infinitives)

Participles ("x-ing" in the Interlinear)

Pattern	Voice	Gender	#	Uses
(Q-Ht)	Active	M/F	S/P	Predicate (as a verb)
	Passive			Attributive (as an adjective)
				Substantive (as a noun)

Parsing: root, verbal pattern, mood = participle, gender, number. Example: √ כתב Qal active participle m.s.

Infinitives
("to-x" in the Interlinear; indeclinable for P/G/#/voice)

Pattern	Type	Additions	Uses
(Q-Ht)	Construct	+/- prefixed preposition;	purpose, result, goal; temporal use;
		+/- pronominal suffix	substantive; or verb complement
	Absolute	None	adverbial; main verb

Parsing: root, verbal pattern, mood = infinitive type (+ any additions, if construct). Example: √ כתב Qal infinitive construct + 3 m.s. suffix

Verb functions

Perfect Tense: represents a completed situation
(Also, the preterite often shows the same uses.)

Aoristic uses: presents action as a whole or momentary

1. Past Time	
Definite past	You *laughed*. (Gn 18:15)
Indefinite past	Whose ox *have I (ever) taken*? (1 S 12:3)
2. Present Time	
Instantaneous	*I lift* my hand. (Gn 14:22)
Epistolary	*I am sending* you (this) present. (1 K 15:19)
3. Repeated Action	
Gnomic	The grass *withers*. (Is 40:7)
Characteristic	Why *do* the nations *rage*? (Ps 2:1)

Perfective uses: presents a state resulting from an action

1. Resultant State	
Present perfect	They *have forsaken* the LORD. (Is 1:4)
Past perfect	Rachel *had stolen* them. (Gn 31:32)
Future perfect	land which *He has given you* (Dt 8:10; a future act in this context)
2. Descriptive State	
Adjectival	*I am old*. (Gn 27:2)
Experiential	*I delight* to do Your will. (Ps 40:9)
3. Future State	
Resolve	*I (intend to) take* it. (1 S 2:16)
Prophetic	Unto us a child *has been born*. (Is 9:5; future when spoken)

Imperfect Tense: represents an uncompleted situation
(Also, the *waw consecutive plus perfect*
often shows the same uses.)

Future action: "*You shall die*, truly." (Gn 2:17)

Repeated action

1. Present progressive	What *are you seeking*? (Gn 37:15)
2. Habitual	pursued you as bees *do* (Dt 1:44)
3. Customary (past)	*They (used to) water* the flocks. (Gn 29:2)
4. Historical (past progressive)	The country *was being destroyed* by flies. (Ex 8:20)

Modal uses

1. Permission	You *may eat*. (Gn 2:16)
2. Deliberation (in questions)	Why *should I be bereaved* of both of you? (Gn 27:45)
3. Obligation	what *you (ought to) do* (Rt 3:4)
4. Desire	if he *(desires to) redeem* you (Rt 3:13)
5. Potential	A blacksmith *was not (able to) be found*. (1 S 13:19)
6. Possibility	whoever *may lap* with his tongue (Jg 7:5)
7. Final (purpose)	that *it might go well* (Dt 4:40)

Volitive uses

1. Injunction	*Purge me* with hyssop. (Ps 51:9)
2. Instruction (in legislation)	That ox *shall certainly be stoned*. (Ex 21:28)
3. Prohibition	*You shall not murder*. (Ex 20:13)

Volitives

Cohortative (first person)

1. Resolve: showing the speaker's will	
Desire	*I desire to eat* meat. (Dt 12:20)
Intention	*I will turn aside* …. (Ex 3:3)
Determination	*I will make* it a wasteland. (Is 5:6)
2. Request: invoking another's will	
Appeal	*Let me cross* your land. (Dt 2:27)
Wish	*May I not be put to shame.* (Ps 25:2)
3. Hortatory (plural): calling on others to participate	
	Let us go after other gods. (Dt 13:3)

Imperative (second person)

1. Command	*Leave* your country. (Gn 12:1)
2. Request	Please *give them*…. silver. (2 K 5:22)
3. Permission	*Go* and *bury* your father. (Gn 50:6; answering a request)
4. Assurance	In the third year *you will sow and reap.* (Is 37:30)
5. Warning	*Sow for yourselves* righteousness. (Hs 10:12)
6. Challenge (irony)	*Go* to Bethel and *sin.* (Am 4:4)
7. Concession	*(Although you) prepare for battle,* you will be broken. (Is 8:9)
8. Exclamation	*Come on!* Let's make bricks. (Gn 11:3)

Jussive (third person; and second for a negative command)

1. A "superior" speaking to an "inferior"		
	Command	*Let there be* light. (Gn 1:3)
	Counsel	The officers shall say ... *"Let him go back."* (Dt 20:5)
	Prohibition	*Do not eat* food. (1 K 13:22)
2. An "inferior" speaking to an "superior"		
	Prayer	LORD God, *do not destroy* your people. (Dt 9:26)
	Blessing	*May* the LORD *bless* you and *keep* you. (Nm 6:24)
	Appeal	*Let him pass over* with my lord the king. (2 S 19:38)
	Desire	*Do not refuse* me. (1 K 2:20)
	Invitation	*Let* the king and his servants *go*. (2 S 13:24)
	Advice	*Let Pharaoh seek* a wise and discerning man. (Gn 41:33)

Qal verb profile

Perfect Tense		P/G/#	Imperfect Tense	
כָּתַב	he wrote	3 m.s.	he will write	יִכְתֹּב
כָּתְבָה	she wrote	3 f.s.	she will write	תִּכְתֹּב
כָּתַבְתָּ	you wrote	2 m.s.	you will write	תִּכְתֹּב
כָּתַבְתְּ	you wrote	2 f.s.	you will write	תִּכְתְּבִי
כָּתַבְתִּי	I wrote	1 c.s.	I will write	אֶכְתֹּב
כָּתְבוּ	they wrote	3 m.p.	they will write	יִכְתְּבוּ
כָּתְבוּ	they wrote	3 f.p.	they will write	תִּכְתֹּבְנָה
כְּתַבְתֶּם	you wrote	2 m.p.	you will write	תִּכְתְּבוּ
כְּתַבְתֶּן	you wrote	2 f.p.	you will write	תִּכְתֹּבְנָה
כָּתַבְנוּ	we wrote	1 c.p.	we will write	נִכְתֹּב

	m.s.	m.p.	f.s.	f.p.
Active participle	כּוֹתֵב	כּוֹתְבִים	כּוֹתֶבֶת	כּוֹתְבוֹת
Passive participle	כָּתוּב	כְּתוּבִים	כְּתוּבָה	כְּתוּבוֹת
Imperative	כְּתֹב	כִּתְבוּ	כִּתְבִי	כְּתֹבְנָה
Cohortative	c.s.	אֶכְתְּבָה	c.p.	נִכְתְּבָה
Infinitive	construct	כְּתֹב	absolute	כָּתוֹב

Hebrew has two infinitives (the Interlinear renders both "to-[do something]"). The *infinitive construct* is a verbal noun which functions as either a verb or noun; it may have words attached (prefixed prepositions or pronominal suffixes). The *infinitive absolute* conveys the verbal idea of the root; it primarily modifies a main verb (usually indicating completeness or certainty).

Syntax

Word order

Contrary to English, typical word order in prose main clauses is *verb-subject-object* (VSO). A separate subject need not be present, since finite verbs — not participles and infinitives — contain an inherent subject pronoun. Shifts from VSO order may indicate emphasis (such as a topic, or a contrast); yet clause type and genre, euphony, narrative breaks, and other factors may be at work. Seemingly redundant structures (like the use of *waw* and repeated pronouns) occur frequently.

Subordinate clauses

Type	*Typical Indicator*
Relative clauses "who/which"	1. אֲשֶׁר 2. definite article on a participle 3. juxtaposition (= appended, unmarked)
Causal clauses "because"	1. כִּי 2. prepositions (יַעַן, אֲשֶׁר, מִן) 3. disjunctive *waw*
Purpose clauses "in order to"	1. infinitive construct plus לְ ("to") 2. *waw* plus a volitive 3. פֶּן ("lest") 4. אֲשֶׁר
Result clauses "so that"	1. כִּי 2. infinitive construct plus לְ ("to") 3. conjoined *waw* consecutive 4. אֲשֶׁר
Temporal clauses "while/ when"	1. כִּי 2. *waw* consecutive plus הִיה 3. conjoined *waw* consecutive 4. unmarked (juxtaposition) 5. prepositions (אַחֲרֵי, עַד, כְּ, בְּ) 6. disjunctive *waw*
Concessive clauses "although"	1. adverbs גַּם, אִם 2. preposition עַל 3. disjunctive *waw*
Conditional clauses "if"	1. assumed real condition (כִּי, אִם, הֵן , or juxtaposition) 2. assumed unreal (לוּלֵא or לוּ)

Disjunctive clauses

In addition to the subordinate clause uses already indicated, *waw* disjunctives may mark three types of independent clauses:

Episode marginal (introductory "Now," or final "Then")	"*Now* the serpent was more shrewd ...." (Gn 3:1)
Parenthetical ("Now")	"*Now* the Canaanites ... were dwelling in the land." (Gn 12:6)
Contrastive ("But")	"[There was a famine in all the other lands] *but* in all the land of Egypt there was food." (Gn 41:54)

Discourse analysis (supra-syntax)

A *discourse* is a structured collection of thoughts; linkages beyond the sentence level establish cohesion in communication. Discourse analysis (or *text linguistics*) is a young and promising science.

Rhetorical features like word-plays, symbols, and irony unite discourses. Besides topical, transitional, and temporal indicators, references (pronouns or demonstrative use of the definite article), repetitions (lexical or thematic), and conjunctions serve as discourse markers.

In narratives, *waw* disjunctives sometimes mark episode margins (introductory or concluding); עַל כֵּן ("therefore") or a shift in genre (narrative to poetry) may indicate closure. In poetry, acrostics and stanzas or shifts in meter or cola patterning may mark out stretches of text.

Selected Bibliography

Aharoni, Yohanan, Michael Avi-Yonah, A. Rainey, and Z. Safrai, eds. *The Macmillan Bible Atlas*. 3d rev. ed., New York: Macmillan, 1993.

Aharoni, Yohanan. *The Archaeology of the Land of Israel*. Edited by Miriam Aharoni. Translated by Anson F. Rainey. Philadelphia: Westminster, 1982.

Alter, Robert and Frank Kermode, eds. *The Literary Guide to the Bible*. Cambridge, MA: Belknap, Harvard University, 1987.

Alter, Robert. *The Art of Biblical Narrative*. New York: Basic, 1981.

____. *The Art of Biblical Poetry*. New York: Basic, 1985.

Archer, Gleason L., Jr. and Gregory Chirichigno. *Old Testament Quotations in the New Testament*. Chicago: Moody, 1983.

Archer, Gleason L., Jr. *A Survey of Old Testament Introduction*. Rev. ed., Chicago: Moody, 1974.

Avi-Yonah, Michael and Ephraim Stern, eds. *Encyclopaedia of Archaeological Excavations in the Holy Land*. Englewood Cliffs, NJ: Prentice-Hall, 1975-78.

Baker, David L. *Two Testaments, One Bible*. Rev. ed., Downers Grove, IL: InterVarsity, 1992.

Baly, Denis. *Basic Biblical Geography*. Philadelphia: Fortress, 1987.

Barber, Cyril J. *The Minister's Library*. 2 vols. Chicago: Moody, 1985.

Barker, Kenneth, ed. *The NIV Study Bible*. Grand Rapids: Zondervan, 1985.

Barthélmy, D., A. R. Hulst, N. Lohfink, W. D. McHardy, H. P. Rüger, and J. A. Sanders, eds. *Preliminary and Interim Report on the Hebrew Old Testament Text Project*. 5 vols. 2d rev. ed., New York: United Bible Societies, 1979-80. [HOTTP]

Barton, John. *Reading the Old Testament*. Philadelphia: Westminster, 1984.

Bavinck, Herman. *Our Reasonable Faith*. Repr. of Eerdmans, 1956 ed., Grand Rapids: Baker, 1977.

Beekman, John and John Callow. *Translating the Word of God*. Grand Rapids: Zondervan, 1974.

Beitzel, Barry. *The Moody Atlas of Bible Lands.* Chicago: Moody, 1985.

Ben-Tor, Amnon, ed. *The Archaeology of Ancient Israel.* Translated by R. Greenberg. New Haven, CT: Yale University, 1992.

Berkhof, Louis. *Systematic Theology.* 4th rev. & enlarg. ed., Grand Rapids: Eerdmans, 1941.

Berkouwer, G. C. *Studies in Dogmatics.* 14 vols. Grand Rapids: Eerdmans, 1952-1976.

Black, David Alan. *Using New Testament Greek in Ministry.* Grand Rapids: Baker, 1993.

Blaiklock, E. M. and R. K. Harrison, eds. *The New International Dictionary of Biblical Archaeology.* Grand Rapids: Zondervan, 1983.

Boice, James Montgomery. *Foundations of the Christian Faith.* Rev. ed., Downers Grove, IL: InterVarsity, 1986.

Bright, John. *A History of Israel.* 3d ed., Philadelphia: Westminster, 1981.

Bromiley, Geoffrey W., ed. *International Standard Bible Encyclopedia.* Rev. ed., Grand Rapids: Eerdmans, 1979-1988.

Brotzman, Ellis R. *Old Testament Textual Criticism.* Grand Rapids: Baker, 1994.

Bullinger, Ethelbert W. *Figures of Speech Used in the Bible.* Repr. of London: Messrs. Eyre and Spottiswoode, 1898 ed., Grand Rapids: Baker, 1968.

Buswell, J. Oliver. *A Systematic Theology of the Christian Religion.* Grand Rapids: Zondervan, 1962-63.

Buttrick, George A., ed. *The Interpreter's Dictionary of the Bible.* Nashville: Abingdon, 1962.

Carson, D. A. *Exegetical Fallacies.* Grand Rapids: Baker, 1984.

Carter, Charles W., ed. *A Contemporary Wesleyan Theology.* 2 vols. Grand Rapids: Zondervan, 1984.

Chafer, Lewis Sperry. *Systematic Theology.* Dallas: Dallas Seminary, 1947.

Childs, Brevard S. *Biblical Theology of the Old and New Testaments.* Minneapolis, MN: Fortress, 1993.

_____. *Old Testament Books for Pastor and Teacher.* Philadelphia: Westminster, 1977.

_____. *Old Testament Theology in a Canonical Context.* Philadelphia: Fortress, 1985.

Clines, David J. A. *The Theme of the Pentateuch.* JSOT Supplement Series 10, Sheffield: JSOT, 1978.

Clinton, Bobby. *Figures and Idioms.* Coral Gables, FL: Learning Resource Center, West Indies Mission, 1977.

Crim, Keith, ed. *The Interpreter's Dictionary of the Bible: Supplementary Volume.* Nashville: Abingdon, 1962.

Danker, Frederick W. *Multipurpose Tools for Bible Study.* Rev. and exp. ed., Minneapolis, MN: Fortress, 1993.

Davis, John J. and John C. Whitcomb. *The History of Israel.* Grand Rapids: Baker, 1969-1971.

de Vaux, Roland. *Ancient Israel.* New York: McGraw-Hill, 1965.

Dockery, David S., Kenneth A. Matthews, and Robert B. Sloan. *Foundations for Biblical Interpretation.* Nashville: Broadman & Holman, 1994.

Douglas, James Dixon, N. Hilyer, F. F. Bruce, Donald Guthrie, A. R. Millard, J. I. Packer, and Donald J. Wiseman, eds. *New Bible Dictionary.* 2d ed., Downers Grove, IL: InterVarsity, 1994.

Edwards, I. E. S., ed. *Cambridge Ancient History.* 3d ed., Cambridge: Cambridge University, 1970-1977.

Eichrodt, Walther. *Theology of the Old Testament.* Translated by J. A. Baker. Old Testament Library, Philadelphia: Westminster, 1967.

Eissfeldt, Otto. *The Old Testament: An Introduction.* Translated by Peter R. Ackroyd. New York: Harper & Row, 1965.

Elwell, Walter A., ed. *Evangelical Dictionary of Theology.* Grand Rapids: Baker, 1984.

Enns, Paul. *The Moody Handbook of Theology.* Chicago: Moody, 1990.

Erickson, Millard J. *Christian Theology.* Unabridged, one vol. ed., Grand Rapids: Baker, 1985.

Fee, Gordon D. and Douglas Stuart. *How to Read the Bible for All Its Worth.* 2d ed., Grand Rapids: Zondervan, 1993.

Fohrer, Georg. *Introduction to the Old Testament.* Translated by David E. Green. Nashville: Abingdon, 1968.

Free, Joseph P. *Archaeology and Bible History.* Revised and expanded by Howard F. Vos. Grand Rapids: Zondervan, 1992.

Freedman, David Noel, ed. *The Anchor Bible Dictionary.* New York: Doubleday, 1992.

Freeman, James M. *Manners and Customs of the Bible.* Repr. of New York: Nelson and Phillips ed., Plainfield, NJ: Logos, 1972.

Freeman-Grenville, G. S. P. *Historical Atlas of the Middle East.* New York: Simon & Schuster, 1993.

Fritz, Volkmar. *An Introduction to Biblical Archaeology.* Sheffield: JSOT, Sheffield Academic, 1993.

Glynn, John. *Commentary and Reference Survey.* Rev. ed., Vol. 2:1. n.p.: n.pub., 1995.

Goldingay, John. *Theological Diversity and the Authority of the Old Testament.* Grand Rapids: Eerdmans, 1987.

Grudem, Wayne. *Systematic Theology*. Grand Rapids: Zondervan, 1994.

Hagner, Donald A. *New Testament Exegesis and Research*. n. p.: Donald A. Hagner, 1992.

Harrison, Roland K. *Introduction to the Old Testament*. Grand Rapids: Eerdmans, 1969.

Harrison, Roland K., Bruce K. Waltke, Donald Guthrie, and Gordon D. Fee. *Biblical Criticism* Grand Rapids: Zondervan, 1978.

Hasel, Gerhard. *Old Testament Theology*. Rev. and expanded 4th ed., Grand Rapids: Eerdmans, 1991.

Hastings, James, ed. *A Dictionary of the Bible*. New York: Charles Scribner's Sons, 1898-1904.

Hayes, John H. and Carl R. Holladay. *Biblical Exegesis*. Rev. ed., Atlanta: John Knox, 1987.

Hayes, John H. and Frederick Prussner. *Old Testament Theology*. Atlanta: John Knox, 1985.

Hayes, John H. and J. Maxwell Miller, eds. *Israelite and Judaean History*. Philadelphia: Trinity Press International, 1990.

Heaton, Eric William. *Everyday Life in Old Testament Times*. New York: Scribner's, 1970.

Henrichsen, Walter A. *A Layman's Guide to Interpreting the Bible*. Grand Rapids: Zondervan, 1985.

Henry, Carl F. H., ed. *Basic Christian Doctrines*. Rep. of Holt, Rinehart and Winston, 1962 ed., Grand Rapids: Baker, 1971.

Hill, Andrew E. and John H. Walton. *A Survey of the Old Testament*. Grand Rapids: Zondervan, 1991.

Hirsch, Eric D., Jr. *The Aims of Interpretation*. Chicago: University of Chicago, 1976.

_____. *Validity in Interpretation*. New Haven, CT: Yale University, 1967.

Hoerth, Alfred J., Gerald L. Mattingly, and Edwin M. Yamauchi, eds. *Peoples of the Old Testament World*. Grand Rapids: Baker, 1993.

Holtz, Barry W., ed. *Back to the Sources*. New York: Summit, 1984.

Horn, Siegfried H. *The Spade Confirms the Bible*. Rev. and enlg. ed., Washington, DC: Review and Herald, 1980.

Inch, Morris A. and C. Hassell Bullock, eds. *The Literature and Meaning of Scripture*. Grand Rapids: Baker, 1981.

Jensen, Irving L. *Independent Bible Study*. Chicago: Moody, 1963.

Johnson, Elliott E. *Expository Hermeneutics*. Grand Rapids: Zondervan, 1990.

Joüon, Paul. *A Grammar of Biblical Hebrew. Translated and Revised by T. Muraoka. Vol. 2, Part Three: Syntax, Paradigms and Indices*. Rome: Biblical Institute, 1991.

Kaiser, Walter C. and Moisés Silva. *An Introduction to Biblical Hermeneutics*. Grand Rapids: Zondervan, 1994.

Kaiser, Walter C., Jr. *Malachi: God's Unchanging Love*. Grand Rapids: Baker, 1984.

_____. *Toward an Exegetical Theology*. Grand Rapids: Baker, 1981.

_____. *Toward an Old Testament Theology*. Grand Rapids: Zondervan, 1978.

_____. *Toward Old Testament Ethics*. Grand Rapids: Zondervan, 1983.

Keel, Othmar. *The Symbolism of the Biblical World*. Translated by Timothy J. Hallett. New York: Crossroad, 1985.

Kitchen, Kenneth A. *Ancient Orient and Old Testament*. Downers Grove, IL: InterVarsity, 1966.

_____. *The Bible in Its World*. Downers Grove, IL: InterVarsity, 1978.

Klein, Ralph W. *Textual Criticism of the Old Testament*. Philadelphia: Fortress, 1974.

Klein, William W., Craig L. Blomberg, and Robert L. Hubbard Jr. *Introduction to Biblical Interpretation*. Dallas: Word, 1993.

Knight, Douglas A. and Gene M. Tucker, eds. *The Hebrew Bible and Its Modern Interpreters*. Chico, CA: Scholars/Fortress, 1985.

Kraus, Hans-Joachim. *Theology of the Psalms*. Translated by Keith Crim. Minneapolis, MN: Fortress, 1986.

Lewis, Gordon R. and Bruce A. Demarest. *Integrative Theology*. 2 vols. Grand Rapids: Zondervan, 1987, 1990.

Livingston, G. Herbert. *The Pentateuch in Its Cultural Environment*. 2d ed., Grand Rapids: Baker, 1974.

Longman, Tremper, III. *Old Testament Commentary Survey*. Grand Rapids: Baker, 1991.

Martens, Elmer A. *God's Design: A Focus on Old Testament Theology*. Grand Rapids: Baker, 1986-1987.

Masom, Caroline and Pat Alexander, eds. *Picture Archive of the Bible*. Batavia, IL: Lion, 1987.

Matthews, Victor H. and Don C. Benjamin. *The Social World of Ancient Israel, 1250-587 B.C.E.* Peabody, MA: Hendrickson, 1993.

Matthews, Victor H. *Manners and Customs in the Bible*. Rev. ed., Peabody, MA: Hendrickson, 1988.

May, H. G. *The Oxford Bible Atlas*. 2d ed., London: Oxford University, 1974.

Mazar, Amihai. *Archaeology of the Land of the Bible, 10,000—586 B.C.E.* New York: Doubleday, 1990.

Mazar, Benjamin, ed. *Views of the Biblical World*. Jerusalem, ISRAEL: International, 1961.

McCarter, P. Kyle, Jr. *Textual Criticism*. Philadelphia: Fortress, 1986.

McKenzie, Steven L. and Stephen R. Haynes, eds. *To Each Its Own Meaning*. Louisville, KY: Westminster/Knox, 1993.

McNeill, John T., ed. *Calvin: Institutes of the Christian Religion in Two Volumes*. Philadelphia: Westminster, 1977.

McQuilkin, J. Robertson. *Understanding & Applying the Bible*. Rev. ed., Chicago: Moody, 1992.

Meeks, Wayne A., ed. *The HarperCollins Study Bible*. San Francisco: HarperSanFrancisco, HarperCollins, 1992.

Merrill, Eugene H. *An Historical Survey of the Old Testament*. 2d ed., Grand Rapids: Baker, 1991.

_____. *Kingdom of Priests*. Grand Rapids: Baker, 1987.

Metzger, Bruce M. and Michael D. Coogan, eds. *The Oxford Companion to the Bible*. New York: Oxford, 1993.

Metzger, Bruce M. and Roland E. Murphy, eds. *The New Oxford Annotated Bible: New Revised Standard Version*. New York: Oxford University, 1993.

Mickelsen, A. Berkeley. *Interpreting the Bible*. Grand Rapids: Eerdmans, 1963.

Miller, Madeleine S. and J. Lane Miller, eds. *Harper's Encyclopedia of Bible Life*. San Francisco: Harper & Row, 1971.

Mills, Watson E., ed. *Mercer Dictionary of the Bible*. Macon, GA: Mercer University, 1991; 3d corr. printing, 1992.

Moo, Douglas J., ed. *An Annotated Bibliography on the Bible and the Church*. Deerfield, IL: Trinity Evangelical Divinity School, 1986.

Murphy-O'Connor, Jerome. *The Holy Land*. 3d ed., New York: Oxford University, 1992.

Negev, Avraham, ed. *The Archaeological Encyclopaedia of the Holy Land*. 3d ed., New York: Prentice Hall, 1992.

Ollenburger, Ben C., Elmer A. Martens, and Gerhard F. Hasel, eds. *The Flowering of Old Testament Theology*. Winona Lake, IN: Eisenbrauns, 1992.

Osborne, Grant R. *The Hermeneutical Spiral*. Downers Grove, IL: InterVarsity, 1991.

Ott, Ludwig. *Fundamentals of Catholic Dogma*. Edited by James Canon Bastible. Translated by Patrick Lynch. Rockford, IL: Tan, 1974.

Parker, Don. *Old Testament Study Aids*. San Bernardino, CA: International School of Theology, 1988.

Paterson, John H., Donald J. Wiseman, John J. Bimson, and John P. Kane, eds. *New Bible Atlas*. Downers Grove, IL: InterVarsity, 1994.

Pieper, Francis. *Christian Dogmatics*. Translated by Engelder Mueller Albrecht. St. Louis: Concordia, 1950-57.

Pritchard, James B., ed. *Ancient Near Eastern Texts Related to the Old Testament*. 3d ed., Princeton, NJ: Princeton University, 1969.

_____. *The Ancient Near East in Pictures*. 2d ed., Princeton: Princeton University, 1969.

_____, ed. *The Harper Atlas of the Bible*. New York: Harper & Row, 1987.

Ramm, Bernard. *Protestant Biblical Interpretation*. 3d ed., Grand Rapids: Baker, 1970.

Rasmussen, Carl G. *The Zondervan NIV Atlas of the Bible*. Grand Rapids: Zondervan, 1989.

Rendtorff, Rolff. *The Old Testament: An Introduction*. Translated by John Bowden. Philadelphia: Fortress, 1985.

Ryken, Leland and Tremper Longman III, eds. *A Complete Literary Guide to the Bible*. Grand Rapids: Zondervan, 1993.

Ryken, Leland. *The Literature of the Bible*. Grand Rapids: Zondervan, 1974.

_____. *Words of Delight*. Grand Rapids: Baker, 1993.

Ryrie, Charles Caldwell. *Basic Theology*. Wheaton, IL: Victor Books, 1986.

_____. *The Ryrie Study Bible: New International Version*. Expanded ed., Chicago: Moody, 1994.

Sailhamer, John H. *Introduction to Old Testament Theology*. Grand Rapids: Zondervan, 1995.

Scott, William R. *A Simplified Guide to BHS*. 2d ed., Berkeley, CA: BIBAL, 1990.

Shedd, William G. T. *Systematic Theology*. Repr. of 1872 ed., Grand Rapids: Eerdmans, 1977.

Silva, Moisés. *God, Language and Scripture*. Grand Rapids: Zondervan, 1990.

_____. *Has the Church Misread the Bible?* Grand Rapids: Zondervan, 1988.

Sire, James W. *Scripture Twisting: 20 Ways the Cults Misread the Bible*. Downers Grove, IL: InterVarsity, 1980.

Smith, Ralph L. *Old Testament Theology*. Nashville, TN: Broadman & Holman, 1993.

Sproul, R. C. *Knowing Scripture*. Downers Grove, IL: InterVarsity, 1977.

Stein, Robert H. *Playing by the Rules*. Grand Rapids: Baker, 1994.

Stern, Ephraim, ed. *The New Encyclopedia of Archaeological Excavations in the Holy Land*. Rev. ed., New York: Simon & Schuster, 1992.

Stuart, Douglas. *A Guide to Selecting and Using Bible Commentaries.* Dallas: Word, 1991.

_____. *Old Testament Exegesis.* 2d, rev. and enl. ed., Philadelphia: Westminster, 1984.

Tate, Randolph. *Biblical Interpretation.* Peabody, MA: Hendrickson, 1991.

Tenney, Merrill C., ed. *Zondervan Pictorial Encyclopedia of the Bible.* Grand Rapids: Zondervan, 1975-1976.

Terry, Milton S. *Biblical Hermeneutics.* Repr. of 1885 ed., Grand Rapids: Zondervan, 1974.

Thiessen, Henry Clarence. *Introductory Lectures in Systematic Theology.* Grand Rapids: Eerdmans, 1949.

Thiselton, Anthony C. *New Horizons in Hermeneutics.* Grand Rapids: Zondervan, HarperCollins, 1992.

_____. *The Two Horizons.* Grand Rapids: Eerdmans, 1980.

Thomas, D. Winton, ed. *Documents from Old Testament Times.* Repr. of 1958 ed., New York: Harper & Row, 1961.

_____, ed. *Peoples of Old Testament Times.* Oxford: Clarendon, 1973.

Thompson, J. A. *Handbook of Life in Bible Times.* Downers Grove, IL: InterVarsity, 1986.

_____. *The Bible and Archaeology.* 3d, rev. ed., Grand Rapids: Eerdmans, 1982.

Tov, Emanuel. *Textual Criticism of the Hebrew Bible.* Minneapolis, MN: Fortress, 1992.

Traina, Robert A. *Methodical Bible Study.* Wilmore, KY: Robert A. Traina, 1952.

Unger, Merrill Frederick. *The New Unger's Bible Handbook.* Revised by Gary N. Larson. Rev. ed., Chicago: Moody, 1984.

_____. *Unger's Bible Dictionary.* Chicago: Moody, 1966.

van der Woude, A. S., ed. *The World of the Bible.* Translated by Sierd Woudstra. Grand Rapids: Eerdmans, 1986.

Vasholz, R. I. *Data for the Sigla of BHS.* Winona Lake, IN: Eisenbrauns, 1983.

Vine, W. E., Merrill F. Unger, and William White Jr. *Vine's Complete Expository Dictionary of Old and New Testament Words.* Rev. ed., Nashville: Nelson, 1985.

Virkler, Henry A. *Hermeneutics.* Grand Rapids: Baker, 1981.

von Rad, Gerhard. *Old Testament Theology.* Translated by D. M. G. Stalker. New York: Harper & Row, 1965.

Wald, Oletta. *The Joy of Discovery in Bible Study.* Rev. ed., Minneapolis: Augsburg, 1975.

Walton, John H. *Ancient Israelite Literature in Its Cultural Context.* Grand Rapids: Zondervan, 1989.

Walvoord, John F. and Roy B. Zuck, eds. *The Bible Knowledge Commentary: Old Testament*. Wheaton, IL: Victor Books, Scripture Press, 1985.

Watson, Richard. *Theological Institutes*. New York: Calton & Sanahan, 1840.

Watson, W. G. E. *Classical Hebrew Poetry*. Sheffield: JSOT, 1984.

Weingreen, J. *Introduction to the Critical Study of the Text of the Hebrew Bible*. Oxford: Clarendon, 1982.

Wight, Fred and Ralph Gower. *The New Manners and Customs of Bible Times*. Chicago: Moody, 1987.

Wiley, H. Orton. *Christian Theology*. 3 vols. Kansas City: Beacon Hill, 1940-43.

Wonneberger, Reinhard. *Understanding BHS*. 2d rev. ed., Rome: Biblical Institute, 1990.

Wood, Leon J. *A Survey of Israel's History*. Grand Rapids: Zondervan, 1970.

Würthwein, Ernst. *The Text of the Old Testament*. Translated by E. F. Rhodes. 2d ed., Grand Rapids: Eerdmans, 1994.

Zuck, Roy, ed. *A Biblical Theology of the Old Testament*. Chicago: Moody, 1991.

_____. *Basic Bible Interpretation*. Wheaton, IL: Victor, 1991.

Index

accents 58, 61, 168
allegorical method of
    hermeneutics 95
allegories, allegorizing 95, 132
alliteration 158
ambiguity 87, 128, 146, 168
analogy of Scripture 22, 111
analytical tool 41
apostrophe 112
aspect 74
assonance 158
authority 217
ballast variant 154
Bible translations 60
biblical Hebrew research
    systems 56
biblical theology 23
bicolon 150
big idea 19
case 14
characterization 121
chiasm, mixed 174
chiasmus 130, 155
chrestomathy 230
circles of context 82
cognates 51, 72, 88
colon 150, 172
compensation 154
componential analysis 79
computer software 56
concentric structure 130, 155
conceptual translation 101,
    102, 113
concordance 43, 44, 51
connotation 68

consonance 158
context 67, 68, 96, 102, 105,
    113
convention 129
covenant theology/covenantism
    184
critical analysis 23
culture 179
dead figures of speech 104
Dead Sea Scrolls 51
decontextualizing 134
delimitation 19
denominators 21
derivatives 43, 73
descriptive versus prescriptive
    189
diachronic 64
diagramming 35
dialogue 124
differentiation 187
discourse analysis 95
dispensationalism 184
distanciation 180, 218
documentary hypothesis 138
double-duty function 154, 155,
    172
dynamic equivalence translation
    theory 180
eisegesis 18
ellipsis 155
emendations 50
epangelicalism 184
etymological fallacy 67
etymology 43, 67, 72
exegesis 18

exemplary preaching 196
exemplifying 133
figure of speech 94, 109, 157
form criticism 162
generational sin 134
genres 20
globalization of hermeneutics 180
grammar 21
grammars 45, 225
grammatical analysis 21
haymaker 211
Hebrew inscriptions 51
hendiadys 100
hermeneutical spiral 18
historical criticism 42
homonyms 59, 128
hyperbole 100, 111, 112
idioms 95
illegitimate totality transfer 68
inclusio 156
inner exegesis 23
inscriptions 87
interlinear 40
irony 95, 110
Kethiv-Qere reading 59
keynotes 208, 220
laments 163, 176
langua 87
leitwort 128
Leningrad manuscript 46
levirate marriage 186
lexical analysis 22
lexical form 43
lexicon 42, 50
literal translation 59
literary analysis 20
literary approach 118
litotes 100
manner 213
Masoretes 6
Masoretic pointing 7
Masoretic text 7

meiosis 100
meter 160
metri causa 161
morphology 41, 43
narration 124
narrative 115
narrator reticence 122
normativeness 185
occasional texts 186
onomatopoeia 158
panchronic 64
paradigmatic relations 65
parallelism 149
parallelism, external 150
parallelism, formal 171
parallelism, incomplete 153
parallelism, inexact 153
parallelism, internal 150
parallelism, normal 150
parallelism, numerical 171
parallelism, positional 171
parallelism, semantic 151
parallelism, thetic 170
parole 87
paronomasia 128
particles 45, 51
parts of speech 21
pleas 163, 176
poetry 146
point of view 121
polysemy 128
popular etymologies 128
prayer 221
preference model of interpretation 147
prescriptive versus descriptive 189
preterite 49
principlization 187
proficiency levels 224
progressive dispensationalism 184
promise theology 184

prose particles 155
psalms of innocence 177
psalms, declarative praise 163
psalms, descriptive praise 163
psalms, hallelujah 177
psalms, penitential 177
psalms, pilgrim 177
psychologizing 134
purpose statement 19
qinah 160
redefining 133
referent 89
referential meaning 86
repetition 127
reverse etymologizing 67
rhetorical question 100
rhyme 159
rhyme, weak 159
rhythm 159
root 41, 42, 43, 49
scenes 120
semantic field 65
semantics 64, 86
Semitic languages 6, 41
sentence roles 21
sermon component retention
    hierarchy 221
sermon idea 199
sermon theme 207
source criticism 42, 118
stanzas 156
strophes 156
style 213
symbols 95, 110
synchronic 64
synonyms 52, 79
syntagmatic relations 66
syntax 21, 41, 155
systematic theology 23
tense 49, 74
tetracolon 150
textual analysis 21
textual form 43

textual idea 199
theme, book 19
theme, sermon 207
theological analysis 22
three "worlds" 201
three questions 204
three roles 202
transparency 67
tricolon 150
type-scenes 129
typology 132
understatement 100, 112
verb patterns 43, 44, 49, 52,
    74, 86
verb tenses 49
verse numbers 43
volitives 49, 75
vowel signs 58
waw 48
waw conjunctive 42
waw consecutive 42, 49, 124,
    126, 173
waw disjunctive 126
Whiting Method 206
word order 155, 173
word pairs 157, 175
word studies 51, 64, 69, 91
word study method 71
word study tools 71
word-play 127, 158, 159
wordbooks 44
words, significant 72

7873